WORLD EMPIRE

CAUCASUS MOUNTAINS

URARTU

A

CASPIAN
SEA

Nineveh
★Calah

sshur

Tigris River

MEDIA

Ecbatana★

Sippar

★Babylon

Nippur

•Susa

River

Ur

CHALDEA

★Pasargadae

KINGDOM OF
ANSHAN

•	City
★	Kingdom capital
	Area of Babylonian Empire
	Boundary of Assyrian Empire
--▶	Boundary of Persian Empire

PERSIAN
GULF

0   250 Miles

0   250 Kilometers

Thus Saith the Lord

ALSO BY RICHARD E. RUBENSTEIN

Rebels in Eden

Left Turn

Alchemists of Revolution

Comrade Valentine

When Jesus Became God

Aristotle's Children

RICHARD E. RUBENSTEIN

THUS SAITH THE LORD

✴

*The Revolutionary Moral Vision
of Isaiah and Jeremiah*

HARCOURT, INC.

Orlando   Austin   New York   San Diego   Toronto   London

Requests for permission to make copies of any part of the work
should be submitted online at www.harcourt.com/contact or mailed
to the following address: Permissions Department, Harcourt, Inc.,
6277 Sea Harbor Drive, Orlando, Florida 32887-6777.

www.HarcourtBooks.com

Library of Congress Cataloging-in-Publication Data
Rubenstein, Richard E.
Thus saith the Lord: the revolutionary moral vision
of Isaiah and Jeremiah/Richard E. Rubenstein.—1st ed.
p.   cm.
1. Ethics in the Bible. 2. Bible. O.T. Isaiah—Criticism, interpretation, etc.
3. Bible. O.T. Jeremiah—Criticism, interpretation, etc. I. Title.
BS1515.6.E8R83   2006
224′.106—dc22   2006009232
ISBN-13: 978-0-15-101219-0   ISBN-10: 0-15-101219-9

Text set in Requiem
Designed by Linda Lockowitz

Printed in the United States of America

First edition
A C E G I K J H F D B

For John Burton, mentor and friend

"I have appointed you as a prophet to the nations."

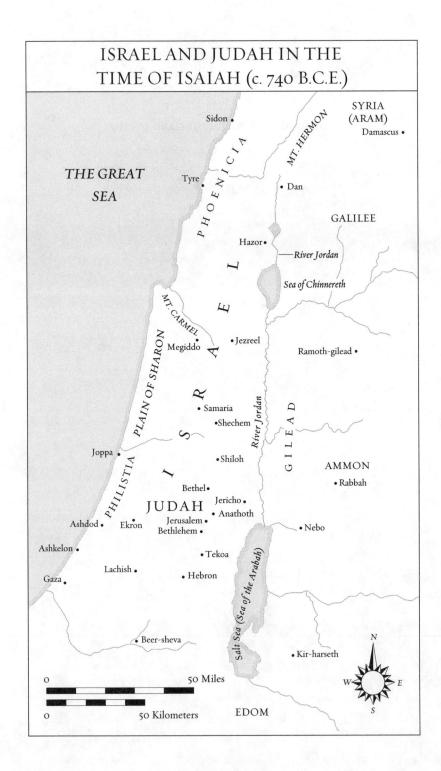

ISRAEL AND JUDAH IN THE
TIME OF ISAIAH (c. 740 B.C.E.)

SYRIA
(ARAM)

Damascus •

Sidon •

MT. HERMON

THE GREAT
SEA

PHOENICIA

Tyre •

• Dan

GALILEE

Hazor •

River Jordan

Sea of Chinnereth

MT. CARMEL

I S R A E L

Megiddo •

• Jezreel

Ramoth-gilead •

PLAIN OF SHARON

Samaria •

• Shechem

River Jordan

G I L E A D

Joppa •

PHILISTIA

• Shiloh

AMMON

• Rabbah

Bethel •

Jericho •

JUDAH

• Anathoth

Ashdod •

Ekron •

Jerusalem •

Bethlehem •

• Nebo

Ashkelon •

• Tekoa

Lachish •

Salt Sea (Sea of the Arabah)

Gaza •

• Hebron

• Beer-sheva

• Kir-harseth

N

W ☀ E

S

0 ────────────── 50 Miles

0 ────────────── 50 Kilometers

EDOM

Contents

*

PREFACE

✳

WHEN I WAS A BOY, I used to attend Sabbath services on Saturday mornings at Temple Israel in Lawrence, New York, not far from my parents' home on Long Island. When my attention wandered from the prayer book, I often found myself staring at three sayings carved in wood and mounted high on the walls overlooking the sanctuary: "And they shall beat their swords into plowshares." "My house shall be called a house of prayer for all peoples." "In quietness and confidence shall be thy strength." All are quotations from the prophet Isaiah.

Even then, these brief phrases had the power to comfort and inspire. They stayed with me long after other childhood remembrances had faded. Perhaps for this reason, it seemed natural to open the book of Isaiah again in the troubled months after September 11, 2001, when America reeled under the impact of a catastrophe that seemed almost biblical in scope. How could people claiming to believe in the One God have committed such heinous attacks? And how should people claiming to believe in the One God respond? These questions concerned me not only as a private citizen, but as a teacher of conflict resolution, with a special interest in studying conflicts involving religion. I could see the terrorist assault provoking a violent American response, and that response provoking further retaliation, in a potentially endless cycle of blows and counterblows. Perhaps the prophets would have something to teach us about how to escape this trap—and, more generally, about how to live in a world so deeply and violently divided.

Delving into the biblical books known in Hebrew as Nevi'im— the Prophets—turned out to be a mind-opening experience. I did not want to ransack the Bible for relevant teachings, a process that almost always writes the interpreter's prejudices into the text. My ambition was to tell the stories of Isaiah, Jeremiah, and their contemporaries by situating them in their own time and place, and to discover on that basis what they might have to say to us more than 2,500 years later.

To do this meant studying the prophets' writings, of course, but it also meant learning about their dangerous and fascinating world. The Hebrew peoples did not live in some out-of-the-way place where they could practice their odd monotheistic religion in peace. Then as now, the volatile, strategically important Middle East was crisscrossed by traders, travelers, soldiers, priests, and people exchanging ideas. In the prophets' time, moreover, it was a region undergoing unprecedented changes because of the rise of a new type of empire, more innovative and aggressive than any seen before. To understand the world of the prophets, I found myself reading Assyrian and Babylonian texts, poring over photos of archaeological finds, and exploring the great collections of West Asian antiquities in New York's Metropolitan Museum of Art, the British Museum, and Berlin's Vorderasiatisches Museum.

This was a real adventure. I recall standing in the beautifully preserved ruins of Sennacherib's palace in the British Museum, examining the vast reliefs that show the Assyrians conquering the Judean city of Lachish in 701 B.C.E. Thousands of defenders died in that battle. One can almost hear their screams as the Assyrian archers, warriors, and siege machines pounded away at the city's walls. Sennacherib later wrote that he had trapped King Hezekiah, the Judean ruler, in Jerusalem, thirty miles away, "like a bird in his cage." Studying the reliefs, I thought about Hezekiah sitting in his palace with the prophet Isaiah, while Lachish burned and the bodies of its defenders were shoveled into a mass grave. In response to questions from the nervous king, Isaiah told him what would happen next. Sennacherib would besiege his city with his incomparable army, but Jerusalem would not fall. "By the road that he came on he will return; he shall not enter the city. It is YHVH who speaks."

How did Isaiah know that? Was he some sort of inspired, ecstatic dreamer, or a sophisticated political advisor, or, somehow, both at the same time? And what was his relationship to his own king, on the one hand, and the Assyrians, on the other? The light that dawned as my research continued was that that Isaiah and Jeremiah were not fundamentalists trying to protect their nation and its traditional culture against foreign enemies. On the contrary, they were sophisticated, innovative thinkers who seized on ideas emanating from the imperial centers, fused them with their own traditions, and used the product—a new ethics and theology of history—to criticize both sides and chart a new course for their people.

This independent stance was a response to the great challenge of their era—the rise of empires determined to bring every nation within reach under their control. The dilemma this created for the Hebrew peoples was similar, in some ways, to that facing the nations now confronted by Western-style globalization. They could accept integration into the new world system— but this would involve adulterating their unique monotheistic culture and sacrificing their political independence. They could resist violently—but this posed a serious risk of massacres, mass deportations, and national extinction. Or they could try to find some way to maintain their identity and values without engaging either in corrupt compromises or suicidal holy wars.

The prophets' genius (or that of the God who spoke to them) was to discover this third way. How they discovered it, and what it may yet mean to us, are the subjects of this book. In telling the story, I decided to focus intensively on a few major figures whose lives and teachings seemed particularly compelling and important: Isaiah, Jeremiah, Isaiah of Babylon (also known as Second

Isaiah), and Jesus of Nazareth. Elijah and Elisha make brief appearances in the first chapter. But the reader will not find much discussion here of Amos, Hosea, Ezekiel, or other figures who might well have been included.

I trust that what the book lacks in comprehensiveness it will make up for in depth and human interest. Now—especially now—we need to contemplate these adventuresome lives, listen to these passionate voices, and think about what they may mean for the future of our nation and our world.

For me, writing this story has been a way of reconnecting with my own religious tradition. I am not a rigorously observant Jew. From time to time I have wondered what role Judaism actually played in my life, compared with other intellectual and cultural traditions. Now the answer seems much clearer, for the God who speaks through the prophets is, above all, the source of ethical creativity—the announcer of "new things," as Isaiah of Babylon puts it. It is He who declares that the old regime of power-based domination and subjection is doomed, that a just and peaceful world order is actually obtainable, and that bringing this new world into existence is the task for which all of us are chosen. Exploring the origins and development of this glowing, demanding vision brought me back to the core of my own unorthodox faith. Almost three thousand years after they first arose to disturb the complacency of Israel, the prophets have not lost their ability to challenge and inspire us.

THUS SAITH THE LORD

CHAPTER I

✳

"If YHVH is God, Follow Him!"
—Elijah, I Kings 18:21

THE TWO KINGS sat side by side on a raised platform overlooking a large open square just outside the gates of Samaria. Both wore their robes of office. Ahab of Israel rested lightly on his ivory-inlaid throne with an ease born of long experience, like an expert cavalryman sitting his horse. Immediately to his right sat his guest, King Jehosophat of Judah, occupying a throne only slightly less ornate than his own. A large crowd of townspeople and farmers ringed the square, many holding up their children or craning on tiptoe for a better look at the two monarchs. But the kings' attention was focused intently on the scene now being played out for their benefit in the open space before the platform.

The name of the place—the Threshing Floor—reflected its main function in the life of Israel's capital. Each year, after the harvests of wheat and barley were brought in, oxen and mules were led round and round the flat, hard-packed surface to trample the stalks of grain or cut them up with threshing plows.[1] At such times, the air would be full of chaff, thrown into the wind by farmers wielding winnowing forks, while the precious grain fell safely to earth. Today, however, the atmosphere was suffused not with dust and straw or the braying of barnyard animals, but with discordant human noise. The square, swept clean of farm debris, was full of prophets, hundreds of them, some dancing ecstatically or chanting with eyes closed, others gesturing wildly and crying aloud in voices that might or might not have been their own.

Those who had never witnessed the nevi'im prophesying en masse might have found the spectacle frightening or absurd—a strange drama performed by demented actors, each enacting a role known only to himself.[2] To the royal onlookers, however, the apparent chaos in the square made perfect sense. They had summoned the prophets to Samaria to help them decide an issue of great public importance. Should Israel and Judah go to war with the kingdom of Syria?[3] Or should the Hebrew-speaking nations keep the peace?

On Ahab's part, this was not a neutral inquiry. For months he had been preparing to attack the powerful Damascus-based regime that was Israel's chief competitor for supremacy in the region. His immediate aim was to recapture Ramoth-gilead, a strategic city formerly occupied by King Solomon in the days of the United Monarchy, but now under the control of the Syrians and their formidable ruler, King ben-Hadad II. Israel and Judah, long at loggerheads, were at last allies, thanks to a diplomatic marriage uniting the two kings' families. Ahab had therefore invited Jehosophat to furnish a certain number of horses and soldiers for the campaign, and the Judean king had agreed—but on one condition. Ahab must first ask his prophets whether or not YHVH—the God worshipped by both monarchs—approved of the proposed war.[4]

Even without this prompting, the king might well have summoned the nevi'im to Samaria before marching off to war.[5] Not only in Israel and Judah, but throughout West Asia, it was customary to confer with religious seers about matters of this sort. From the Iranian plateau to the Mediterranean coast, every substantial ruler employed a phalanx of prophets whose special vocation was to discover whether the national god or gods favored a proposed policy, and to advise the king accordingly.[6] Prophecy was not a gift reserved to a handful of gifted individuals; it was an ancient craft whose practitioners probably numbered more than one thousand in Israel alone. Some nevi'im were attached to the court and lived in the capital. Others performed cultic duties in smaller towns where there were temples, shrines, or sanctuaries. Although a few practiced as individuals, most were members of guilds or brotherhoods that transmitted the techniques of receiving divine messages from father to son (and, in some cases, from mother to daughter).[7] For YHVH's followers, certain arts favored by the seers of other nations—fortune-telling, divination, necromancy, and magic, for example—were prohibited by Mosaic Law.[8] Even so, as the impassioned performers on the Threshing Floor were now demonstrating, there were many acceptable ways to enter that receptive, transcendent state in which one's heart was opened to God's true intentions.

Seated on his reviewing stand, Ahab waited for a pause in the prophetic hubbub, then rose from his throne, quieting the crowd. "Should I march to attack Ramoth-gilead," he asked in a loud public voice, "or should I refrain?"

The response was immediate—and unanimous. "March to Ramoth-gilead and conquer!" the prophets howled as one. "YHVH will deliver it into the power of the king."[9] One ecstatic wearing a headdress equipped with iron horns ran through the crowd snorting like a bull and whipping his head from side to side as if to gore some invisible enemy, while the others scrambled to get out of his way. "YHVH says this," he shouted, pointing at the horns. "With these you will gore the Syrians until you make an end of them."[10]

Satisfied, Ahab settled back on his throne. The advice was welcome, although not unexpected. The nevi'im generally told the king what he wanted to hear, particularly when what he wanted was approval of a war. This was not because they were mere sycophants (although some, no doubt, would say anything to please him), but because the deity who spoke to them in dreams and visions, in audible voices and sudden convictions of absolute certainty, was, among other things, a warrior god. It was YHVH, after all, who had afflicted the Egyptians and drowned their charioteers in the sea; YHVH who instructed Joshua to raze the cities of Canaan and ordered Israel's Judges to conduct merciless wars against their idol-worshipping neighbors; YHVH who punished King Saul for not exterminating the Amelkites, upheld David's sword in battle, and sanctified the conquests of Solomon. As interpreted by the prophets of Ahab's time, God generally preferred the clean, simple violence of a holy war to the dangerous ambiguities of peaceful diplomacy.

Ahab, as it happens, was a skilled practitioner of both arts. He had ruled in Samaria for more than two decades—a lengthy reign by the standards of the small, unstable states of the region. The crown of Israel was more fragile than most. In the fifty-odd years since the breakup of the United Monarchy, seven rulers had ascended the throne of the northern kingdom, and three of these had had their reigns cut short by assassination.[11] Even so, by 852 B.C.E., the year that Jehosophat visited Samaria, Israel had become a far more powerful player than Judah in regional and international politics.[12] Ahab's kingdom outstripped Jehosophat's in population, agricultural productivity, military power, and strategic location.[13] His father, King Omri, had been a famous warrior—so impressive on the battlefield, in fact, that the Assyrians referred to Israel for more than a century as "the House of Omri."[14] Equally important, the old king had married his son, Ahab, to the Tyrian princess, Jezebel, thus cementing an advantageous alliance with the region's leading traders, the Phoenicians of the Mediterranean coast.

King Ahab continued and extended his father's work. On the diplomatic front, he cultivated the Phoenician alliance and ended a half century of hostility between Israel and Judah by marrying his daughter to Jehosophat's eldest son.[15] His military accomplishments were, if anything, even more notable. Only one year before Jehosophat's current visit, the mighty Assyrian army had marched from its Mesopotamian bases into northern Syria—the first attempt by the Assyrians to extend their empire westward. In response, Ahab had dispatched 2,000 chariots and 10,000 foot soldiers to fight side by side with ben-Hadad of Syria and other regional rulers in a grand coalition against the invaders.[16] The great battle at Qarqar on the Orontes River pitted some 50,000 defenders against a somewhat smaller but better equipped force led by the young Assyrian emperor, Shalmaneser III. Despite a large toll of casualties on all sides, the result was favorable to the allies. Shalmaneser was forced to withdraw to his homeland to lick his wounds and reorganize his forces.[17]

At some later time, perhaps, the Assyrians would return—or perhaps not. Ahab was concerned with more immediate matters. Ben-Hadad, his ally at Qarqar, was his only real rival for supremacy in the region. Before uniting to defend their territories against Shalmaneser, he and the Syrian king had fought two short wars, each begun by a Syrian attack on Israel, and each won by the Israelites against heavy odds.[18] The second war ended with a smashing victory by Ahab's troops outside the town of Aphek in the Golan Heights. The Bible states that the Israelites slaughtered 100,000 Syrian foot soldiers in a single day, after which the walls of Aphek collapsed, killing the surviving fighters who had taken refuge there.[19] Probably more accurate, and certainly more revealing, is the report that, disregarding the advice of certain unnamed prophets, Ahab decided to spare ben-Hadad's life and to conclude a peace treaty with him.

Now ben-Hadad had fled and taken refuge within the town in an inner room. "Look," his servants said to him, "we have heard that the kings of Israel are merciful kings. Let us put sackcloth around our waists and ropes on our heads and go out to the king of Israel; perhaps he will spare your life." So they wrapped sackcloth around their waists and put ropes on their heads and went to the king of Israel, and said, "Your servant ben-Hadad says, 'Spare my life.'" "So he is still alive?" [Ahab] answered. "He is my brother."[20]

After acknowledging ben-Hadad as a brother king and allowing him to live, Ahab treated him as a potential ally. The Syrians surrendered several cities in the Galilee that they had taken from his father, and granted Israel trading rights in Damascus similar to the rights won earlier by the Syrians to set up bazaars in Samaria. Then the Israelite monarch permitted his captive to return to Damascus, accompanied by the surviving remnants of his army.

Smart politics? One might well think so, considering that the two kings would soon be fighting together against the Assyrian menace. A praiseworthy act of kindness? So it would seem, since the alternative would be to imprison or slaughter defenseless captives. Yet the brotherhood of prophets immediately condemned Ahab's leniency as dangerous and contrary to the will of God. "YHVH says this," a spokesman told the king: "Since you have let the man escape who was under my ban, your life will pay for his, your people for his people."[21]

The ban referred to is *herem,* a word meaning excommunication, but also a divine sentence of doom. According to the anonymous prophet, YHVH had doomed the Syrians because they belittled him by calling him "a god of the mountains and not of the plains," and by assuming that Israel could therefore be defeated in a battle fought in the open country above Galilee.[22] This arrogant insult altered the character of the war, converting it from a struggle between rival monarchs to a contest between rival gods. That is, it was a holy war, one won by YHVH, who had delivered a superior enemy into Ahab's hands.[23] What was called for in such cases was not a diplomatic deal between fellow monarchs, but the ritual destruction of captives, a practice commanded by the laws of Deuteronomy.[24] When Ahab freed captives under the ban, he defined himself, rather than YHVH, as the victor. As a result, he himself—all Israel, in fact—would be doomed by an angry God.

No record exists of how the king replied to this challenge, if he replied at all, but it is easy to imagine his response. The harsh laws of Deuteronomy (themselves of uncertain date) were purportedly formulated to govern the behavior of the Hebrews conquering Canaan at YHVH's command, not later battles fought by kings on their own initiative to secure territorial or trade advantages.[25] Not every war fought by Israel qualified as a holy war. Therefore, if the Syrians had *not* insulted YHVH as the prophets alleged they had, the struggle between ben-Hadad and Ahab would be an ordinary secular war, and the rule of *herem* would be irrelevant. Implicitly, Ahab's actions denied the prophets' version of events and their interpretation of the character of the war—hence, the curse pronounced by their representative. Especially in light of this controversy, one can imagine a nervous King Jehosophat withholding his approval of the joint expedition against Syria until the brotherhood had blessed it on behalf of YHVH. War was risky enough without running the additional risk of offending God!

The Biblical account does not reveal why Ahab decided to attack Ramoth-gilead, but we know that the town was a strategic strongpoint and a gateway to northern Gilead, a rich grain-bearing region inhabited by many Israelite settlers.[26] It may be that it was one of the cities that ben-Hadad was supposed to return but did not—or Ahab may simply have decided to take advantage of the Syrians' preoccupation with the Assyrian threat in order to expand his own holdings. The boundaries between nations like Israel and Syria were vague and disputable; kings took what they could get, and wars of territorial expansion were normal for the region. So far as Ahab was concerned, the prophets' exhortation to "march and conquer" decided the matter. But Jehosophat, says the book of Kings, wanted more assurance still.

One of the court prophets, Micaiah ben-Imlah by name, was notorious for his refusal to curry favor with the king. "I hate him," Ahab admitted, "because he never has favorable predictions for me, only unfavorable ones."[27] Hauled into the square at Jehosophat's insistence, Micaiah confronted his sovereign alone. No one dared speak as the king leaned forward to question him directly.

"Micaiah, should we march to attack Ramoth-gilead, or should we refrain?"

"March and conquer," the prophet replied perfunctorily. "YHVH will deliver it into the power of the king."

Ahab shook his head impatiently. "How often must I put you on oath to tell me nothing but the truth in the name of YHVH?"

For a long moment, Micaiah remained mute, his head bowed in thought.

Then he raised his eyes to Ahab's and chanted in an unexpectedly sad and melodious voice:

> I have seen all Israel scattered on the mountains
> like sheep without a shepherd.
> And YHVH said, "These have no master,
> let each go home unmolested."[28]

The meaning of this was clear. YHVH had *not* blessed the battle and would not protect Israel's "shepherd," a term used to describe the king since the days of King David.[29] But every other prophet had declared the anti-Syrian campaign a holy war. How could this discrepancy be explained? Micaiah would not accuse his fellow prophets of sycophancy or charlatanism. Instead, he explained, he had seen a vision of YHVH on this throne, surrounded by "all the array of heaven." In his vision, YHVH asks for a volunteer to trick Ahab into marching to his death at Ramoth-gilead, and one of the heavenly creatures offers his services. "I will become a lying spirit in the mouths of all his prophets," the creature says. "Now see how YHVH has put a lying spirit into the mouths of all your prophets here," Micaiah told Ahab in conclusion. "But YHVH has pronounced disaster on you."[30]

Micaiah's listeners would not have considered this vision insulting to God merely because it portrayed him as tricky and vindictive. The YHVH of the ninth-century prophets was not a serene, distant ruler, but a deity as proud and bellicose as the kings who ruled in his name.[31] Nevertheless, the seer's explanation earned him a beating and a prison sentence. The beating was administered by the same prophet who had earlier played the part of a bull goring the Syrians, and who did not like being called a liar even if the lie was allegedly God's work. The sentence was imposed by the governor of Samaria, whom Ahab ordered to imprison Micaiah and "feed him on nothing but bread and water until I come back safe and sound."[32] If the king intended by this punishment to intimidate and silence the stubborn naysayer, the tactic failed of its purpose. "If you come back safe and sound," Micaiah replied obstinately, "YHVH has not spoken through me!"[33]

One can well imagine Ahab riding off toward Ramoth-gilead at the head of his army feeling "gloomy and out of temper."[34] Clearly, he had underestimated the prophet's gumption. Had he also underrated his foresight? Perhaps it would be best, in the battle to come, if he fought in the uniform of an anonymous warrior rather than in his all-too-visible royal regalia. While pondering such matters on the long ride north and east, it would not be surprising if his thoughts turned to another prophet who had dared to challenge him openly, and who had predicted his fall—a seer so powerful, so weirdly charismatic, and so antagonistic to his regime that the king called him "my enemy" and "the scourge of Israel."[35] Ahab was not a coward or a superstitious man, but it sometimes seemed to him that despite his successes on the battlefield and at the diplomatic table, his whole reign had been shadowed by the forbidding presence of Elijah the Tishbite.

"As YHVH lives, the God of Israel whom I serve, there shall be neither dew nor rain these years except at my order."[36]

King Ahab had reason to recall these stern and presumptuous words, delivered years earlier before a shocked crowd of courtiers in his throne room at Samaria. With them Elijah steps into history—or into legend, since he lived at a time when written records memorialized the deeds of kings, while the exploits of extraordinary commoners were told and retold as tales.[37] Even in his own lifetime, this formidable figure enjoyed the reputation of a wonder-worker—not just YHVH's messenger, but a man of power fully authorized to act in his master's name. Elijah was not a writer or poet, a court functionary, or (so far as we know) a member of any prophetic guild. He was not even a resident of Israel proper, but a native of Tishbe, a town in the rough frontier colony of Gilead. With his wooly cloak, leather loincloth, and warrior spirit, the longhaired prophet seemed a throwback to an earlier era, when the mantle of prophecy fell on men like Joshua, Gideon, and Samuel—violent rigorists inspired to wreak holy terror on the worshippers of foreign gods.

We do not know what originally brought Elijah to Samaria.[38] Tradition has it that he simply turned up at Ahab's court—a place he despised as a hotbed of Baalist idolatry—to predict that a drought would occur and to declare his God-given ability to con-

tinue or to stop it.[39] More likely, the king summoned him to court
after the drought had begun, to secure YHVH's help in bringing
rain to the parched land.[40] In agrarian kingdoms like Israel, not
that far removed from nomadism, few natural events were more
alarming than a failure of the winter and early spring rains. After
one dry season, people resorted to stored stocks of grain, fruit,
and meat, or went hungry. Two rainless seasons, and the nation's
foreign trade withered along with its barren olive trees and shriv-
eled grapevines. A three-year drought desiccated the grasslands,
forcing farmers to slaughter their livestock and producing all the
horrors of a general famine. Civilization itself could not survive
a dry spell much longer than this. As Isaiah pictured them some
time later, the results of a devastating drought and a foreign invasion might well look the same:

That day, where a thousand vines used to be,
worth one thousand pieces of silver,
all will be briar and thorn.
Men will enter it with arrows and bow,
Since the whole country will revert to briar and thorn.
On any hillside hoed with the hoe
no one will come
for fear of briars and thorns;
it will be pasture for cattle and grazing for sheep.[41]

How to save the people from such a disaster? Throughout the
region, a traditional function of prophets was to intervene with
the gods to bring an end to droughts, floods, infestations, and
other indicators of divine displeasure.[42] No doubt the hundreds
of Phoenician seers brought to Israel by Queen Jezebel were daily
invoking the aid of Baal and Asherah, the male and female deities
whom they worshipped as gods of rain and fertility. The king
would surely have asked Elijah and other prophets of YHVH to

help as well, especially since the Tishbite had the reputation of being able to influence the processes of nature.[43] Elijah's refusal to cooperate—in fact, his substitution of a frightful curse for the sought-after blessing—amounted to a declaration of war on Ahab's regime. No rain or dew until I (acting for YHVH) say so! This was not only to assert the Hebrew God's absolute power to bring rain or withhold it, but also to allege the impotence of Jezebel's nature gods.[44] Little wonder that after refusing to assist the king and denigrating the queen's religion, Elijah fled the country and headed for the trans-Jordanian frontier.

For more than two years, while the crops failed and the land burned, Ahab hunted for him. We are told that the king put the rulers of neighboring nations under oath and made them swear that they had no knowledge of the prophet's whereabouts.[45] At the same time, the search for scapegoats within Israel intensified.

No one doubted that the drought was a form of divine punishment, but was it the result of YHVH's rage against Baalist idolators, or Baal's rage against the arrogant Yahwists? Acting on the latter theory, Jezebel persecuted the prophets of YHVH, some of whom sought refuge in the mountains or left the country as Elijah had done. Acting on the former, militant Yahwists may have subjected the Baalist priests to violent attacks.[46] This internal struggle added urgency to Ahab's hunt for Elijah; past Israelite regimes had been overthrown for lesser reasons than this. Moreover, the king was, after all, a follower of YHVH. His own name and those of his children were based on forms of "YHV," the shorthand name for God. The prophet's claim to be able to end the drought had to be taken seriously. Punishing him was now irrelevant; the point was to find him and persuade him to remove the curse.

In the third year of the drought Elijah returned to Israel voluntarily, because he knew that the rains were about to begin. In the Biblical account, this knowledge takes the form of a divine word: "Go, present yourself to Ahab; I am about to send down rain on the land."[47] Modern readers may wonder if the prophet, who had spent a good deal of his time in exile in seafaring Phoenicia, may have had other sources of information about great thunderstorms moving eastward across the Mediterranean. In any event, Ahab greeted his return with relief as well as indignation. First, the two men exchanged insults; then they entered into negotiations.

Ahab spoke first. "So there you are, you scourge of Israel!"

"Not I," Elijah replied fearlessly. "I am not the scourge of Israel; you and your family are, because you have deserted YHVH and gone after the Baals."[48]

By "desertion," Elijah was referring to the fact that Ahab had permitted his wife to import her religion into Israel. He had built a Baalist temple for her in Samaria, allowed her to fill it with Phoenician priests and priestesses, erected a phallic pole for the worship of Asherah, and apparently remained neutral in disputes between the Baalists and the prophets of YHVH. Elijah did not allege that the royal couple had tried to replace the worship of YHVH with that of Baal; merely (but, to Elijah, of course, not just "merely") that they had accorded other gods divine status.[49] The drought was therefore YHVH's response to an outrageous insult: the worship of other gods on his territory. Having thus saddled the king with responsibility for Israel's suffering, Elijah demanded that he convene a popular assembly on Mount Carmel and require the prophets of Baal and Asherah to attend as well. Ahab's compliance was a token of his desperation, and, perhaps, of his fear of YHVH. Anything to end the drought and the instability that it had provoked!

So began the famous contest of the gods, in which Elijah challenged the Baalist prophets to prepare a bull for sacrifice on their altar, while he alone offered up a similar sacrifice on the broken-down altar of YHVH. The winner would be determined by a divine act: The genuine deity, the god who was truly God, would consume the acceptable offering with fire. Elijah's choice of Mount Carmel as a site for this test of strength was telling. The mountain, overlooking what is now the harbor of Haifa, was the highest point on the vaguely defined Israel-Phoenician border: some 2,000 feet in elevation. The existence at the summit of a functioning Phoenician altar and a ruined Israelite altar suggests that it was disputed territory or land that had recently changed hands. (Building altars in those days was a traditional way of symbolically claiming land.)[50] The contest was not intended to settle a territorial dispute, however, or even to end the drought, but to resolve an intense, long-term conflict between two Israelite factions: the diplomatic compromisers, represented by Ahab, who believed that recognizing YHVH as supreme God did not require forbidding the worship of other gods; and the "YHVH alone" fundamentalists like Elijah, who considered this toleration of other deities idolatry.

Elijah's strategy on the mountain was one of radical simplification. At sunrise he addressed the assembled crowd, which probably consisted of one or two thousand people at most, including the "450 prophets of Baal and 400 prophets of Asherah" maintained by Queen Jezebel.[51] He began by posing a rhetorical question: "How long will you keep hopping on the two boughs?"—that is, wavering like a bird unable to choose between forked branches.[52] According to the prophet, a definitive choice between deities was urgent and unavoidable. One imagines his adamant either/or echoing loudly in the morning air: "If YHVH is God, follow him; if Baal, follow him!" What could be simpler or less ambiguous? Yet the response of the assemblage was silence—a silence that requires explanation.[53]

Were the onlookers simply afraid to reply? Perhaps. Caught between Elijah's implacable gaze and that of Jezebel, uneasy Israelites may well have hesitated, knowing that an incorrect choice could result in their persecution on grounds of idolatry, or, at the very least, a prolongation of the drought. But there were less obvious reasons for their reticence. The alternatives presented by Elijah must have seemed intolerable to many, since each carried with it such grave disadvantages.

Could Israel choose to follow Baal rather than YHVH? For virtually all Israelites (as the prophet must have known), that option was inconceivable. Obviously the God encountered by Moses on Mount Sinai was the Hebrew peoples' incomparable liberator, lawgiver, and battle leader: the divine king of Israel and of Judah. The real question for Ahab and his subjects was not whether Baal should be worshipped as God—of course he should not—but whether affirming YHVH's supremacy required that Israel deny Jezebel and others the right to worship other gods. Elijah's answer has often been called monotheistic, and so it was in the sense that he insisted that YHVH alone was entitled to recognition by Israel's inhabitants, including even her foreign queen. Whether the same God was supreme outside Israel and Judah was not a matter that concerned him. His consuming interests—the spiritual purity and national identity of Israel— were exclusively local.

For this reason, we can imagine how alarming Elijah's intransigence must have seemed to the regime and its defenders, particularly the court officials, wealthy landowners, merchants, soldiers, and others who stood to benefit from the current status quo. Although framed as a defense of Hebrew tradition, the prophet's refusal to tolerate Baalism in any form actually represented a frontal attack on the system of alliances that had made Israel the leading commercial and military power in its region. In a society still based on tribal and clan loyalties, diplomatic marriage was a normal feature of peacemaking. Since one's birth into a particular ethnic or national community defined one's gods, religious conversion was a rarity. From King Solomon's time onward, therefore, the nation's rulers had assumed that while YHVH was clearly Israel's Lord, other gods might also be entitled to recognition, especially by their foreign devotees.

It was accepted international practice for kings like Ahab to permit their foreign wives to worship their own deities in temples provided by the state.[54] In commerce, too, as well as in politics and religion, the hallmark of peaceable relationships was reciprocity. Just as YHVH was supreme in the territory of Israel, with Baal and Asherah playing supporting roles, Baal was considered the chief god in Tyre, and Hadad in Damascus, where resident Hebrew shopkeepers and traders were allowed to worship their own God at their own altars. At least for upper-class Israelites, the advantages of such arrangements were obvious.[55] As a result of the treaty with Tyre, Israel gained amicable foreign relations with a key Phoenician city-state, access to the coastal plain, a ready market for its agricultural exports, a share of the spice trade, and a flood of useful and beautiful craft products.[56] In fact, one could argue that relationships of this sort were essential to the advancement of civilization. Not only did they expose Israel to sophisticated foreign cultures, they enhanced the nation's ability to generate an economic surplus. The surplus could then be used to finance the building of secure, fortified cities, as well as to create a powerful military infrastructure, support a growing class of priests, scribes, and administrators, reinvest in agriculture, and expand the nation's international reputation and influence.[57]

What accounts, then, for the silence of the crowd on Mount Carmel? Why even consider Elijah's policy of "Yahweh alone," which threatened to isolate Israel diplomatically and unleash a bloody struggle against foreign and domestic idolators? The answer may be that prosperity and power, which benefited the elite more than the common people, came at a high cultural price. Internally, the shift from subsistence farming to farming for export was concentrating wealth in fewer hands, increasing the power of the state, and disrupting traditional institutions of justice and welfare.[58] Externally, peaceable relations with Israel's neighbors threatened to integrate Hebrew culture into a regional environment that was polytheistic and, to rigorists like Elijah, hopelessly corrupt. Perhaps, if the practice of Baalism had been limited strictly to Jezebel, her courtiers, and a few foreign traders, it might not have represented a serious problem for faithful monotheists—but there is considerable evidence that native Israelites as well as foreigners dallied with the nature gods and goddesses.

Although the exact extent to which they practiced polytheism openly or in secret cannot be determined, many Israelites seem to have paid obeisance to the ancient fertility gods while continuing to recognize YHVH as their spiritual king.[59] Israel's ethnically diverse population may have contained fairly large numbers of recently conquered Canaanites who continued their traditional worship of the Baalim.[60] Scraps of pottery from the ninth century B.C.E. containing personal names show most Israelite names containing the Yahwist initials "YV" or "YHV," but many others contain letters representing Baal. Also significant is an inscription on a storage jar dating from the same period that reads, "I bless you by YHVH of Samaria and his Asherah."[61] Numerous female figurines, possibly representing the goddess, have also been discovered by archaeologists.[62] Some of Ahab's subjects clearly believed that YHVH had a female consort (in a subordinate role, of course), while others may have considered YHVH and Baal different names for the same supreme God.[63]

Even so, one wonders what made this monolatry (the worship of a supreme God along with the recognition of other gods) so problematic. Three interrelated factors, all brought dramatically into play by the great drought, suggest an answer: national identity, sin, and punishment. During the reign of Ahab, "competing states were emerging at the same time in neighboring Damascus,

Phoenicia, and Moab—each with powerful cultural claims on population groups on the borders with Israel."[64] To the extent that the Hebrew peoples behaved like Syrians, Phoenicians, or Moabites, they might lose that particular national identity and sense of chosenness that made them feel uniquely blessed, and which legitimized their claim to rule the lands promised by YHVH to their ancestors. Furthermore, like many ancient fertility cults, Baalism sexualized religion, generating a worrisome cultural and theological clash with the more ascetic values of the Hebrews.[65] The worship of the Baals, even as minor gods and goddesses, seems to have involved adherents in forbidden practices like the frequenting of male and female sacred prostitutes.[66] Other pagan traditions long practiced in the region—child sacrifice, for example—also served as symbols of alien sin and temptation to a nation struggling to preserve its identity during a period of greatly increased contact with other peoples.[67]

To those feeling guilty about such cultural backsliding, the long drought must have seemed a logical and justifiable expression of YHVH's rage. To embrace the Tyrian alliance, to make peace with another people and its gods, represented a betrayal of both the nation and its jealous God—a "desertion," in Elijah's terms, punishable by death. Tapping into these feelings of fear and shame, the prophet offered the spectators on Mount Carmel the possibility of self-purification through repentance—and through violence.

In the biblical account of the contest, Elijah begins by ridiculing the prophets of Jezebel as they perform their "hobbling dance" around their altar, calling on Baal to accept their sacrifice. "Call louder, for he is a god: he is preoccupied or he is busy, or he has gone on a journey [alternatively, "He has gone to the toilet"]; perhaps he is asleep and will wake up."[68] It is not clear whether this means that Baal does not exist, or that he is powerless in the land consecrated to YHVH, but no matter—the taunt stings either way. The Baal worshippers respond by shouting louder and mutiliating themselves with swords and spears, "as their custom was."[68] But though they continue to perform until late afternoon, when the sacrifice is formally offered, "no voice, no answer, no attention" repays their efforts.

Now it is Elijah's turn to perform. He gathers the crowd closer and rebuilds the ruined altar of YHVH using twelve stones to symbolize the twelve Hebrew tribes and their historic (but now declined) power and unity. He raises the altar high and digs a trench around it, dismembers a bull, and lays the sacrifice on the wood. Then, while the crowd gapes, he douses it again and again with water, until the water overflows the altar and fills the trench. "Answer me, YHVH," he cries, "answer me, so that this people may know that you, YHVH, are God and are winning back their hearts."[70]

If the prophets of Baal could not manage to burn a sacrifice displayed on bone-dry wood, how will Elijah succeed in igniting a soaking-wet altar surrounded by the equivalent of a small pond? YHVH responds with a miracle—or, as we might say, a miracle of nature. The great thunderstorm expected by the prophet has not yet reached the harbor, but the atmosphere is electric in the cooling evening air. A bolt of lightning, precursor of the storm, strikes the wet construction that he has erected at the highest point on the seacoast. The "fire from heaven," considered a manifestation of divine power throughout the ancient world, consumes the sacrifice and the wood, and "licks up" even the water in the trench.[71] As the people fall on their faces crying "YHVH is God! YHVH is God!" Elijah seizes the opportunity to cleanse the nation of foreign pollution. He incites the crowd to capture the Baalist prophets—"Do not let one of them escape!"—and has them taken down the mountain to the river Kishon, where they are butchered like cattle.[72] The Biblical account attributes this massacre to Elijah alone, but since the victims numbered in the hundreds, the frenzied, exalted crowd must have joined in with a will.

Now it is time for another sort of purification. Elijah hears a far-off rumbling and tells Ahab to have dinner in his tent while he climbs back to the top of Mount Carmel. There he assumes a symbolic fetal position and waits until "a cloud, small as a man's hand" rises from the sea, announcing the birth of the storm.[73] Then he rises, and like a great king sending a message to some subordinate, dispatches his servant to tell Ahab to make for the Jezreel Valley before the deluge arrives. Too late. No sooner has the king mounted his chariot than the thunderstorm explodes, drenching the mountain and everyone on it in life-giving rain. Once again, according to the tale, Elijah becomes a wonder-worker possessed with superhuman ability. Gathering up his hairy cloak to free his legs, he runs in front of Ahab's chariot, faster than the king's horses, all the way to the outskirts of Jezreel.[74]

NOW AHAB WAS mounted again behind two warhorses, the reins in his charioteer's hands, his mail coat glistening. This time no prophet ran before him, for he rode with the combined armies of Israel and Judah to confront the Syrians at Ramoth-gilead. The troops of Ahab and Jehosophat filled the landscape as far as the eye could see.[75] More than 1,000 chariots, each drawn by two horses, led the advancing forces. Each vehicle carried at least one warrior in addition to the charioteer, and some carried two: a bowman and a fighter armed with a shield and a lance or spear. Some 10,000 foot soldiers followed this vanguard, together with a small force of mounted cavalrymen, additional archers and slingers, siege weapons, the supply train, and several thousand reserve horses. The entire force stretched out for more than six

miles, giving the farmers and their families on the road to Gilead
something to wonder at and talk about long afterward.

If these spectators hoped to catch a glimpse of their king as
the great parade passed by, however, they were disappointed. On
this expedition, Ahab was not wearing his royal uniform or riding in his usual position at the head of the chariot corps. He had
given Jehosophat that honor, and the Judean king, normally his
second in command, was making the most of the opportunity.
Dressed in full regalia, the sun glinting off his gold-plated breast-
plate, he looked every inch the supreme war leader. Ahab followed some distance back in his anonymous armor, his face
composed but his spirit profoundly uneasy.

Why go into battle wearing this disguise, with his heart quak-
ing like that of a frightened recruit? The ostensible reason was the
prediction made a few weeks earlier by Micaiah ben-Imlah that he
would fall in battle with the Syrians. "If you come back safe and
sound," the prophet had said, "YHVH has not spoken through
me." But Micaiah invariably preached disaster. His words would
not have disturbed Ahab nearly so much had they not awakened
echoes of another prophecy, this one pronounced by a far more
credible source—his old nemesis, Elijah. A fortune or misfortune
told was one thing, a curse quite another, especially when uttered
by a man of power. What made Ahab cringe inwardly as he recalled his last encounter with the prophet was that Elijah had not
just predicted his downfall but had condemned him. Worst of all,
he knew in his bones that the condemnation was justified.

What had possessed him, in the first place, to negotiate for
the vineyard of his wealthy neighbor, Naboth? The vineyard ad-
joined the grounds of his palace in Samaria. For some reason,
Ahab wanted—no, he needed—a garden planted on that parcel
of land. A garden producing fresh vegetables for his and Jezebel's
table—was that so much to ask? He offered Naboth better land
in exchange for the vineyard; he offered a generous cash payment;

but the old fool would not consider parting with it on any terms, not even to please his king. He held the antiquated view that land belonged to one's ancestral family and that no part of it could ever be bought, sold, or exchanged.[76] For some reason—was it the insult to his authority? Naboth's reliance on an absurd and out-dated law?—Ahab found himself unable to accept the refusal. He had returned to the palace unable to eat or sleep, his malaise so disturbing to Jezebel that when he finally revealed the reason for it, she had flashed out, sarcastically, "You make a fine king of Is-rael, and no mistake! Get up and eat; cheer up, and you will feel better; I will get you the vineyard of Naboth of Jezreel myself."[77]

Recalling that evening, Ahab felt remorse pierce him like an arrow.[78] Legally, he was guiltless in the affair of the vineyard. He had had no idea that his clever, unscrupulous wife would write letters in his name, sealed with his seal, commanding the city's council of elders to frame his hapless neighbor for blasphemy and sedition. Knowing that two eyewitnesses were necessary to secure a conviction in a capital case, she had ordered the council to find two liars who would testify publicly that Naboth had cursed God and threatened the king in their presence.[79] Since no official de-pendent on the royal family's favor would dare disobey such a command, the outcome was foreordained. Naboth was duly ac-cused, convicted, and stoned to death outside the city walls—the usual punishment for such serious crimes.

Ahab remembered Jezebel telling him immediately after-ward, as he lay wearily on his couch, that his neighbor had died a felon, and that his property was therefore the crown's by forfeit. "Get up!" she had said with an air of superiority that bordered on contempt. "Take possession of the vineyard which Naboth of Jezreel would not give you for money, for Naboth is no longer alive, he is dead."[80]

What had he felt upon hearing this announcement? Joy? Yes. Dread? That, too. But three years later, on the road to Ramoth-

gilead, what struck him most forcibly (again, that sharp bite of remorse) was that he had not felt at all shocked or surprised. He
had known nothing—yet he knew everything. When his wife
promised him Naboth's vineyard, he did not ask how she would
acquire it. When she announced the man's death, he did not in-
quire about his crime or the circumstances of his conviction. His
silence spoke for him. Just get me that vineyard, my love, and I
won't ask how you did it. Procure the murder of an innocent man,
pervert the court system, do what you will, and I will think about
something else.

Of course, without knowing, he had known. When, to his astonishment, he had found Elijah waiting for him in the dead
man's vineyard, he could offer no defense to the prophet's accusation—an indictment all the more chilling for being delivered in
a quiet, almost intimate tone. Observing the two men whisper-
ing together intently, workers in the vineyard might have thought
that they were old friends sharing a secret.

"YHVH says this," Elijah had said, his mouth close to Ahab's
ear. "You have committed murder; would you now you take possession as well? For this—and YHVH says this—in the very place
where the dogs lapped up Naboth's blood, the dogs will lap up
your blood too."[81]

Ahab had responded in the voice of a guilty conspirator. "So
you have found me out, O my enemy."

"Yes, I have found you out," Elijah had replied. "Because you
have committed yourself to doing what is evil in the sight of
YHVH, I will bring disaster upon you. I will make a clean sweep
of you. I will wipe out every male belonging to the family of Ahab,
fettered or free. All of Ahab's line who die in the town shall be
devoured by dogs, and all who die in the open country shall be devoured by the birds of the sky."

Horrible! Even now, sweating in his suit of armor, the recollection of that curse froze the king's blood. Not only to have one's

line extinguished, but to have them eaten by wild creatures! If they were not accorded a decent burial, even their memories would be blotted out. Moreover, by naming Ahab's male heirs, Elijah's prophecy clearly aimed to end the dynasty founded by his father, Omri. Grimacing painfully, the king bowed his head as if to YHVH himself, but Elijah was not yet finished.

"The dogs shall devour Jezebel in the field of Jezreel."

Sickened by guilt and fear, Ahab had gone into mourning for Naboth and, prospectively, for his own wife and family. He tore his clothes, dressed in sackcloth, fasted, and meditated according to the Hebrew custom—one way of acknowledging responsibility publicly for the judicial murder. In recognition of this repentance, says the story, YHVH delayed the punishment of his family until his son had become king.[82] This "amendment" may have been inserted later on to account for the events that occurred after Elijah's death. Or the prophet himself, acting as God's representative, may have decided against an outright assault on the dynasty, since he seems to have nurtured the hope of "winning back hearts" for YHVH and reforming the regime from within.[83] In any case, when Ramoth-gilead finally came into view and Ahab saw King ben-Hadad's chariots drawn up in the plain before its walls, he must have wondered whether either his repentance or his disguise would protect him from the judgment of an angry God.

The Syrian chariots moved forward quickly to intercept the invading force before it closed in on the city. Ahab expected as much and ordered his chariot commanders to concentrate their strength in the center. As the two armies drew together, however, ben-Hadad's commanders began to maneuver strangely. Rather than attacking en masse, they divided their forces and made lightning forays into the forward ranks of the Israelite chariot corps, wheeling about and withdrawing when they encountered serious resistance. It was as if they were determined *not* to fight, at least not yet.

But of course! Ahab of Israel was one of the outstanding military leaders of his generation. Three times he had met ben-Hadad in battle, and three times he had defeated him. At Qarqar, he had even helped drive the great Assyrian army from the field. If he were the Syrian king, thought Ahab, he would order his commanders to delay an all-out attack on the Israelite army. He would command them to avoid engaging with anyone but Ahab himself, to find the Israelite king, and to kill him.

In a few minutes, Ahab's hunch was vindicated. Catching sight of King Jehosophat with his royal armor ablaze, the Syrians shouted to one another and closed in on their prey. Jehosophat quickly recognized that he was under attack. As his charioteer turned to confront the onrushing Syrians, he hoisted his spear, shook it, and gave the Judean war cry. The Syrian commander in the lead immediately reined in his horses, and waved the other attackers off. This was not the king of Israel. Royally outfitted or not, he was not the man targeted for death by King ben-Hadad.[84]

Ahab's disguise had worked. Ben-Hadad's quest had been fruitless. Now the Syrians had no choice but to defend the city. They engaged the Hebrew armies full force on the plain before Ramoth-gilead, and the fighting continued all morning, with first one side and then the other gaining the advantage. Ahab's disguise did not prevent him from doing what he did best; his chariot left a trail of dead and wounded Syrians in its wake. His own war cry rang out, and he was just about to strike another blow when he suddenly gasped and addressed his charioteer in an altered tone of voice. "Turn the horses around and get me behind the lines; I'm wounded."[85] Twisting about, the charioteer saw the shaft of a Syrian arrow jutting out between the metal plates of Ahab's armor. Apparently by chance, the king had been struck in the chest, and the arrow had penetrated deeply.[86]

At least where his own troops were concerned, Ahab's disguise meant nothing. Everyone on the Israelite side and many of

the Judeans knew him on sight. Now a more important deception was required; the men who had followed him into battle for
years, and who considered him invincible, must not know that he
was seriously wounded. Ahab ordered the driver to withdraw to
a spot behind the active fighters, on high ground within plain
view of the bulk of the army. His retainers propped him up in the
rear of the vehicle facing the Syrian forces and held him there,
upright, throughout the afternoon, while the battle raged and the
blood from his wound flowed steadily into the bottom of the
chariot. Ahab's life ebbed with the setting sun. Finally, there was
no longer any possibility of disguise. At sundown a shout ran
through the camp: "Every man back to his town, every man back
to his country; the king is dead!"[87]

The army disintegrated overnight, ending the campaign
against Ramoth-gilead and fulfilling Micaiah ben-Imlah's
prophecy. The king's body was returned to Samaria, where he was
buried with all the honors due a monarch, statesman, and war
hero. Those who shared Elijah's vision, however, saw the story of
Ahab ending not with honor but in disgrace. Years later, they recalled how his war chariot was washed in the public pool just outside the town, close to the site of Naboth's execution. The waters
of the pool dissolved the blood coagulated at the bottom of the
chariot, and stray dogs lapped up the bloody water, fulfilling the
first part of Elijah's prophecy. When the prostitutes of the town
bathed in the pool as well, as was their custom, the king's degra-
dation, at least in the eyes of the Yahwists, was complete.[88]

FROM THE CONTEST of the gods on Mount Carmel to his symbolic triumph at the pool of Samaria, Elijah's epic story was one
of repeated victories. Yet, one cannot say that the prophet ever
struck a decisive blow against the regime he detested. Under his
leadership, a certain type of monotheism—zealous, ascetic, and

intensely nationalistic—had become a force to reckon with in the
northern kingdom. Very likely, although Elijah is pictured in stories as a loner, a collective movement had already begun to crys-
tallize around him during his lifetime.[89] Even so, while he lived,
the movement stopped short of challenging the Omrid dynasty's
right to rule. It was as if the prophet sensed that to overthrow the
existing system, as corrupt, compromising, and power hungry as
it was, would take an unprecedented bloodbath. Elijah's prefer-
ence was to deal with sinful kings face-to-face in the hope of res-
cuing them and the nation from YHVH's wrath. He condemned
only individuals, not the system itself.[90] It would be left to his disciple, Elisha, to raise the struggle to a more massive and destructive level.

Elisha! A name evocative of miracles and of terror; a figure
creepily familiar in an era of religious politics and fundamental-
ist violence. One cannot help but wonder what the young militant really thought of his legendary master. His holy cause—the
return of Israel to pure monotheism—was Elijah's. What drove
Elisha, however, was a calculus of means: the conviction that this
goal could not be achieved without overthrowing the Omrid dynasty, putting an end to the system of treaties and diplomatic
marriages supported by the monarchy, and ridding Israel of all
foreign priests and prophets. Revolution, not reform, was the answer. To rid Israel of the hated Omrid regime, allies would be
needed: dissident aristocrats and army officers, zealous prophets,
angry farmers, perhaps even foreign kings.[91] The movement
therefore required a new type of leader—not just a charismatic
figure, but one with a highly motivated, well-organized following,
a stomach for mass violence, and a willingness to plunge into the
murky waters of political conspiracy.

For better or worse, these were Elisha's strengths. From the
start of his prophetic career he had maintained close ties with
members of the prophetic brotherhoods, living with them as

their leader, sharing their experiences, and solving their everyday problems.[92] In modern terms, we would call him a party man— one far more inclined than Elijah to work with and through others to achieve his purposes. One might also call him a cult leader. His hold over his followers was bolstered by his reputation for exercising a wide range of supernatural gifts, including clairvoyance, the ability to blind his enemies, hypnotic powers, extrasensory perception, and magical skills, as well as healing powers and control over the processes of nature.[93] His fame as a seer, healer, and magician extended beyond Israel to Tyre and Damascus. And his taste for holy violence was equally legendary. According to one well-known story, when some small boys mocked him by calling him "baldhead," he cursed them in the name of YHVH, and they were forthwith savaged by wild bears.[94]

Elisha's first challenge was to establish his absolute authority over the Yahwist movement. Precisely because his program was so much more radical than Elijah's, it was necessary for him to cloak himself, literally and figuratively, in the great prophet's mantle. Two stories circulated, one deriving his legitimacy as leader from Elijah, the other founding his revolutionary program directly on the word of God.

The first story—one of the most celebrated in the Bible— climaxes with Elijah's miraculous ascension into heaven.

> Now as they went on, talking as they went, a chariot of fire appeared and horses of fire, coming between the two of them; and Elijah went up to heaven in the whirlwind. Elisha saw it, and shouted, "My father! My father! Chariot of Israel and its chargers!" Then he lost sight of him, and taking hold of his clothes he tore them in half.[95]

In addition to illustrating the prophet's special status in the eyes of YHVH and his disciple's grief at the loss of his revered master, this tale made a political point. According to Elisha, Elijah had asked him beforehand, "What can I do for you before I am taken from you?" In reply, Elisha had requested that he be treated as the prophet's son and heir.[96] Elijah had then stated, "If you see me while I am being taken from you, it shall be as you ask; if not, it will not be so."[97] Having had the vision, in short, validated the disciple's claim to the leadership. Immediately afterward, he was empowered to perform a miracle himself: He divided the waters of the Jordan by striking the river with his master's cloak, and the brotherhood of prophets bowed to him as its leader.[98]

The second story begins with Elijah's escape from Israel after his massacre of the Baalist prophets at Mount Carmel. With Queen Jezebel swearing revenge upon him, the prophet fled in despair to Mount Sinai, where, according to tradition, he heard the voice of YHVH in the sound of a "gentle breeze."[99] In the Biblical account, Elijah indicts the "sons of Israel" before God for apostasy. The people "have deserted you," he complains, "broken down your altars and put your prophets to the sword. I am the only one left and they want to kill me."[100] YHVH's response is to condemn the entire Omrid dynasty and its supporters. He orders Elijah to anoint a Syrian official called Hazael king of Syria, to anoint a Hebrew army commander called Jehu king of Israel, and to name a farmer named Elisha as Elijah's own successor. Then he predicts (and authorizes) a storm of violence:

> Anyone who escapes the sword of Hazael will be put to death by Jehu; and anyone who escapes the sword of Jehu will be put to death by Elisha. But I shall spare seven thousand in Israel: all the knees that have not bent before Baal, all the mouths that have not kissed him.[101]

The events referred to in this encounter—a coup d'état and war of aggression by Hazael of Syria and a bloody rebellion by

Jehu—actually took place in Elisha's lifetime.[102] For some time, the prophet had cultivated powerful connections in Damascus, where he had a reputation as a famous healer.[103] When ben-Hadad invited him to come to the capital to consult with him about a serious illness, he saw his chance. While there, he met with an army officer named Hazael, described in a contemporary Assyrian inscription as "the son of a nobody" (that is, not an aristocrat)—an ambitious plotter whom he had determined to place on ben-Hadad's throne.[104] Whether this was his first meeting with the Syrian we do not know, but it seems likely that the two conspirators had met before. In the biblical story, Elisha advises Hazael to tell the king that he will recover from his illness, although, he confesses, "YHVH has shown me that he will certainly die." Then his face changes mysteriously—he sees the future—and he weeps.

"Why," Hazael asked, "does my lord weep?"

"Because I know all the harm you will do the Israelites: you will burn down their fortresses, put their picked warriors to the sword, dash their little children to pieces, rip open their pregnant women."

"But how can your servant, who is a mere dog, achieve anything so great?"

"In a vision from YHVH," Elisha replied, "I have seen you king of Syria."

The would-be king lost no time carrying out his implied mandate. Returning to ben-Hadad's sickroom, he informed the king that Elisha had predicted his complete recovery. The next day, taking advantage of the old man's helplessness and trust, Hazael returned to his room, placed a wet blanket over his face, and suffocated him.[105]

Shortly after assuming power in Damascus, Hazael fulfilled the rest of Elisha's brutal prophecy. At a major battle at Ramoth-gilead, his forces succeeded in wounding King Jehoram of Israel and forcing the withdrawal of the Hebrew forces.[106] Then, after an Israelite general named Jehu had seized power in Samaria, he captured Israel's trans-Jordanian possessions, invaded Israel, and ravaged the country down to the coastal plain, reducing both Israel and Judah to the status of vassal states.[107] Newly discovered archeological evidence suggests that in the years after 835 B.C.E., Hazael "controlled the upper Jordan valley and significant areas in northeastern Israel—and devastated major Israelite administrative centers in the fertile Jezreel valley as well."[108] But the most remarkable and controversial discovery was made in 1993 at Tel Dan, site of the ancient city of Dan in northern Israel. There, etched into the broken pieces of a black basalt monument, are fragmentary phrases written in Aramean that, reconstructed, read as follows:

[I killed Jeho]ram son of [Ahab] king of Israel, and [I] killed [Ahaz]isahu son of [Jehoram kin]g of the House of David. And I set [their towns into ruins and turned] their land into [desolation].[109]

The inscription, it seems clear, is from an obelisk or statue erected at Dan by Hazael of Syria. Its great interest for historians lies particularly in the phrase "House of David," for this is the only extrabiblical evidence so far discovered of the existence of a Davidic dynasty. But another feature is particularly significant for our story: Hazael's claim to have killed the Israelite and Judean kings. According to the Bible, it was not the Syrian king but Jehu—and, just behind the scenes, Elisha—who was responsible for these two murders—and for a plethora of homicides afterwards.

King Jehoram of Israel, we are told, was injured, not killed, at the battle of Ramoth-gilead. He retired to Jezreel to tend his wounds, leaving in charge his chief commander, Jehu. Seizing this opportunity, Elisha dispatched a young member of the brotherhood of prophets to go up to the Israelite camp, take Jehu into a private room, and anoint him king of Israel. The fledgling prophet did as he was instructed. He poured oil over Jehu's head, declared him king, and ordered him, in Elisha's words, "to strike down the family of Ahab your master." When Jehu's officers discovered what had happened, "they all took their cloaks and spread them under him on the bare steps; they sounded the trumpet and shouted, 'Jehu is king!'"[110]

The would-be monarch moved quickly to take advantage of Jehoram's weakness. After ordering his men to stay in camp, he made for Jezreel with a troop of hand-picked horsemen, driving his chariot "like a madman." At length, his chariot was spotted by the watchmen manning the tower on the city wall. The injured king sent messengers out to greet him, but Jehu refused to parley with them. Sensing trouble, Jehoram left his sickbed, harnessed his chariot, and drove painfully out to meet him in the company of King Ahaziah of Judah, who had been staying with him in the city. The confrontation between the wounded king and the furious usurper set a tone of horror that would color politics in Israel for decades to come.

As soon as he saw his chief commander, Jehoram offered the ritual greeting: "Is all well, Jehu?" The general's reply must have sickened him. "What a question! When all the while the prostitutions and countless sorceries of your mother Jezebel go on."

At this, Jehoram wheeled and fled, saying to Ahaziah, "Treason, Ahaziah!" But Jehu had drawn his bow; he struck Jehoram between the shoulder blades, the arrow went through the king's heart, and he sank down in his chariot. "Pick him up," Jehu said to Bidkar, his equerry, "and throw him into the field of Naboth of Jezreel."[111]

Aghast, the Judean king, Ahaziah, lashed his horses and tried to escape, but Jehu's men hunted him down as well and wounded him. Gravely injured, he managed to drive the team to Megiddo, a city of refuge, but died there of his wounds a day or two later.

Meanwhile, Jehu returned to Jezreel to deal with the queen mother. Threatened with almost certain death, Ahab's widow rose to new heights of dignity, courage, and vituperation. First, in token of her position and beauty, Jezebel "made up her eyes with kohl and adorned her head." Then, as Jehu came through the gateway in his chariot, she appeared at the window of her palace, high above the courtyard, and greeted him with undisguised contempt. "Is all well . . . you murderer of your master?"

That was enough for Jehu. At his bidding, three of her eunuchs threw her down into the courtyard where "her blood spattered the walls and the horses; and Jehu rode over her." After a time, he gave an order to bury her since, after all, she was a king's daughter. But nothing could be found of her but her skull, feet, and hands. The dogs had eaten her body, fulfilling the terrible prophecy of Elijah the Tishbite.[112]

We are left with a question: Did Jehu kill the Israelite and Judean kings? Or, as Hazael boasted on his monument at the city of Dan, did he, the Syrian conqueror, kill them? The likely answer is both. Given Elisha's manipulative string-pulling and his contact with both men, Hazael probably viewed Jehu as his agent, or at least as part of the same conspiracy against the Israelite regime, and may well have supported his rebellion.[113] In any event, the violence unleashed by these assassinations now unrolled with terrifying fatality. Jehu ordered the surrender of Samaria and, to awe the city's residents and break their will, demanded the severed heads of the late king's seventy sons. The city elders murdered the princes and brought their heads to Jezreel in baskets, where they were displayed in two heaps at the entrance to the city gates. "Jehu then killed everyone of the House of Ahab surviving in Jezreel, all his leading men, his close friends, his priests; he did not leave a single one alive."[114] But this was just the beginning. On the way to Samaria, Jehu and his troops met the Judean king's brothers and killed them as well. Then, after arriving at the capital, he massacred all the survivors of Ahab's "family"—again, a term including friends, relatives, chief officials, priests, and political supporters.[115]

The final act of Jehu's rebellion echoed Elijah's purge of Baalist prophets at Mount Carmel, but on a larger scale. The new king invited all the prophets of Baal and Asherah residing in Israel to attend a sacred service at the temple in Samaria built by Ahab for Jezebel. Summoned by messengers, the Baalists arrived en masse. We do not know their exact number, but they "packed into the temple of Baal until it was full from wall to wall." Jehu himself offered a sacrifice on the temple altar as a ruse. Then, having stationed eighty men outside to catch anyone trying to escape, he had his soldiers massacre all the celebrants, leaving not a single person alive. They completed their work by burning the pole sacred to Asherah and demolishing the temple, "making it into a latrine, which it still is today."[116]

So ended the revolution fomented by Elisha. As one historian notes, "Elisha was directly behind this act of horror. It was he who designated as king this eager partisan of uncontaminated Yahwism, and it is hard to imagine that he could have been blind to the fact that in the struggle against Baal and his worshippers, Jehu was to wade through a sea of blood."[117] In at least one sense, the revolt was successful: The Omrid dynasty was overthrown, and Baalism as a cult supported by the Israelite court was eliminated. One might also say that Elijah and Elisha provided monotheists ever after with models of militant faith and resistance to idolatrous authority. But, as Hebrew prophets for the next two centuries were to testify, the worship of other gods among the common people continued; new dynasties in Israel and Judah proved just as high-handed and oppressive as the Omrids had been (if not more so); and at least one Judean king set up altars to Baal and Asherah in the Jerusalem Temple itself.[118] The philosopher Martin Buber summarizes the consequences with his usual insight:

> The worship of the Baal was broken down, but the prophetic protest shows us not only that the ancient sexual rites flourished in the very shadow of the temple, but also that people treated with JHVH Himself as with a mighty Baal, from whom they wished to buy at the price of many offerings the unfettered freedom of profane life.[119]

Not only did idolatry continue in new forms, but the great international dilemma confronting the Israelite nation remained unsolved. How could YHVH's followers retain their unique spiritual and national identity without engaging in perpetual holy war against domestic idolators and foreign unbelievers? In theory, they could simply sever all contacts with the profane world around them, but, as events were now to show, isolation was never a real option either for the Israelites or their neighbors. Jehu's massacres "swept away the foreign alliances which entailed the danger of religious compromise," and Israel's trade with the Phoenician city-states declined to a trickle.[120] The Omrid queen mother of Judah seized power in Jerusalem, and relations between Israel and Judah deteriorated to the point that the Hebrew kingdoms once again became bitter enemies.[121] Meanwhile, Syria's King Hazael defeated both Jehu and his son, occupying large portions of Israel and forcing the king of Judea to buy him off with the temple treasures. By 800 B.C.E., Israel's army had been reduced to "fifty horsemen, ten chariots, and ten thousand foot soldiers." "The king of Syria had destroyed them," says the Bible, "making them like the dust that is trampled under foot."[122]

Clearly, national isolation meant weakness and defeat. But

Omrid-style diplomacy opened the door to the importation of polytheistic religious cults. What, then, was the alternative? If Israel had possessed the military and economic capacity to become a great empire, Jehu might have been tempted to impose Yahwism on the region by force. But a startling development—the return of the Assyrians to Syria-Palestine—demonstrated the futility of such dreams. Not long after Jehu assumed power in Samaria, Shalmaneser III returned to the West, and his invincible army marched on Damascus. In a desperate attempt to avoid defeat and occupation by Hazael's troops, Jehu offered to make Israel a vassal state of Assyria, to pay Shalmaneser tribute, and to assist him against his enemies. Early in his reign, he journeyed to the Assyrian capital of Nimrud, on the Tigris River, with a retinue bearing silver, gold, and other items of tribute, and prostrated before the emperor. This act of submission bought Israel a brief respite from Hazael's depredations, but trouble in their Mesopotamian homeland soon forced the Assyrians to withdraw, and Israel's affliction continued for another generation.

Midway through the next century, led by an emperor of a new type, the Assyrians would return in force, and everything would change—even the definition of monotheism and the role of its prophets. For the moment, however, it is worth recalling that Jehu's submission to Shalmaneser, so humiliating to Israelite nationalists, earned that king a strange distinction. Go today to the British Museum in London and enter its huge collection of Assyrian artifacts. There, in an unassuming floor exhibit, side by side with other steles and obelisks, you will discover a shiny black monument about six feet tall. Circling the slender structure in vivid relief are representations of five processions, each one displaying human figures in profile. The figures carry baskets or other objects, or lead tethered animals to present to another figure who holds the symbols of high office. This is the Black

Obelisk of Shalmaneser III, which celebrates the receipt of tribute from five subject peoples.

In the second row of figures from the top, a bearded man in
foreign dress prostrates before the emperor. He is identified in the
Assyrian annals as "Yaua": Jehu, king of Israel.[123] The cuneiform
caption over the procession describes the tribute borne by the Israelites: "Silver, gold, a golden vase, a golden dish, golden buckets,
a load of tin, a staff for the hand of the king, wooden hunting
spears."[124] This is the only contemporary pictorial representation
that we have of any figure in the Bible. On Shalmaneser's obelisk,
carved almost 3,000 years ago, the murderous usurper whom
Elisha made king of Israel achieves artistic immortality.

CHAPTER II

✳

"What Are Your Endless Sacrifices to Me?"

—ISAIAH 1:11

I N THE COLD JANUARY of 733, wrapped in his winter cloak, King Ahaz of Judah walked just outside the walls of Jerusalem on the Fuller's Field road. He had finally yielded to the wishes of the bodyguards who insisted on accompanying him on his tour, but he kept them at a distance while he crouched down near a spring-fed pool, inspecting the conduit that led to a system of cisterns and storage pipes located just inside the walls.[1] Yes—the conduit was clean and well protected. It would continue to function during the siege so long as his archers and slingers kept the enemy away from the pool, which they should easily be able to do. With a supply of fresh water guaranteed, the city could probably hold out for several months, at least—long enough to permit the Assyrians to return to the region and to dispose of the armies now marching toward his capital.

Ahaz's bodyguards would not have interfered with his inspection, of course, but he did not want any distractions while he pondered the grave situation confronting the city and his regime. Moreover, he had asked his trusted advisor, Isaiah ben-Amoz, to attend him, and was determined to conduct that conversation in private. Now twenty-one, having occupied the throne for scarcely one year, the boyish king faced the most serious crisis in his nation's history. An attack on Judah by King Rezin's powerful Syrian army would have been difficult enough to repulse, but Rezin had allied himself with Ahaz's co-religionists, the Israelites, and both armies were now closing in on Jerusalem after devastating the rest of the country.

What had triggered this crisis initially was an assassination. Five years earlier, Ahaz recalled, Israel's King Menahem had submitted to the authority of the Assyrian emperor—a fearsome character known to the Hebrews as King Pul. To keep him from attacking Samaria and occupying the northern kingdom, Menachem had paid an enormous bribe, extracted from Israel's men of substance. Virtually every other ruler in the region had done the same.[2] This was not the result of cowardice. Many knowledgeable people, including Isaiah, believed the Assyrian army to be the most effective fighting force ever assembled. The prophet himself had written a frightening poem about it:

> Its arrows are sharpened,
> its bows all bent,
> the hoofs of its horses are like flint,
> its chariot wheels like tornadoes.

> Its roar is the roar of a lioness,
> like a lion cub it roars,
> it growls and seizes its prey,
> it bears it off, and no one can snatch it back.

> Growling against it, that day,
> like the growling of the sea.
> Only look at the country: darkness and distress,
> and the light flickers out in shadows.[3]

After submitting to King Pul, it was doubly dangerous to break with him, since he was known to punish rebellion even more mercilessly than resistance. Even so, there were many patriots in Israel (and, Ahaz well knew, in Judah) who preferred to fight the arrogant conqueror rather than pay him tribute and submit to his dictates. When King Menahem died, he was succeeded by his son, also a member of the pro-Assyrian party, but the young man was quickly assassinated by an army officer named Pekah—a violent opponent of Assyrian expansionism. Pekah went immediately to Damascus and concluded an alliance with Syria's King Rezin. Both rulers then demanded that Judah join their coalition and prepare to defend the region against an inevitable Assyrian attack.

In 734, when the Israelite-Syrian delegation arrived in Jerusalem with its list of nonnegotiable demands, Ahaz's father, although in poor health, was still on the throne. King Jotham, who was not on good terms with either of the rebel kings, sent the delegation packing without giving them a reply.[4] At around the same time, news came that King Pul was marching west with an enormous army to put down the rebellion and reestablish his control over the region. Furious and desperate, the Israelite and Syrian rulers launched a two-pronged invasion of Judah. Either Jotham would cooperate, or they would replace him with a puppet king of their own.[5] The old man never had a chance to change his mind. In the midst of the crisis, he died, and Ahaz inherited the throne.[6]

What was the young king to do? While waiting for Isaiah to arrive, he reviewed the alternatives. His instinct, like his father's, was to refuse to join the coalition, but there was great division in Judah, with many of his subjects (especially those outside Jerusalem) and even some court advisors favoring a battle to the death against the hated Assyrians.[7] By now, the forces of Pekah and Rezin had advanced deep into the country, inflicting a series of grave defeats on the Judean army, taking large numbers of soldiers and civilians as prisoners, and capturing the approaches to the capital. One Israelite champion alone had already killed Ahaz's brother, the controller of the palace, and the army's top general.[8] There were reports that to secure divine aid in averting a siege, the king had made his own son "pass through the fire"— an ancient Caananite custom, forbidden by Hebrew law, requiring the ruler to sacrifice his firstborn son to avert a national disaster.[9] If he had done so, however, the magic had proved useless. There was virtually nothing left of the country but Jerusalem and its immediate environs.

Food was not yet scarce in Jerusalem, but the mood of the city was bleak and contentious. The horrors of a long siege were well understood. When the last scrap of food was consumed, people in extremis—even believers in YHVH—had been known to kill and eat their own children.[10] Two motives could make the sufferings of a long siege bearable: the zeal to defend one's independence and way of life, and the fear of a great massacre if the city were to fall. In the present case, however, the Israelite and Syrian attackers were offering to rid the entire region of Assyrian domination, and there would be no mass murder of civilians if the city were to surrender. The people of Jerusalem had little love for the Israelites, who had entered the capital forty years earlier, destroyed part of the city wall, and pillaged the treasures of the temple.[11] But, if one had to choose between conquerors, better to lose one's independence to fellow Hebrews than to Assyrian idolators. Better King Pekah than King Pul.

Ahaz was well aware of this sentiment. Holding out against Pekah and Rezin was not a popular course of action—not even in the capital, where he had his strongest base of support. He could relieve Jerusalem in a moment (and avert the threat of an internal revolt) by adhering to the anti-Assyrian coalition. But the Assyrians were smashing their way toward an inevitable confrontation with the rebel kings. If Ahaz saved Jerusalem now by joining the rebellion, how long would it be before King Pul's legions appeared at her gates with their battering rams and battle towers? Then the Judeans might lose much more than their capital. The survivors of that siege could well be exiled to the far corners of the Assyrian empire.

The worried king was grateful, yet a bit uneasy, to see Isaiah striding briskly down the road toward him with a small boy in tow. Grateful, since the prophet had been giving sound advice to the royal family since the days of Ahaz's grandfather, King Uzziah. Uneasy, because one never quite knew what the volatile prophet might say or do.

Despite his intense, authoritative manner, Isaiah was not much older than the king—thirty or thirty-five at most. For the past decade, ever since the end of Uzziah's reign, he had been preaching to large crowds in the temple and advising Judean kings privately on political matters.[12] His stature, of course, was undeniable. Even without his aristocratic credentials and keen intellect, the brilliance and passion of his rhetoric (which a growing number of disciples were now transcribing in written form) would have won him an honored place among Jerusalem's cultural elite.[13] Of course, being a prophet, he was moody and sometimes spoke in obscure, symbolic language. But what Ahaz found most disconcerting was that even as a prophet he was impossible to classify.

Like his countrymen, the king was familiar with prophets of two types. Some—the court prophets—were responsible insiders who advised the ruler how to rule more justly, and how to make decisions of which YHVH would approve. King David's chief advisor, Nathan, had been just such a man: highly principled and courageous, but deeply loyal to the monarchy he served.[14] Others, however, like the prophets Elijah and Elisha, were intemperate, visionary outsiders, often from the rural hinterlands, whose mission (or obsession) was to expose the injustice, corruption, and idolatry of wicked regimes and prophesy their destruction. These independent prophets also held out the hope of future salvation for those remaining true to YHVH, but this was not much use to kings like Ahaz, who craved solutions to urgent problems existing entirely in the present.

Was Isaiah a court prophet and political realist like Nathan, the sort of person on whom a ruler could rely without losing either his crown or his soul? He had certainly played that role in the past. Or was he a utopian visionary like Elijah—a prophet who would just as soon see the king and his supporters destroyed as saved? His recent speeches in the temple had sounded a note almost this uncompromising.[15] With most of Judah in flames and the city preparing for a siege, the crowds in the capital were flocking to Jerusalem's holiest place for words of consolation, explanation, and advice. What they heard from Isaiah, however, sent them away shaking their heads and muttering, as if they had been given an insoluble puzzle to solve.

Standing in the temple court, the prophet spoke in a furious rapture, alternating vituperative criticism of Judah's ruling class with fantastic visions of future peace and security. His speeches were not exactly subversive—he was no Elisha, calling for an overthrow of the regime—but, to a king needing a morale-booster during a time of great trouble, they were not helpful. In fact, considering the country's desperate situation, the words of its leading prophet seemed strangely unresponsive to the nation's immediate needs. When Isaiah chanted, "Your land is desolate, your towns burned down, your fields—strangers lay them waste before your eyes," he seemed almost triumphant, as if an angry, vengeful deity were speaking through his lips.

The daughter of Zion is left
like a shanty in a vineyard,
like a shed in a melon patch,
like a besieged city.

Had YHVH not left us a few survivors,
we should be like Sodom
we should now be like Gomorrah.[16]

What possible good could it do at this critical juncture for worshippers to be told that they were "a sinful nation, a people weighed down with guilt" who deserved punishment for turning away from God?[17] In most of his speeches, the prophet avoided such blanket condemnations. His chief targets were the irresponsible leaders he had been denouncing ever since King Uzziah's time, in particular, idolatrous and dissipated aristocrats,[18] corrupt officials who filled their own pockets by exploiting the poor and neglecting the weak,[19] and greedy landowners "who add house to house and join field to field until everywhere belongs to them and they are the sole inhabitants of the land."[20] Recently, his criticism displayed a ferocity that would not have been tolerated in a man of lesser rank. "Your princes are rebels," he thundered, "accomplices of thieves. All are greedy for profit and chase after bribes. They show no justice to the orphan, and the cause of the widow is never heard."[21]

The common people could only agree—but since Isaiah was not calling for revolution, it was hard to see what practical use they could they make of these denunciations. Did he really expect the rich and powerful to stop oppressing the poor and weak because he urged them to? And, if they did so, would Rezin and Pekah lift the siege of Jerusalem? Would King Pul return to Assyria?

The king asked himself the same questions. Religion, he understood, offered two explanations for a disastrous military defeat: Either the god of the conquered people had shown himself weaker than the god of the conqueror, or the national god was taking vengeance on his people because of some insult he had suffered. The first explanation, of course, was impossible for monotheists to accept—and, in any case, YHVH was also the God of the Israelite invaders. The second, that YHVH had been insulted, made more sense. Even in polytheistic nations, military reverses were often attributed to some misdeed or error performed by a high official—a priest's failure to offer the correct sacrifice, for example, or a king's neglect in celebrating the deity's holiday properly.[22] This at least offered the possibility of undoing the error by rectifying the observance or offering up some scapegoat to avert the god's wrath. For Ahaz to make his son "pass through the fire," even though illicit under Hebrew law, was exactly the sort of service that one expected religion to perform in a crisis like this.

But what did Isaiah have to say about propitiating an angry God? Nothing useful. On the contrary, rather than suggesting some form of sacrifice or worship that would help a terrified people avoid the nightmare of a long siege, he informed the priests of the temple that their sacrifices, holidays, and even their prayers were utterly useless. "What are your endless sacrifices to me? says YHVH. . . . Bring me your worthless offerings no more, the smoke of them fills me with disgust."

> When you stretch out your hands
> I turn my eyes away
> You may multiply your prayers,
> I shall not listen.
> Your hands are covered with blood,
> wash, make yourselves clean.
>
> Take your wrongdoing out of my sight.
> Cease to do evil.
> Learn to do good,
> search for justice,
> help the oppressed,
> be just to the orphan,
> plead for the widow.[23]

Again, the poor people, widows, and orphans! How could this be taken seriously? It was one thing to say that YHVH was insulted because some people continued to worship idols. At least that suggested a remedy: People could take their little Baal figurines and Asherahs out of their closets and destroy them (as many were already said to be doing). But if God was angry because Judah's rulers were not virtuous—because they were acting as men of power acted everywhere—how could the country be saved? To relieve the despair that this sort of criticism might produce, the prophet also offered hope: YHVH's punishment could be averted by a change in his people's behavior. "If you are willing to obey, you shall eat the good things of the earth, but if you persist in rebellion, the sword shall eat you instead."[24] In time, he predicted, a just king of Judah—a "shoot from the stock of Jesse"—would rule with integrity and faithfulness, and all civil discord would cease.[25] Even so, to demand a radical change of attitude on the part of priests and princes seemed both unrealistic and, to Ahaz, uselessly long range. It was not softheartedness toward the weak, but military strength and diplomatic agility that would save Jerusalem from the enemies now approaching her gates. If Isaiah did not understand this, thought the king, it was hard to see what was to be gained by talking to him.

Now the prophet was at his side. Ahaz noted with interest that he had brought his son with him—a boy he had named Shear-yashub, "a remnant will repent." As he knew, the nevi'im were often inspired to give their children symbolic names and then to display them as a way of delivering some important message. By taking his first-born son to meet the king, Isaiah was not only warning him, but also offering him a sign of hope for the survival of Judah and its ruling house.[26] This impression was confirmed by his first words: "Pay attention, keep calm, have no fear."[27] The prophet spoke in a warm, natural tone, authoritative and comforting—the voice of a trusted counselor. Perhaps he would have some useful advice to give after all.

"Do not let your heart sink because of these two smoldering stumps of firebrands," he continued, "or because Syria, Israel, and Pekah have plotted to ruin you."[28] He paused a moment, his face assuming a masklike rigidity, and then chanted in an altered voice that seemed, somehow, to emanate both from deep within him and from outside:

> *The Lord YHVH says this:*
> *It shall not come true; it shall not be.*
> *The capital of Syria is Damascus,*
> *the head of Damascus, Rezin;*
> *The capital of Israel, Samaria;*
> *the head of Samaria, Pekah.*
>
> *Six or five years more*
> *and a shattered Israel shall no longer be a people.*
> *But if you do not stand by me,*
> *you will not stand at all.*[29]

The style was oracular, but, to Ahaz, the message was perfectly clear. The siege of Jerusalem would not succeed. Just as Rezin was king in Damascus and Pekah in Samaria, Ahaz was king in Jerusalem, where he would remain, if only he stood fast. The northern kingdom was headed for destruction, but, as YHVH had promised, the House of David would survive in Judah. Ahaz appreciated the inspired wordplay that expressed the condition essential for this survival: If you don't stand firm (*im lo ta'aminu*), you won't stand at all (*ki lo te'amenu*).[30] He clasped Isaiah's arm in gratitude and returned to his palace strengthened in his conviction that joining the Syro-Israelite coalition could lead only to disaster. But unanswered questions remained, chief among them the problem of whether or not to call on the Assyrians for aid and to accept the status of one of the Great King's vassals.

Isaiah's words implied that this was unnecessary, since YHVH himself would save Jerusalem from the two "stumps of firebrands." The Assyrians would probably arrive in time to force Pekah and Rezin to lift their siege. Even so, could Ahaz take the risk of waiting? Wasn't it his duty to his people, as well as to his own house, to win the emperor's favor and ensure his army's quick return? The answer seemed obvious. A few days after his conversation with Isaiah, the king had his scribes draft a message to King Pul requesting immediate assistance and ordered the temple officials to begin collecting gold and silver treasures to send to him. But if he thought that he could interpret the prophet's words to serve his own purposes, he was mistaken.

When Isaiah appeared unannounced at the door of the royal palace, the palace guards, assuming that he had been invited, stood aside. He went immediately to the throne room, where the king was meeting with court officials, and began speaking to him in a tone usually reserved for particularly stubborn teenaged children. If Ahaz doubted YHVH's power to deliver him from the Syrians and Israelites, said Isaiah impatiently, let him ask for a sign "coming either from the depths of Sheol or from the heights above."

"No," the king answered, with some embarrassment, "I will not put YHVH to the test."

"Listen now, House of David," the prophet burst out angrily. "Are you not satisfied with trying the patience of men without trying the patience of my God, too? The Lord himself, therefore, will give you a sign. It is this. The young woman is with child and will soon give birth to a son whom she will call Immanuel—God is With Us. On curds and honey will he feed until he knows how to reject the bad and choose the good. For before this child knows how to reject the bad and choose the good, the land whose two kings terrify you will be deserted."[31]

Ahaz smiled. He was delighted to learn that one of his wives would soon bear him a son and heir.[32] Another sign of life for Judah and continuity for the House of David! Moreover, if Isaiah's prediction was accurate, the Assyrians would return to deal with Syria and Israel sooner than he had thought. While the child was still on an infant diet of curds and honey—that is, within a year and a few months—King Pul would defeat the rebel kings and depopulate their nations. This vision was encouraging, to say the least, but it did not resolve Ahaz's doubts. As everyone knew, even the greatest prophets were fallible. They often made mistakes, especially where predictions involving precise time periods were involved.[33] National security required a more substantial guarantee, the sort of guarantee that only real-world power—Assyrian power—could provide.

Reading Ahaz's transparent face, Isaiah recognized that his attempts at persuasion were falling short. Now his tone became more ominous. What the king failed to understand was that the force he hoped to tame and channel for his own purposes was uncontrollable by nature. Assyrian power could no more be held in check than an infestation of insects or a devastating flood.[34] If the king and his supporters relied on King Pul rather than on YHVH and their own defenses, the results would be disastrous.

The Lord will bring up against you
the mighty and deep waters of the River
(the king of Assyria and all his glory),
and it will overflow out of its bed
bursting all its banks;
it will inundate Judah, flow over, pour out,

flooding it up to the neck,
and its wings will be spread
over the whole breadth of your country, O Immanuel.[35]

Did Ahaz really think that he could employ the Assyrian emperor as his own instrument, like some mercenary employed to fight his local battles? The "barber" hired by the king to "shave" Syria and Israel would shave the Judeans instead, from head to toe.[36] Not only would they humiliate Ahaz's warriors, they would end by impoverishing the country, wrecking its agriculture, and reducing its people to a nomadic state.[37] Inviting them in as protectors—an insult to YHVH and his protective power—would be the height of folly.

Fairly soon, the Assyrians would destroy the rebel axis. Enduring the Israelite-Syrian siege while waiting for this to happen was a risk worth taking, since calling for Assyrian aid would obligate the nation unconditionally to the emperor. It would make Judah part of the Assyrian world order, subject to King Pul's every whim, and tempted constantly either to apostatize or to rebel. Clearly, Ahaz would eventually have to negotiate with the Assyrians. Considering their great power, he would have to make significant concessions. But it was essential, if Judah's national and religious identity were to be maintained, to avoid trading her independence for an illusory security. The only sound policy was to defend Jerusalem against Pekah and Rezin, maintain the nation's neutrality in foreign policy, and thoroughly reform its corrupt administration.

Isaiah looked searchingly at Ahaz, but the king would not meet his gaze. It was as if each man were thinking in a different language. Like most statesmen, Ahaz saw the realm of international politics as the "real world": a complex network of transactions whose common currency, now as always, was military and economic power. Like virtually all rulers, he calculated the costs and benefits of this or that course of action in terms of this common currency. What should a responsible leader do when trapped between two hostile forces, one regional and relatively backward, the other far-flung and, for all practical purposes, invincible? Common sense answered: Join forces with the stronger power, use its strength to cripple one's local enemies, and become part of its new order. The situation, after all, was either/or: Either one was for the Great King of Assyria or against him. Neither a fool nor a bad man, Ahaz preferred the risks of submission to those of resistance. Not only was Assyrian power the answer to Judah's immediate problem, it might also be the key to her future.

Isaiah had another view of the situation altogether, but he could see that it was useless to continue the discussion. The king's mind was clearly set in its predetermined mold. He would not join the Syrian-Israelite coalition, but he would continue to play the game of power politics. The prophet bowed imperceptibly, nodded to the officials, and withdrew. A few weeks later, with the armies of Pekah and Rezin in plain view of the walls of Jerusalem, Ahaz sent messengers to the Assyrian emperor with a fortune in silver and gold taken from the temple and the palace. His message was brief. "I am your servant and your son. Come and rescue me from the king of Syria and the king of Israel who are making war against me."[38]

ISAIAH RETURNED to his house in Jerusalem too distracted to speak to his wife or the disciples who waited there to hear about his interview with the king. Now, for the first time, he understood the meaning of a disturbing vision that had come to him almost a decade earlier, in the last year of King Uzziah's reign, when the old man lay dying of leprosy in a separate apartment reserved for those with incurable diseases.

While in a trancelike state, he had seen YHVH seated on a

high throne in the temple—a throne so huge and lofty that the skirts of his gown filled the sanctuary. Surrounding him were six-winged creatures of flame—seraphim—who cried out to one another in thunderous voices, "Holy, holy, holy is YHVH of the Hosts. His glory fills the whole earth."[39] Immediately, the prophet was stricken with a profound sense of unworthiness—a feeling of shame mixed with terror, since he had violated the most ancient of taboos by looking directly at the Lord.[40] "I am a man of unclean lips and I live among a people of unclean lips," he moaned aloud, "and my eyes have looked at the King, YHVH of the Hosts." But a seraph flew to him bearing a live coal that he had taken from the altar, touched it to the prophet's lips, and announced that his sin was forgiven.[41]

Thus purged, Isaiah heard the Lord ask, "Whom shall I send? Who will be our messenger?" "Here I am," he had answered. "Send me." He might not have volunteered so quickly had he known in advance the dreadful contents of the message entrusted to him:

> Go, and say to this people
> Hear and hear again, but do not understand;
> see and see again, but do not perceive.
> Make the heart of this people fat,
> its ears dull;
> shut its eyes
> so that it will not see with its eyes,
> hear with its ears,
> understand with its heart
> and be converted and healed.

"Until when, Lord?" Isaiah could not help pleading. And God had answered: "Until towns have been laid waste and deserted, houses left untenanted, countryside made desolate, and YHVH drives the people out." Only a remnant—a "holy seed"—would survive to repopulate the land of Judah.[42]

What did this strange commission mean?[43] Was YHVH so angry with the Judeans that he actually ordered the prophet to make sure they would not repent, so that he could oversee their destruction? This seemed to be the plain sense of his words. But since God's power is unlimited, why not destroy them whether they repented or not? The answer to this question, Isaiah understood, was that YHVH is a God of justice, and just rulers do not sentence repentant wrongdoers to death. But—here was the crux of the matter—since he is just, how could he order his servant to obstruct the people's repentance? What made the problem especially troublesome was that the words the prophet agreed to speak were not his own but YHVH's. In effect, God seemed to be asking him to collaborate in setting up the Judeans for annihilation—all of them, except for the small remnant that he promised to save.

At the time he had this unsettling vision, Isaiah understood at least what it did not mean. God was not asking him to tell the people soothing falsehoods, so that they would remain complacent. He did not put a "lying spirit" into Isaiah's mouth as he had done in the case of the prophet Micaiah.[44] Nor was he merely predicting that the prophet's listeners would remain complacent no matter what he told them.[45] YHVH's words must mean exactly what they said. Somehow, by speaking as God inspired him to speak, Isaiah would blind his people to the very dangers that he warned them about. Something in the message itself or the way he delivered it would ensure that his words would be disregarded. Isaiah did not *want* this to happen. He would try his best to save his people. But the God-voice resounding in his deepest consciousness warned him that disaster could not be averted, and might even be hastened, by telling people the truth.

Now, fresh from his struggle with Ahaz, he could make more

sense of this troubling experience. He had told the truths vouch-safed to him by YHVH: that Judah would be punished for her leaders' corruption and injustice, and that the nation would be saved from its enemies without calling on King Pul's assistance. As he delivered these messages, he could almost see the king's heart becoming "fat" and his ears "dull." This was not realistic ad-vice, Ahaz was obviously thinking. At best, it was poetic preach-ing. In fact, Isaiah's impractical words seemed to confirm what he and his courtiers had always understood—that the world is di-vided into two realms, a real world of relationships based on power, and a spiritual world of ethical ideals and moral precepts. Prophets like Isaiah inhabited the latter world, responsible states-men the former.

Of course, the king was not such an unbeliever as to suppose that the two realms never intersected. He did seem to worry a bit when Isaiah warned that Judah would be punished for her sins. But he interpreted this as a declaration that YHVH had super-natural powers and might conceivably use them. If one insulted one's god or violated his laws persistently enough, the deity might retaliate. By the same token (gods being capricious beings), he might even save a people foolish enough to avoid allying them-selves with the most powerful empire on earth. On the other hand, if Judah's leaders acted as though only the spiritual world existed—if they did not recognize the realities of power—they would default on their obligation as the people's shepherds to provide them with national security. Then, they *would* deserve divine punishment.

Staring through his window at Jerusalem's purple hills, Isaiah felt his lips tighten with frustration. This division of the universe into spheres of power and morality, one obeying the laws of his-tory and the other the Law of God, was exactly what YHVH in-spired him to deny. Two spheres meant two gods, at least. Those who excluded history and politics from the purview of YHVH's constant activity were actually worshipping him alongside Baal, Marduk, Chemosh, and the other gods of power. But everything the prophet had witnessed since experiencing his vision convinced him that the real world was not exempt from God's Law or subject merely to an occasional divine intervention. YHVH not only ruled in heaven, he also ruled the entire human family through all its travails and triumphs on earth.

Did Ahaz really think that the corruption of a nation's leadership had no historical consequences? He had only to consider what had happened to Israel and Judah since the 740s, around the time that Isaiah began preaching, when Israel's internal politics, which had always been consumed by the pursuit of wealth and power, became incredibly violent. First, an obscure army officer called Shallum murdered King Jereboam II's son and heir, and the century-old dynasty founded by Jehu became extinct. One month later, Shallum was killed by Menahem and his followers, who submitted to the Assyrians in order to shore up their own tenuous hold on power.[46] Menahem's son was assassinated by Pekah. And Pekah's alliance with Syria had provoked the current war with Judah and the coming Assyrian intervention.

Did the present crisis have nothing to do with the idolatrous worship of privilege and power? When Isaiah denounced the officials of his own country for their neglect of the poor, the landowners for adding "field to field," or the judges for selling justice for money, he was not merely predicting that some sort of supernatural disaster might befall them for violating God's Law. The principle that he affirmed was simultaneously spiritual and political. With or without a specific divine intervention, unjust government incubates disaster. Activities that brutalize and corrupt the leadership divide and weaken the community, exposing it to violent internal conflicts, disastrous wars, and self-destructive alliances. Power is real, Isaiah understood, but it does not have the last word. The laws of history are governed by the Law of God.

Equally important, history does not stand still, like a board on which the counters of power are arrayed. International politics is more than a strategic game played by pieces of various sizes and strengths; it is part of an historical process in which everything is subject to transformation, including the board, the pieces, and the rules of the game itself. That transformation, Isaiah recognized, is the creative work of YHVH, the God of history. King Ahaz and his men of power beheld the Assyrian emperor, King Pul, with a mixture of fear and envy, and saw only a more formidable version of themselves. Isaiah knew King Pul's real name— Tiglath-pileser III. And, thanks to his visions, he understood that this brutal conqueror was fulfilling the will of YHVH to open a new chapter of world history.

Who was Tiglath-pileser? The prophet had studied his career closely. Although he claimed to be descended from kings, he was probably a dissident general who seized the throne by force around the year 745 during a chaotic period in the Assyrian capital.[47] Royally born or not, he soon proved much more than another Mesopotamian warlord. Putting an end to two decades of disunity and imperial decline, he reorganized the empire's administrative structure; built a vast network of roads to facilitate military movements, communication, and trade; rebuilt the army; and equipped his troops with devastatingly effective weapons. Iron had been in use for some time in the region, but the Assyrians were the first to mass-produce iron weapons and to make them available to large armies.[48] In the entrance halls of their palaces, the Great Kings had battle scenes carved to awe and terrify their visitors. There, etched in stone, victorious troops in body armor wielded iron swords, shields, and lances; drew new-model bows that fired armor-piercing arrows; drove armored chariots; and utilized a new generation of siege weapons to break the resistance of walled cities under attack. (The same artworks made sure to picture the Assyrians' enemies defending their cities bravely before being led away in chains or flayed alive.)[49]

If the battle required large numbers, Isaiah well knew, Tiglath-pileser was capable of putting up to 400,000 well-armed troops in the field.[50] But it was his battering rams, catapults, battle towers, mines, and other siege weapons that were most potent, since by altering the balance of power in warfare, they helped to create a new type of empire. Before this, a nation attacked by a foreign army could almost always survive by retreating to its fortified cities and (so long as there was fresh water available) holding out until the invaders ran out of food, came down with unfamiliar diseases, or were recalled to deal with problems elsewhere.[51] For this reason, most military campaigns on foreign soil had the character of raiding parties; the invading troops despoiled the countryside, plundered unprotected towns, and then returned home. Now that this defensive advantage in warfare was eliminated, conquest had a different meaning. A superpower like Assyria could occupy an enemy's major cities, demobilize or absorb the defeated army, and subject the whole country to its rule.

Under Tiglath-pileser, for the first time, it became possible to incorporate conquered territories into one's empire as provinces to be administered by imperial appointees.[52] No longer was the emperor a mere looter on a grand scale. Now, without obvious exaggeration, he could style himself "king of the world."[53] But how to maintain control over a domain that already extended from the Caucasus Mountains to the Mediterranean coast, and that included subject nations of every sort? The Great King's answer was a combination of attractive rewards and terrifying punishments. He was prepared to leave subject rulers on their thrones, so long as they recognized his supreme authority and fulfilled the elaborate duties of a vassal.[54] The great advantage of accepting vassal status (at least for men of substance) was the incorporation of one's nation into the growing Assyrian world economy.[55] The chief disadvantage—in addition to frequent calls for conscript troops and workers, and the payment of exorbitant sums by way of tribute—was the price that might be paid for disobedience. To ensure the loyalty of his subjects, Tiglath-pileser had invented a new form of state terror: the mass deportation and resettlement of subject populations.

The Assyrian system was devastatingly simple. If a vassal king rebelled or refused to pay tribute, the emperor would remove him, declare the land an Assyrian province, and appoint a governor to rule it. Ordinarily this was enough to ensure obedience. In cases of serious or repeated rebellion, however, he would escalate the punishment. The nation's rulers, men of wealth, skilled workers, and their families would be carried off—not merely into exile, which might give them some hope of returning, but to some corner of the empire where they would disappear permanently into the native population.[56] To ensure their extinction as a homogeneous group, the deportees were broken into smaller groups and resettled in widely scattered locations where communication with their countrymen was difficult or impossible.[57] Similarly, when conquered people from elsewhere in the empire were brought in to replace them, the conquerors made sure that they, too, were drawn from diverse backgrounds, lest they begin to act like a coherent, potentially rebellious nation.[58]

Huge numbers of people were transported in this way from place to place. Throughout the period of Assyrian rule, the total number of people forcibly driven from their homelands probably amounted to more than four million.[59] This brutal and ingenious policy deprived the rebellious nation of educated decision-makers, military leaders, priests, traders, and skilled workers, leaving behind only the more passive and manipulable peasantry. Equally important, it gave the conquerors an unheard-of capacity to place deportees where their skills were most needed. Conquered people were used "to fill new towns on the borders . . . to repopulate abandoned regions and develop their agriculture; to provide the Assyrians not only with soldiers and troops of laborers . . . but also with craftsmen, artists, and even scribes and scholars."[60] Since their talents were in demand, and since they were destined for social assimilation, most deportees were not enslaved, abused, or treated as pariahs. Even so, the Assyrians wielded a terrifying new political weapon. For the first time in history, those facing superior military forces were threatened not only with defeat, domination, and possible loss of their national independence, but with their extinction as a culture.

Isaiah understood very well that Israel and Syria, having re-belled unforgivably against Assyrian authority, were likely to be ravaged and depopulated. That is why he had told Ahaz that "a shattered Israel shall no longer be a people." But by accepting the duties of an Assyrian vassal, the Judean king was exposing his own people to the same danger if they later attempted to rebel. No, not if—*when* they attempted to rebel.

Why would rational people even consider running such a ter-rible risk? One might as well ask why the Israelites and Syrians were now awaiting a confrontation with the most powerful army in the world. Despite the Assyrians' unstoppable military ma-chine, rebellions against their authority were endemic through-out the empire. In part, this was because imperial domination inevitably corrupted local officials, threatened native cultural and religious traditions, and divided societies into opposed groups of collaborators and resisters. But the spirit of revolt was also in-flamed by the Assyrians' notorious violence and arrogance as im-perial masters. Paradoxically, the very measures of state terror they had designed to crush the spirit of revolt incited unquench-able hatred against them. If the price to be paid for resisting their domination was national extinction, there were always some to argue that serving them slavishly posed an equivalent threat to the nation's identity, and that a brave fight to the death was preferable to surrender.[61]

The apparent alternatives presented by the Assyrian empire were these: either to accept incorporation, with all the national humiliation, cultural pollution, and skewed development that this entailed; or to resist imperial power at the possible cost of one's existence as a people. But collaboration with the Assyrians and rebellion against them, Isaiah recognized, were not true alternatives at all. They were complementary aspects of a vicious cycle of repression and revolt. Somehow, there must be a way to escape this destructive wheel of violence. The very existence of the new international system created by Tiglath-pileser suggested that YHVH had plans for Judah and the world that he had not yet revealed—that he was making use of the Assyrian juggernaut for some purpose of his own. Meditating on this question, the prophet could not help recalling the vision that had inspired him in King Uzziah's last days, when Tiglath-pileser had already appeared in eastern Syria in his terrible glory, and all the monarchs of the region were bowing before him.

Isaiah had then seen YHVH as a king of kings—an emperor—sitting on an unimaginably high throne surrounded by courtly servants, his glory covering the entire earth. If he had never before been envisioned in quite this way, this is because until the rise of Tiglath-pileser there had never been an earthly ruler who could claim to rule the entire world, and whose regal "glory" (a word used commonly by the emperor's scribes) was said to overwhelm his enemies.[62] The six-winged seraphim that had flanked the Lord in Isaiah's temple vision were enhanced versions of the two- or four-winged protective spirits that guarded the Great King's throne in reliefs carved into the walls of Assyrian palaces.[63] They chanted God's praises as the Great King's choristers chanted his. And the very words that Isaiah would use to announce God's messages to his people—"Thus says YHVH"—

were the same as those used by Assyrian heralds to announce the emperor's messages to his subjects: "Thus says the King."[64]

In fact, the prophet's role as YHVH's messenger—a role greatly changed since the days of Elijah and Elisha—also mirrored that of the Assyrian monarch's heralds. Like them, Isaiah "stood in the court of the Great King, participated in the deliberative processes of the court, received the declaration of the king's wishes from the king's own mouth, and then carried the [message] to its destination."[65] Under Assyrian rule, furthermore, the king's commands were announced not only to vassal kings and princes but also to their subjects—that is, to all the people subject to imperial authority. And all the people were held responsible, on pain of death or exile, for heeding and obeying them. In the same way, Isaiah delivered YHVH's messages not just to rulers (as the court prophets had previously done) but to all the people, who, again, were to be held collectively responsible for putting them into effect.[66]

The point, of course, is not that Isaiah equated God with the Assyrian emperor. It went without saying that YHVH was infinitely greater in every respect than the Assyrian monarch. But there is little doubt that the authority of a human king exercised on a scale previously unheard of, a power capable of annihilating national boundaries and reorganizing society on an international basis, fired the prophet's imagination and profoundly influenced his thinking about God, history, and his calling.[67] Even now, reflecting on the failure of his interview with King Ahaz, he could understand that history does not stand still or repeat itself, always returning to some starting point. Nor is it the product of blind power. The work of an all-powerful deity, history moves forward inexorably, destroying old institutions and patterns of behavior, creating new ones, and in turn destroying those to clear the way for something newer still, and more acceptable to God.

Tiglath-pileser's conquests were clearly YHVH's work, Isaiah concluded. But since YHVH is a God of justice and righteousness, not a god of war, the power of any emperor must prove evanescent.[68] What stabilizes political authority over the course of time, he understood, is not a government's command of force, but its justice and integrity—or, as we might say, its moral legitimacy. "Zion will be redeemed by justice," he had sung, "and her penitents by integrity. Rebels and sinners together will be shattered, and those who abandon YHVH will perish."[69] The dialogue with Ahaz had been hopeless, just as the God of his vision had predicted, because the king would not—could not—understand that history and ethics could not be pried apart. YHVH had decided to realize his will through history by proportioning the long-term political strength of nations to their moral character.

Precisely for this reason, the apparent winners in the current game of power politics would not long enjoy their preeminence. Not only would Israel be annihilated because of her rulers' arrogant adventurism, internal violence, "infamous laws," and "tyrannical decrees," but Assyria would fall as well, consumed by her own overweening pride and addiction to violence.[70] The good news was that the process by which power undermined power would not continue indefinitely. A repentant minority would come to understand that a government founded on personal virtue, social justice, and the pursuit of peace could be stable and lasting.[71] At that point, real-world authority would be suffused by ethics—that is, by the word of YHVH—and the historical transformation would be complete.

Now it was time for Isaiah to rejoin his wife and children and to greet his disciples. Soon, he would try again to make his king and countrymen understand what God required of them in this new age. Israel was clearly doomed. If his vision had been accurate, so (except for the holy remnant) was Judah. But he would not stop trying to save his beloved people.

CHAPTER III

✳

"Blessed Be My People Egypt"
—ISAIAH 19:25

I T SEEMED THAT Isaiah's time as a person of influence in Jerusalem was over.

The prophet had warned King Ahaz not to ask the emperor of Assyria for aid and had predicted disaster for Judah were she to become an Assyrian vassal state. Earthly power, he had asserted, was only a tool in the hands of YHVH, who would judge nations according to their righteousness, not their strength of arms. Only by establishing a reign of justice at home, by caring for the poor and weak, rooting out greed and corruption, and submitting to God's Law, could the Judeans hope to save themselves from the whirlwind that was about to descend on the Israelites. Speaking at the temple and in the marketplace, he bitterly criticized the young king's failure of leadership and the greed of the ruling elite:

> *Oh my people, oppressed by a lad,*
> *ruled by women.*
> *O my people, your rulers mislead you*
> *and destroy the road you walk on.*

> *YHVH rises from his judgment seat,*
> *he stands up to arraign his people.*

YHVH calls to judgment
the elders and the princes of his people:

"You are the ones who destroy the vineyard
and conceal what you have stolen from the poor.
By what right do you crush my people
and grind the faces of the poor?"
It is the Lord YHVH of Hosts who speaks.[1]

As for the common people, Isaiah spoke with undisguised contempt of their rudeness, violence, and immorality:

The people bully each other,
neighbor and neighbor;
a youth can insult his elder,
a lout abuse a noble,
so that everyone tries to catch his brother
in their father's house, to say,
"You have a cloak, so you be leader,
and rule this heap of ruins."[2]

Jerusalem's "haughty" and flirtatious women also came under his rhetorical lash, as did dissolute drinkers, liars, land specu-lators, and idolators—but it soon became apparent that few Jerusalemites were listening.[3] Ahaz's foreign policy, his adminis-tration's greed, and the people's immorality had not produced the disastrous results foreseen by the prophet. In fact, the opposite seemed to be the case. Power politics had saved Judah, not de-stroyed it. Government corruption was what it had always been, but business was booming. And in the great relief sweeping over a nation spared from destruction, popular immorality seemed no more than a natural expression of healthy animal spirits.

Tiglath-pileser certainly did not prove to be the menace that

Isaiah had warned against in his speeches on the Assyrian danger. In fact, by destroying Judah's traditional enemies, he established the nation as the strongest power in the region. When he received King Ahaz's call for help, the emperor was in Gaza, smashing a rebellion there and sealing the Egyptian border off against a possible intervention by the pharaoh.[4] In response to the king's message, he brought his troops northward so quickly that Pekah of Israel and Rezin of Syria had no chance to organize a joint defense against him. They abandoned the siege of Jerusalem and withdrew their forces in great haste to avoid being cut off from Samaria and Damascus. The Assyrians then poured into Israel, seized virtually all its territory, and destroyed its fortified cities one by one. Tiglath-pileser incorporated his new conquests into the empire as provinces and deported useful elements of the northern kingdom's population.[5] Then, with Pekah bottled up in Samaria, he turned his attention to western Syria, which he occupied in 733, and Damascus, which fell to his iron-clad forces in 732 after a yearlong siege. In short order, he put the Syrian king to death and impaled his chief advisors on stakes, deported the city's men of rank and skilled workers, and created four Assyrian provinces out of what had once been the Syrian nation.

In Samaria, meanwhile, probably with the Great King's connivance, Pekah's reign came to a bloody end. In the same year that Damascus fell, the Israelite king was assassinated by a pro-Assyrian faction led by a usurper called Hoshea.[6] Tiglath-pileser accepted Hoshea's submission and permitted him to remain the ruler of his tiny kingdom so long as he followed Assyrian orders. He was far more generous to King Ahaz, who had earlier pledged him the fealty of a "servant and son." Ahaz went to Damascus to do homage to him and was overwhelmed by the splendor of his court, as well as by the modernity of the Syrian metropolis. He admired an altar that he saw there so much, in fact, that he sent orders to the high priest of Jerusalem to copy it and place it near the great altar of the temple.[7] He soon became one of the emperor's favorites, and Judah prospered as a result.

Events during the next few years seemed to bear out the wisdom of Ahaz's decision to become an Assyrian vassal—and the foolishness of Isaiah's worries. Judah's regional enemies were crushed, her hegemony was recognized in trans-Jordan and Philistia, her trade expanded greatly, and Jerusalem prospered. "The royal citadel of Jerusalem was transformed in a single generation from the seat of a rather insignificant local dynasty into the political and religious nerve center of a regional power."[8] The king and his advisors tolerated Isaiah's occasional appearances at court, but Judah's important officials clearly considered him a has-been, while the common people to whom he preached—with the exception of a few admirers and disciples—treated him as an irritating crank.

Understanding that it was time for him to retire from public life, the prophet left Jerusalem. It is not known where he spent his years outside the public eye, but one imagines him living with his disciples in one of the prophetic communities that could be found in settlements throughout Judah. There he gathered his followers, bound up his writings and the reports of his speeches that others had compiled, sealed them, and entrusted them to his closest disciples. The writing down of prophecies—something new in the history of the Hebrew peoples—would ensure that what Isaiah had said during the Syria-Israelite crisis would be preserved and heard again when times changed. Until then, he told his friends with calm resignation, "I wait for YHVH who hides his face from the House of Jacob. In him I hope."[9]

ISAIAH WAS STILL in retirement in 727 when Tiglath-pileser died, and his son, Shalmaneser V, became the ruler of Assyria. As in times past, whenever the Great King died it sent a wave of unrest throughout the empire, inspiring discontented vassals and conquered people everywhere to dream of regaining their lost independence. The news circulating about Shalmaneser was that he was not nearly the leader his father had been. Plots against him therefore blossomed, not least among the Israelites who had seen their territory shrink to Samaria and a few surrounding hill towns during Tiglath-pileser's devastating campaign against them.

King Hoshea of Israel had been the old emperor's faithful vassal, but now he was pressed on all sides to join other city-states that were fomenting rebellion against his untested successor. Soon, the pressure became irresistible. In 726, he withheld paying the annual tribute—a symbolic declaration of independence—and sent messengers to the Egyptian pharaoh seeking his support for an armed uprising. But Shalmaneser gave the plan no chance to mature. He marched immediately on Israel, occupied the territory around Samaria with little resistance, and besieged the city.

The hilltop capital was well located and heavily fortified. Its people held out for three agonizing years, but the end was inevitable. In 722 the Assyrians entered Samaria, tore down its walls, imprisoned Hoshea in chains, and began the deportations that would send at least 30,000 of its most productive residents to cities in northern Syria, Mesopotamia, and the lands far east of the Tigris River.[10] The deportees were replaced by people from at least five different provinces of the empire who "took possession of Israel and lived in its towns."[11] The subjugation of Israel was a significant international event—important enough to induce two Assyrian emperors to compete for the title of conqueror of Samaria. Although the Bible and some ancient documents name Shalmaneser as the victor, that emperor died in the year the city fell, and his successor, Sargon II, was probably responsible for finishing the job and deporting its inhabitants.[12] In any case, Sargon's chronicles claim full credit for the conquest:

The inhabitants of Samaria, who agreed and plotted with a king hostile to me not to endure servitude and not to bring tribute to [the god] Assur and who did battle, I fought against them with the power of the great gods, my lords. I counted as spoil 27,820 people, together with their chariots, and gods, in which they trusted. I formed a unit with 200 of their chariots for my royal force. I settled the rest of them in the midst of Assyria. I repopulated Samaria more than before. I brought into it people from countries conquered by my hands. I appointed my commissioner as governor over them. And I counted them as Assyrians.[13]

Israel, once the most powerful state in Syria-Palestine, was no more. More significantly, perhaps, the people who had governed it, owned its most productive land, and served it as merchants, soldiers, priests, scribes, artisans, and skilled workers disappeared into myriad alien cultures, never again to emerge as an identifiable community.[14] Ten of the twelve tribes of Israel were thus "lost" to history, although the total number of people deported by Tiglath-pileser and his successors probably comprised no more than a fifth of the population of the northern kingdom.[15] The remaining Israelites, now residents of the new Assyrian province of Samerina, stayed on the land, cohabiting with the variegated collection of foreigners imported to serve as their masters. The Bible recounts how the new settlers had some bad luck at first, which was attributed to their ignorance of "the god of the country." The Assyrians therefore returned one of the deported priests to the holy city of Bethel to teach the foreigners how to placate YHVH. "They worshiped YHVH and served their own gods at the same time," reports the scribe. "They still follow their old rites even now."[16]

The extent to which the Judeans mourned the fall of Israel is not certain, since they left no record of lamentation. Clearly, they recognized their historical and religious connections with the northerners, but for three centuries the two countries had been cold friends or violent enemies, and Judah was still grieving for her sons lost in the bloody Syrian-Israelite invasion. Moreover, the immediate effects of the Israelite collapse on the southern kingdom were by no means adverse. Jerusalem and the agricultural hinterland experienced "an unprecedented population explosion," probably caused by an influx of thousands of refugees from the north, many of whom were skilled workers trying to escape deportation.[17] Archeological evidence suggests that in the period after Samaria's fall, new settlements multiplied, the production of olive oil and wine increased, trade blossomed, and "Judah experienced not only sudden demographic growth but also real social evolution. In a word, it became a full-fledged state."[18] At the same time, the existence of several hundred thousand YHVH-worshippers in Assyrian-controlled Israel ignited dreams of potential reunification under Judean leadership. When King Ahaz's son, Hezekiah, assumed the kingship in 715, one of his first acts was to command a national celebration of the Passover holiday and invite the Hebrews residing in Israel to come to Jerusalem to participate. (Few, however, accepted his invitation.)[19]

While Ahaz was still king in Jerusalem, Isaiah remained inactive as a court advisor, but the events of the day affected him deeply. The fall of Samaria did not surprise him; he had repeatedly predicted it, comparing the northern kingdom to a fig ripe for the picking, "no sooner in the hand than swallowed," and referring to Assyria as YHVH's chosen agent of destruction.

> See, a strong and mighty one, sent by the Lord,
> like a storm of hail, a destroying tempest,
> like a storm of torrential, overflowing waters;
> with his hand he throws them to the ground.

There will be trampled underfoot
the haughty crown of Israel's drunkards,
and the faded flower of its proud splendor
overlooking the lush valley.[20]

The great question was: What difference was there between Israel and Judah? If Israel had not been specially favored by God—if, in fact, YHVH had used Assyria as his "rod" to deliver an annihilating judgment against that nation—why would he not subject Judah to the same treatment? One answer, in theory, might be the moral superiority of the southern kingdom's leadership to that of Israel; but Isaiah denied vehemently that there was any such difference. If anything, YHVH was even more disappointed with Judah, which he had lovingly cultivated as his own vineyard, but which yielded only "sour grapes."[21] Alternatively, one could rely on God's covenant with David and David's descendants—a promise to sustain the Judean dynasty that Isaiah took very seriously. But YHVH could preserve Davidic rule in Jerusalem while the rest of the country was ravaged and its people killed or deported.[22] This was, indeed, the fate that the prophet predicted for the country, using the same metaphors of storm and flood that he had earlier applied to Israel. You have taken refuge in lies and made falsehoods your shelter, he warned Jerusalem's elite, but "hail will sweep away the refuge of lies and floods overwhelm the shelter."[23]

Ahaz's answer to the Assyrian threat was to stay the course—to strengthen his ties with the Assyrians and play the role of the good vassal to the hilt. The great problem with this position, Isaiah understood, was that it was untenable over the long run—and perhaps in the short run as well. There were two lessons to be learned from the earthshaking events of the 720s. The first was that the success of Assyrian arms and the continued expansion of the empire did not depend on the particular talents or personality of any emperor. The administrative and military system created by Tiglath-pileser would survive him. Under his successors, the army remained for all intents and purposes invincible. Rebellions were ruthlessly suppressed, and the number of people deported from their homelands rose to the hundreds of thousands.[24]

The second lesson was that a stable peace was impossible under Assyrian rule. However great the disparity of power between the emperor and his conquered subjects, the latter could not help struggling for their identity and independence at every opportunity, and sometimes when there was no opportunity at all. What Hoshea had done by breaking with Shalmaneser V might have seemed irrational, but it was not at all uncommon. The imperial system ensnared every participant, from the emperor and his governors to hotheaded local tribesmen, in an endless cycle of repression and rebellion. This being so, it was as foolish for Ahaz to believe that he could control the forces of revolt as it was to believe that he could control the Assyrian army. Some Judeans might prosper under the rule of Sargon II, but others were ruined by the tyrant's exactions and the growing gap between rich and poor in a rapidly changing society. How long before these latent insurrectionary forces would write finis to the king's docile policy?

In 720, near the end of Ahaz's reign, Isaiah reappeared quite unexpectedly in Jerusalem. To say that his reemergence on the public stage was dramatic is a considerable understatement. What happened was this:

Sargon II had no sooner deported the rebel Israelites than he found himself confronted by a series of new uprisings, the most serious of which was a takeover of Babylon by a charismatic Chaldean chieftain from a city in southern Iraq.[25] This canny leader, Merodach-baladan, had purchased the loyalty of the fierce Elamites, who attacked a large Assyrian garrison before Sargon

had time to respond, won a rare victory, and established themselves in such force that the emperor was forced to leave Babylon
in their hands for the next decade.[26] Meanwhile, anti-Assyrian
revolts broke out in other regions, including the West, where a
Syrian prince led a multicity uprising that included (amazingly
enough) some of Samaria's new leaders.[27] Rumblings of unrest
were felt in Phoenicia and Philistia as well, abetted by Egyptian
agents who were seeking to weaken the Assyrian position in
Palestine. After centuries of decline, the empire of the pharaohs
had fallen into the hands of an energetic Ethiopian dynasty that
hoped to rid itself of the Assyrian presence on its border and to
reestablish Egyptian influence in the Fertile Crescent.[28]

When the Egyptians sent a delegation to Jerusalem to solicit
Judean participation in the rebellion, Isaiah could no longer remain in seclusion. More than a decade earlier he had advised Ahaz
not to invite the Assyrians in, but maintaining any sort of national
life and religious independence now required that open revolt be
avoided at all costs. The residents of the capital were therefore astonished, one bright morning, to discover the famous prophet,
now middle aged, walking its crowded streets without his sandals
or the usual sackcloth covering around his waist. He was "naked
and barefoot," a state of undress that sent a message easily com-
prehended by his fellow Jerusalemites: Isaiah was modeling an enslaved prisoner of war.[29] To those who asked, he explained that
YHVH had commanded him to appear in this costume as "a sign
and portent for Egypt and Ethiopia—so will the king of Assyria
lead away captives from Egypt and exiles from Ethiopia, young and
old, naked and barefoot, their buttocks bared, to the shame of
Egypt. You will be frightened and ashamed about Ethiopia in
which you trusted, and about Egypt of which you boasted."[30] He
also preached an oracle against Ethiopia, diplomatically praising
the "people tall and bronzed" from "a nation always feared," but
predicting the utter defeat of their international schemes.[31]

For a long time (the Bible says three years), in all seasons, Isaiah haunted the streets in this humiliating garb as a sign to King Ahaz and his people that playing the game of power politics against Assyria would cost them their homeland and what remained of their freedom. In effect, the prophet reestablished himself in Jerusalem, this time as an independent preacher rather than a member of the court. As if to vindicate his vision, Sargon marched his army west to smash the rebellion in Syria, defeat an Egyptian army on the Sinai border, and reconquer the cities of Philistia. "These major victories were followed by massive operations in which the rebel states were reoccupied and the offenders punished; large numbers of people were transported to Assyria and captured peoples from other regions settled in their place."[32]

The Judeans could congratulate themselves on their prudence in avoiding seditious entanglements and remaining in the Assyrian camp—but then, quite suddenly, everything changed. In 715, King Ahaz died, and his gifted son, Hezekiah, inherited the throne. Isaiah took off his slave costume, donned his prophet's robes, and returned to court to advise the new king. During the next fifteen years, he would experience the most dizzying hope, the most shocking disappointments, and the most profound visions of his career.

FIRST, THERE WAS HOPE. Hezekiah—the child Isaiah had called Immanuel twenty years earlier—was king. Clearly, the boy was brilliant. He had been groomed by his father during a period of coregency to be a masterful ruler. And he was passionately interested in religious reform. Very early in his reign, he repaired the temple and purified the sanctuary, established Passover as the principal national holiday, and celebrated it magnificently. Immediately afterward, he ordered a mass campaign to smash the idol-worshippers' pillars and sacred poles, reorganized the clergy, and attempted to centralize worship in Jerusalem.[33]

The Bible gives no indication of how Isaiah felt about these changes. Ordinarily, a reform of cult practices without a corresponding transformation in ethical behavior would leave him cold. But he nurtured a tantalizing hope that Hezekiah might be the long-sought "virtuous king" who would lead Judah into a new age of integrity, justice, and peace.[34] "For there is a child born for us," he chanted at the young king's coronation, "a son given to us, and authority has settled on his shoulders, and this is the name they give him:

> *"The Mighty God is Planning Grace;*
> *Eternal Father, Prince of Peace."*
> *Wide is his dominion*
> *In a peace that has no end,*
> *For the throne of David*
> *And for his royal power,*
> *Which he establishes and makes secure*
> *In justice and integrity.*[35]

Isaiah established close relations with Hezekiah, hoping to help keep him out of the whirlwind of international power politics, but a violent system drew the king inexorably into its orbit. He was, after all, the ruler of a prosperous, growing nation with territorial ambitions of its own—and Sargon had been compelled to return to the East to expel the Chaldean chief, Merodach-baladan, from Babylon. In his absence, Hezekiah flexed his muscles, expanding Judean influence in Philistia and sending his agents north to renew contacts with the Hebrew population there.[36] When anti-Assyrian revolts broke out in two Philistine cities, he avoided direct participation—a wise decision, since Sargon soon dispatched an army under one of his top generals to

smash the rebels and restore order. But he supported the uprisings in minor ways, for example, by imprisoning a pro-Assyrian
king expelled by insurgent forces from one of the cities.[37]

To Isaiah's dismay, an anti-Assyrian party was clearly gaining
strength in Jerusalem. In an effort to quell the growing insurrectionist sentiment, the prophet threw himself into political activity, denouncing the leaders of the movement at court, but events
soon reduced his influence almost to the vanishing point.[38] In 710,
Sargon succeeded in recapturing Babylon and driving Merodach-
baladan into the marshes of southern Iraq. Five years later, Sargon
died in battle in the mountains of northern Persia, and the crown
prince, Sennacherib, ascended the throne. Although Sennacherib
had long been groomed to succeed his father, the transition was
once again a signal for widespread rebellion. The Babylonians
rid themselves of Sargon's administrators and brought back
Merodach-baladan. The kings of Tyre and Sidon declared their
independence, followed by a number of rulers in Syria and Philistia. And in Judah, despite Isaiah's protests, Hezekiah began making preparations for war.

The king strengthened Jerusalem's fortifications, rebuilt its
citadel, and had a tunnel cut through solid rock to furnish the city
with a secure supply of fresh spring water.[39] When Merodach-
baladan sent an embassy from Babylon to encourage him to open
a second front against the Assyrians, Hezekiah received them
warmly, disregarding Isaiah's warning that "the days are coming
when everything in your palace, everything that your ancestors
have amassed until now, will be carried off to Babylon."[40] Even
worse from Isaiah's point of view, he sent an embassy to Egypt
carrying gifts to the pharaoh to solicit his support.

Enraged, the prophet broke openly with his royal protégé. He
preached against "those rebellious sons—it is YHVH who speaks—
who carry out plans that are not mine and make alliances not
inspired by me, and so add sin to sin. They have left for Egypt

without consulting me, to take refuge in Pharaoh's protection, to shelter in Egypt's shadow. Pharaoh's protection will be your shame, the shelter of Egypt's shadow your confounding."[41] Not only was Egyptian aid unreliable, but the strategy of playing one empire off against another left everyone, the "protectors" as well as the "protected," trapped in the universe of brute power. "Woe to those who go down to Egypt," the prophet thundered,

> *to seek help there,*
> *who build their hopes on cavalry,*
> *who rely on the number of chariots*
> *and on the strength of mounted men,*
> *but never look to the Holy One of Israel*
> *nor consult YHVH. . . .*

> *The Egyptian is a man, not a god,*
> *his horses are flesh, not spirit;*
> *YHVH will stretch out his hand*
> *to make the protector stumble;*
> *the protected will fall*
> *and all will perish together.*[42]

Soon enough, the protector stumbled. After driving Merodach-baladan once more from Babylon, Sennacherib marched through Syria to Phoenicia with a huge army, the largest ever seen in the West, subjugating all the cities that had defied him and receiving tributes from terrified rulers throughout the region. At Eltekeh, south of modern Jaffa, he met a combined force of Egyptians, Ethiopians, and Philistines and destroyed them. Barely pausing for rest, he then invaded Judah, taking (according to his own account) forty-six fortified towns, leveling them, and deporting thousands of their inhabitants.[43] A graphic representation of one of those conquests taken from the walls of his palace in Nineveh shows, stage by stage, his brutal assault on Lachish, the nation's most important city after Jerusalem.[44] Sennacherib's troops wield battering rams to breach the walls and erect ramps, up which hordes of storming troops, archers, and slingers advance to take the city. The defenders fight back, hurling torches to set the siege machines on fire, but their efforts are fruitless. Modern excavations of the site have uncovered a pit in which at least 1,500 bodies were thrown, together with quantities of Assyrian garbage.[45] The Assyrians had the high officials of the city tortured and executed, but most of those captured at Lachish were enslaved and deported.

At the end of his Judean campaign, the emperor (no doubt with considerable exaggeration) reported the deportation of 200,150 people to Assyria.[46] In the same document in which he boasts of these deportations, Sennacherib speaks of "Hezekiah, the Jew," who "did not submit to my yoke. . . . Himself I made a prisoner in Jerusalem, his royal residence, like a bird in a cage."[47] The siege of Jerusalem began in 701.[48] While Sennacherib was still besieging Lachish, Hezekiah had sued for terms, stripping the temple treasures to pay an enormous bribe, but the Great King was unrelenting.[49] He sent a high official, his cup-bearer in chief, to parley with Hezekiah's chief officers on a hill within earshot of the soldiers manning the ramparts of Jerusalem. In an attempt to demoralize the defenders, turn them against the king, and secure a quick surrender, the Assyrian official spoke in a loud, taunting voice, and in Hebrew:

> Say to Hezekiah, thus says the Great King of Assyria: What makes you so confident? Do you think empty words are as good as strategy and military strength? We know that you are relying on that broken reed—Egypt—which pricks and pierces the hand of the man who leans on it.
>
> You may say to me: We rely on YHVH our God, but are they not his high places and altars that Hezekiah has

suppressed? Come, make a wager with my lord the king of Assyria: I will give you two thousand horses if you can find horsemen to ride them. How could you repulse a single one of the least of my master's servants?

And lastly, have I come up against the country to lay it waste without warrant from YHVH? YHVH himself said to me: "March against the country and lay it waste."[50]

The Judean officials protested, demanding that the official speak in Aramaic (the educated classes' lingua franca) rather than in Hebrew, but he replied scoffingly, "Do you think my lord sent me here to say these things to your master or to you? On the contrary, it was to the people sitting on the ramparts who, like you, are doomed to eat their own dung and drink their own urine." Then, shouting in Hebrew, he addressed the soldiers on the walls directly.

Do not let Hezekiah delude you! He will be powerless to save you. Do not let Hezekiah delude you by saying YHVH will save you. Has any god of any nation saved his country from the power of the King of Assyria? Where are the gods of Hamath and Arpad? Where are the gods of the land of Samaria? Did they save Samaria from me? Tell me which of all the gods of these countries have saved their countries from my hands, for YHVH to be able to save Jerusalem?[51]

Listening to a verbatim report of the envoy's speech, Hezekiah was devastated. In a few brief sentences, at a time when un-avenged insults brought lasting disgrace, the Assyrian had succeeded in denigrating his allies, his religious reforms, his military prowess, and his God. He went into the temple, prostrated, and begged YHVH to punish the Assyrians for this outrage. Then he turned for advice to his old friend and chief critic, Isaiah. Eventually, the city must fall. Should he surrender it now for the sake

of its people? His own death or exile and that of his chief supporters would be preferable to the horrors of a long siege and the
inevitable destruction that must follow it.

Isaiah must have thought that time had reversed itself, and
that he was addressing Hezekiah's father thirty-five years earlier.
His first words were "Do not be afraid." His advice: Defend
Jerusalem. As for the insolent Assyrian king, "I am going to put a
spirit in him, and when he hears a rumor he will return to his own
country and in that country I will bring him down with the
sword."[52] After receiving a second threatening message from Sennacherib, the king prayed again for help, and Isaiah replied with
an oracle excoriating the Great King. How dare Sennacherib take
credit for deeds designed and carried out by YHVH himself?
God had commissioned Assyria to punish the kingdom of Israel,
but "in [the Assyrian's] heart was to destroy, to go on cutting nations to pieces without limit."[53] Sennacherib's great mistake was
to believe that his triumphs were the result of his own strength
and intelligence. "By the strength of my own arm I have done
this," he boasted, "and by my own intelligence, for understanding
is mine."

> I have erased the frontiers of peoples
> and plundered their treasures.
> I have brought their inhabitants down to the dust.
> As if they were a bird's nest, my hand has seized
> the riches of the peoples.
> As people pick up deserted eggs
> I have picked up the whole earth,
> with not a wing fluttering,
> not a beak opening, not a chirp.[54]

But this was to mistake the agent for the principal, the "axe" for
"the man who wields it." And so, Isaiah concluded, "YHVH of

the Hosts is going to send a wasting sickness on his stout warriors; beneath his plenty, a burning will burn like a consuming fire."[55]

Why did the prophet advocate the defense of Jerusalem? Part of the answer, of course, is that he believed that YHVH would fulfill his promise to King David and his descendants by saving the city.[56] As usual, however, he did not simply bank on the occurrence of a miracle; to Isaiah, faith was also a guide to the accurate evaluation of historical risks. Yes, Sennacherib commanded the world's most powerful military force and was a specialist at taking fortified cities. But Jerusalem was very strongly defended; the emperor had serious problems elsewhere in his empire; and Isaiah may have heard reports of an outbreak of plague—a "wasting sickness"—among the invading troops. (For soldiers far from home to die of local illnesses to which they are not immune has been a common occurrence from ancient times until quite recently.)[57] Most important, the conquest of Jerusalem would almost certainly be followed by the same sort of deportations that had stripped Samaria of its ruling class and skilled workers and put an end to the ten northern tribes. It was not Judean nationalism that made this such an appalling prospect for Isaiah—in a world dominated by great empires, he had no hopes of Judah ever becoming a powerful nation—but something else.[58]

YHVH had revealed himself to David's ancestors and had promised to sustain his descendants—but why? What was Judah's mission, if not to be a great and prosperous nation? The answer could be uncovered if one interrogated contemporary history with a mind and spirit laid open to visions—that is, with a prophet's imagination. History, for Isaiah (and henceforth for us), was not the story of a particular chosen people. It was *world* history: a vast, ongoing drama encompassing all the nations—a saga in which every people had a role to play. YHVH had not only selected the Hebrews to implement his plans, he had also selected Assyria, Egypt, and the myriad other nations about which the prophet preached so knowingly.[59] Although Israel has its own special role to play, all these nations are morally equal. As different as their customs and beliefs may be, it is impossible to distinguish between them on any true scale of virtue or vice. All— the Hebrew peoples included—are destined to suffer for their commitment to violent, unjust power. All will be rewarded for turning back to justice, integrity, and peace.

Isaiah remained fascinated by Assyria, the world leader, whose mission, as he now interpreted it, was to punish sinful nations by annihilating national frontiers. Relatively soon, the Great King's empire would fall, as would that of Babylon and all other world conquerors. But the empire-building, nation-smashing activities of the Assyrians—even their policy of mass deportations—were revelatory. They revealed, first of all, that just as God is One, the earth's inhabitants are one. The correlative of monotheism is the unity of mankind. And second, the Assyrians' behavior demonstrated the inefficacy of coercive power to create that unity. They could create the conditions for international community, for example, by building magnificent roads to facilitate travel between distant parts of the empire. But roads used for conquest and rebellion could not provide a stable basis for peaceful intercourse among people. Only when the power of all nations is subordinated to YHVH's universal ethics will the highways become a blessing.

These thoughts produced one of Isaiah's most moving and beautiful orations. After delivering a prophecy predicting the decline of Egypt, he was inspired to imagine a time when the Egyptians would "turn to YHVH who will listen to them and heal them." "In that day," he said, no doubt thinking of the Assyrians' famous roads, "there will be a road from Egypt to Assyria. Assyria will have access to Egypt and Egypt will have access to Assyria. Egypt will serve Assyria." But that was not all. Israel (meaning the Hebrew peoples) would have a crucial part to play in the creation

of a new type of world order. "In that day," the prophet proclaimed, "Israel, making the third with Egypt and Assyria, will be
blessed in the center of the world. YHVH of the Hosts will give
his blessing in the words, 'Blessed be my people Egypt, Assyria my
creation, and Israel my heritage.'"[60]

"My people Egypt, Assyria my creation, Israel my heritage"—
no one in Israel or Judah, or, so far as we know, in any other land,
had imagined the world of competitive nations transformed and
blessed by a God who cared for all of them. Isaiah reached the
same visionary conclusion when he considered another Assyrian
innovation: the use of iron weapons to create the world's most
terrifying military machine. Iron is a perfect symbol of transformation, since it can be heated until it becomes malleable and is
reshaped into a new form. Because of this mutability (symbolic
of the mutability of all human institutions), the instruments of
war could be transformed into instruments of peace, provided
that YHWH's ethics were recognized as prior to the claims of
power. There would come a time, the prophet proclaimed, when
"the mountain of the Temple of YHVH shall tower above the
mountains and be lifted higher than the hills," when "all the nations will stream to it," and when YHVH himself (or those inspired by him) would "adjudicate between many peoples."

> These will hammer their swords into plowshares,
> Their spears into sickles.
> Nation will not lift sword against nation,
> There will be no more training for war.[61]

That was why YHVH would save Jerusalem—so that Judah
might fulfill her mission to take the word of God to the nations,
and so to help them settle their differences without the need for
war. Some readers of these famous words have suggested that Isaiah's vision of universal peace was eschatological—that is, that he

was speaking of a time at the end of history, or after the end of history, when the earth would be transformed and God would rule without human assistance.[62] But this is not at all consistent with the prophet's deep conviction that God *already* works his will through history, and that history's most fundamental law is a law of transformation. To Isaiah, the idea of a peaceful resolution of international conflicts was not at all posthistorical or utopian.[63] The political history of his own time demonstrated the hopelessness of trying to establish a stable world order on the basis either of imperial might or violent rebellion. What would finally organize international politics, he was certain, would not be some sort of pax Assyriana but "a peace that has no end."[64] The Assyrian "king of the world" could not realize such a peace, but those following the world's true king could do so—and not at the end of history, but in the course of it.

And so, because he had faith in YHVH's promise to David and in Judah's God-given mission—and because, practical man that he was, he believed that Jerusalem might withstand a siege—Isaiah counseled Hezekiah not to surrender the city. All this counseling was said to have taken place at night. In the morning, something strange was discovered to have happened. The Assyrian army was gone. (One cannot help being reminded of the experiences recounted by survivors of the Holocaust, who awakened one morning in Auschwitz or Buchenwald to find that their guards had disappeared and that the gates of the camp were wide open.)[65]

Two versions of the story circulated. According to one, all that observers could find in the abandoned Assyrian camp were corpses, struck down during the night by the "angel of YHVH."[66] Could a plague have struck the army? One Egyptian account quoted by the Greek historian, Herodotus, states that Sennacherib's army was forced to retreat by an infestation of mice—a possible reference to bubonic plague, which is carried by rats.[67] A second version, supported by Assyrian documents, holds that Sennacherib heard a report of trouble at home, as predicted by Isaiah, and withdrew his forces to deal with serious unrest in Babylonia.[68] It is possible that both accounts are correct—that a combination of illness in his army and problems in the East convinced Sennacherib that it was not worth taking Jerusalem, since he had already crippled Judah by destroying its towns, seizing its richest lands, and collecting an enormous tribute from Hezekiah.

In any case, Sennacherib returned to his homeland, where he created a magnificent new capital at Nineveh. On the walls of his palace he commissioned sculptures in relief describing his conquest of Lachish and other Judean cities. The inscription on one wall reads, "Sennacherib, king of the world, king of Assyria, sat upon his throne and passed in review the booty taken from Lachish."[69] The emperor survived another twenty years before being assassinated in 681, possibly by his son, Esarhaddon, or the crown prince's brothers.[70] Esarhaddon and his son, the famous Ashurbanipal, would realize the Assyrian dream of conquering Egypt, but their dominion, as Isaiah had predicted, did not last long. Less than a century after Sennacherib's victory over Judah, the mightiest empire in world history suddenly collapsed, to be replaced by a new breed of world conquerors, the Babylonians.[71]

Jerusalem was spared—a happy denouement that had a strange and deleterious effect on the course of prophecy in Judah. Isaiah's prediction was vindicated. Against all odds, YHVH had protected Jerusalem and the temple, and had preserved the House of David. The conclusion drawn by many Judeans, including high-ranking clerics and government officials, was that no matter what the circumstances, God would always come to the rescue of Jerusalem and her rulers. In this way, the highly unorthodox Isaiah, who had challenged the accepted wisdom of his time, became the unwitting founder of a new orthodoxy. The prophet who had bitterly criticized two Davidic kings and the temple clergy was now cited as authority for the proposition that kings and priests were the chosen of God and under his special protection. His references to a "remnant" of the people who would be saved in a national catastrophe were interpreted as denoting the Jerusalem elite. And the crucial idea that YHVH was the God of the whole earth, who would one day bless Assyria and Egypt as well as Israel, was qualified by the notion that he was particularly attached to one city and one temple, which he would always defend against invaders and despoilers. One day, the Judeans would pay dearly for this attempt to domesticate Isaiah.

As for King Hezekiah, he lived quietly until 687 B.C.E., when he died of natural causes and was succeeded by Manasseh, one of the legendary "bad kings" of the Bible. Manasseh gave up the struggle for national independence and returned Judah to the status of a loyal Assyrian vassal. According to the book of Kings, he "worshipped the whole array of heaven and served it"—a reference to Mesopotamian worship of the sun, moon, and stars—as well as introducing altars and statues of alien gods into the temple itself and practicing the magical arts.[72] Manasseh may also have suppressed the prophets, since there is no record of prophetic activity during his reign, and the Bible charges him with "flooding" Jerusalem with innocent blood.[73] An old tradition suggests that Isaiah was martyred by the wicked king, but there is no evidence that he lived long after Sennacherib's retreat. After the lifting of the siege, he seems to have made one speech denouncing the city's residents for celebrating inappropriately when they should have been mourning their dead, repenting for their arrogance, and giving thanks to YHVH.[74] After this, hoping for a great change in human affairs, but dissatisfied to the last, the aged prophet disappears from history, leaving the sealed record of his visions in the hands of his disciples.

CHAPTER IV

✳

"The Heart Is More Devious Than Any Other Thing"
—JEREMIAH 17:9

THE PROPHET JEREMIAH had a scribe named Baruch who transcribed his words in writing, and, on occasion, read them aloud in his name. He had a few influential allies who came to his aid on several of the occasions when his life and freedom were threatened by the authorities. He may also have had disciples, although there is no evidence of this in his writing. But he cannot have had many close friends.

Read his book—that profuse collection of his speeches, sayings, soliloquies, and stories, some written in poetry and some in prose, so angry and eloquent, grief stricken and self-pitying, so impassioned, and yes, so provoking, despite brilliant flashes of visionary hope, that one can imagine oneself saying, upon seeing him in the street, "Oh, not him again! I hope he won't notice me." Today Jeremiah would surely be considered a fanatical figure, either dangerous or ridiculous, depending on how seriously one took his message. He paid a heavy price for refusing to change his tune to accommodate other people's sensibilities and practical interests. He pays it even now for letting us see him not only as YHVH's spokesman, but also as a fallible human being.

Formally, Jeremiah's book is like Isaiah's, an anthology rather than a story chronologically told, alternating grim warnings of disaster with messages of hope and consolation, but its tone of voice and perspective are unmistakably his own.[1] One cannot imagine Isaiah writing anything quite like this:

> *Who will turn my head into a fountain*
> *and my eyes into a spring for tears,*
> *so that I may weep all day, all night,*
> *for all the slain of my daughter—my people?*[2]

Or this:

> *You have right on your side, YHVH,*
> *when I complain about you.*
> *But I would like to debate a point of justice with you.*
> *Why is it that the wicked live so prosperously?*
> *Why do scoundrels enjoy peace?*[3]

Or this:

> *You have seduced me, YHVH, and I have let myself be seduced;*
> *You have overpowered me: you were the stronger.*
> *I am a daily laughingstock,*
> *Everybody's fool.*[4]

This voice seems, in many ways, shockingly contemporary. Like a modern novelist, the prophet exposes his innermost feelings to public view, converses and argues with God as with an intimate friend, and plays the role of a leading actor in his own story. And he does all this in language that fairly sizzles with passion. "We meet in Jeremiah—perhaps for the first time—with what we today should describe as lyric poetry," says one commentator. "It is because of this as much as anything that his preaching has such a uniquely personal note."[5] Of course, emotion also suffuses Isaiah's preaching. As the Assyrians sweep down on Judah

and successive kings ignore his advice, his words express impa-
tience, anguish, wrath, and sometimes hope or exaltation. But
Isaiah attributes these feelings to YHVH directly, not to himself.
Rarely does he use the word "I," and never does he speak as if the
vicissitudes of his own career or emotional life have great historical significance. In Jeremiah's writing, by contrast, there is no
lack of I. "I weep"; "I complain"; "You have seduced me, YHVH";
"Heal me, YHVH, and I shall be really healed"; "Let my perse-
cutors be confounded, not I."[6]

The shift from Isaiah's relative impersonality to this intensely
personal, moody, confessional style of expression is startling.
Jeremiah's sensibility may have been influenced by cultural trends
emanating from Babylon, long the chief center of West Asian civilization.[7] But if he was inspired by intellectual developments in
the imperial heartland, he clearly used them (as Isaiah did) for
prophetic purposes of his own. According to theologian Martin
Buber, "No word of Jeremiah is simply personal. . . . His 'I' is so
deeply set in the 'I' of the people that his life cannot be regarded
as that of an individual."[8] Buber has a point; Jeremiah did identify his own personal struggles with those of his people. More
than this, however, he was the first prophet to conceive of those
people not only as the collectivity known as Israel, but also as an
aggregation of individuals—men and women like himself, whose
moral and political decisions, made by each person, would decide
the nation's fate.

Isaiah had described a world-historical drama, directed by
YHVH, in which Israel had a vital role to play. Jeremiah pro-
moted the individual—a complex, devious, willful, conflicted,
yearning, potentially heroic creature like himself—to a position
at the center of this great story. In his view, repentance—literally,
"turning back" to God—was the key to national salvation.[9] Repentance could save people not only by placating an angry deity,
but also by altering people's thinking and behavior in ways that

increased their chances of surviving and prospering in the world. This sort of radical personal change was not a pipe dream. It *could* take place, but only if each person experienced a movement of the heart sufficiently strong and sincere to overcome contrary impulses toward self-gratification and self-destruction.[10] Jeremiah thus saw the great conflicts of history, including the rise and fall of empires, turning on the hinge of conflicts taking place within the individual. Not only did his *I* reflect the life of his people, their *I*s reflected his own individuality. He was so passionate a lover and hater because he dealt with all collectivities, including Israel, one person at a time.

When his prophetic career began, Jeremiah was a teenager living in his hometown of Anathoth, some three miles north of Jerusalem.[11] The year was 627 B.C.E. Alone with his thoughts, he heard YHVH say,

> *Before I formed you in the womb I knew you;*
> *Before you came to birth I consecrated you;*
> *I have appointed you as a prophet to the nations.*

One can easily imagine the son of a priest (for the boy was descended from a long line of priests, perhaps originating in King David's time) feeling that his spiritual vocation was predetermined.[12] In his vision, YHVH tells him that he was, quite literally, born to be a prophet—that his career is part of God's plan. But, for him, this revelation creates a painful conflict. His immediate response is to resist it. "Ah, Lord YHVH," he objects, "look, I do not know how to speak: I am a child!"[13]

God immediately recognizes this as an excuse, not a statement of fact, and responds like a stern and loving father:

> *Do not say, "I am a child."*
> *Go now to those to whom I send you*

and say whatever I command you.
Do not be afraid of them,
for I am with you to protect you—
it is YHVH who speaks!

Then, as if recognizing that further persuasion is necessary, he takes one more step. "YHVH put out his hand and touched my mouth," recalls Jeremiah, saying,

> *There! I am putting my words into your mouth*
> *Look, today I am setting you*
> *over nations and over kingdoms,*
> *to tear up and to knock down,*
> *to destroy and to overthrow,*
> *to build and to plant.*[14]

At first glance, this experience of Jeremiah's resembles Isaiah's inaugural vision, when the older prophet saw YHVH in the temple surrounded by seraphs and undertook the burden of preaching God's word to a people who would not comprehend it.[15] But something new happens here at Anathoth. When Isaiah was called on to prophesy, he was already a grown man and an advisor to the Judean court, not a raw, volatile youth. Beholding YHVH in the temple, he was overcome by such strong feelings of shame that a seraph had to purify him by touching his "unclean lips" with a live coal. Once cleansed, though, he volunteered for his difficult mission, telling God, "Here I am; send me." Jeremiah, by contrast, is appointed to his office and refuses at first to accept the commission. This is not because he feels unworthy to stand in the presence of YHVH. A member of the priestly caste, he talks to God (in fact, talks back to him) as if he has met him many times before. Even so, he resists the call to preach, and the touch on his lips—not by a seraph but by God himself—is needed to overcome that recalcitrance.

Why did Jeremiah hold back, since God had promised him protection and power, and he knew that there was no escaping his mission? Perhaps because he was aware of what it meant, in the year 627, to be a "prophet to the nations." The emperor Ashurbanipal had just died, triggering dissension in his Assyrian homeland, a great uprising in Babylon, and a wave of rebellions throughout the empire. The international system created more than a century earlier by Tiglath-pileser trembled on the brink of unexpected change. In Jeremiah's vision, YHVH tells him what to expect in this time of political upheaval. "The North is where disaster is boiling over for all who live in this land," he declares. Hostile kingdoms will surround Jerusalem, and Judah will be punished for her people's idolatry and wickedness.[16] God commands Jeremiah to "confront all this land: the kings of Judah, its princes, its priests and the country people." He is to urge them to repent of their sins or else face total destruction. They will abhor this message and oppose him violently, but YHVH will make him "a fortified city, a pillar of iron, and a wall of bronze," and will protect him against his enemies.[17]

Persuaded by this promise, at least for the present, Jeremiah accepted his destiny. We do not know where he lived during the first decades of his career, but it seems likely that he traveled in the rural areas preaching against the corrupt social and religious practices prevalent among his countrymen.[18] Yet he was not at peace in his new vocation. In fact, the pattern of his inaugural vision would repeat itself throughout his career. Time and again, he would resist speaking God's word and then speak it, refuse to carry out his mission and then fulfill it, as if unable to find solace either in rebellion or surrender. "Each time I speak the word," he complained, "I have to howl and proclaim: 'Violence and ruin!'"

The word of YHVH has meant for me
insult, derision, all day long.
I used to say, "I will not think about him,
I will not speak in his name any more."
Then there seemed to be a fire burning in my heart,
imprisoned in my bones.
The effort to restrain it exhausted me,
I could not bear it.[19]

Clearly, the man of God was no model of saintly humility. He shared the sensibility of an age that valued reputation as much as life itself, and that considered ridicule an unforgivable offense. Nor could he control his own poetic imagination, which made the sufferings he predicted for his people as real for him, and as heartrending, as any current catastrophe.[20] Moreover, to prophesy as YHVH had commanded meant breaking with his own priestly family and caste. Ever since Isaiah's time, it had become increasingly clear that independent prophets and the priests or prophets of the temple might well come into fierce conflict, especially if the unattached prophet felt compelled to question the state's legitimacy or the efficacy of temple rituals.[21] Isaiah had challenged the clergy strongly, but he remained to the end a member of the Jerusalem establishment. Jeremiah felt YHVH asking him to take a further painful step: to challenge the elite's very right to exist.

Was this impassioned young man, perhaps, critical of the established priesthood even before receiving his vision? Was he already in rebellion against his own clerical family? Given the intensity of his scorn for salaried priests and adulterous prophets, indeed, for all those he considered hypocritical compromisers, one suspects that his prophetic calling may have liberated him to express feelings of anger and disappointment that had been building for some time. "For all, least no less than greatest, all are out for dishonest gain," he would soon proclaim. "Prophet no less than priest, all practice fraud."[22] (In retaliation for this sort of preaching, Jeremiah was later threatened with violence by members of his own family and residents of his hometown.)[23] Like the radicalized youth of later centuries, he saw officialdom's insincere promises and rationalizations, mechanistic rituals, and sleazy compromises as symptomatic of a wholly corrupt system. Again, like them, he set out to realize in his own life the ethical ideals to which his elders gave mere lip service, thereby exposing the hypocrisy of the Jerusalem establishment.[24] Finally, he discovered in sexual imagery a way to express deep feelings of revulsion for the system's failings—and his own.

One of Jeremiah's favorite metaphors, borrowed from the work of the Israelite prophet Hosea, was that of Judah as an unfaithful wife or a prostitute who goes "whoring" after false gods.[25] In his preaching, this negative imagery sometimes rises to a level of intensity that seems almost scatological:

> I will also pull your skirts up as high as your face
> And let your shame be seen.
> Oh! Your adulteries, your shrieks of pleasure,
> Your vile prostitution!
> On the hills, in the countryside,
> I have seen your abominations.
> Woe to you, Jerusalem, unclean still!
> How much longer will you go on like this?[26]

The prophet Isaiah, one recalls, had at least one wife and several children. Not so Jeremiah, who reports that YHVH warned him, "You must not take a wife or have son or daughter in this place."[27] The reason given for this ban was that a nation fated to be destroyed was not a fit place to raise a family.[28] One suspects, however, that the decision to remain chaste had personal roots as well.

Associating the older generation's corruption with sexual promiscuity, the young radical found himself drawn, by contrast, to a life of ascetic self-denial.[29] The same voice that told him to leave his familial home and profession also commanded him to remain single, outside the compromising structure of spousal and clan relations; to remain a lover of God and of his people, but not of women; and to accept social isolation as the price to be paid for carrying out his mission.

As always, the prophet accepted the charge. And, as always, he complained about the misery it caused him. In his travail, Jeremiah sometimes disclaimed personal responsibility for his fate as a prophet. He described God's message as an overpowering force—"a fire imprisoned in my bones"—that compelled him to speak whether he wished to or not.[30] But his painful vocation was not forced on him. He chose it continually, as he himself recognized in comparing God's call (most daringly) to a sexual seduction. "You have seduced me, YHVH, *and I have let myself be seduced.*"[31] The metaphor exactly captures the mixture of voluntary choice and persuasive pressure that Jeremiah felt had characterized his appointment. He is not only our first lyric poet, therefore, but the first prophet to have a lover's quarrel with God. Repeatedly, he accuses YHVH of tormenting and disappointing him:

> *Why is my suffering continual,*
> *my wound incurable, refusing to be healed?*
> *Do you mean to be for me a deceptive stream*
> *with inconstant waters?*

And, as always, the God-voice in his heart responds with chastening forgiveness.

> *If you come back,*
> *I will take you back into my service;*

and if you utter noble, not despicable, thoughts,
you shall be as my own mouth.[32]

This is the social meaning of the volatile *I* that appears for the first time in Jeremiah's work. In his struggle to master his own weaknesses, this prophet is a stand-in for Judah, modeling in his own thoughts and affections the movement of alienation and return, rebellion and repentance, which he believes is possible—and urgently necessary—for his people. The choice is always his (which is to say, ours), not God's. One might even say that this talent for dramatizing the violation and renewal of the covenant with YHVH was why he was appointed to prophesy in the first place. If Isaiah is the prophet of the inspired intellect, uncovering the hidden meanings of external events, Jeremiah is the prophet of the suffering and unconquerable will. After each episode of humiliation, each bout of near despair, he chooses once again to be "seduced," thereby demonstrating in the flesh the possibility of a return to God and to one's original sense of mission.

THE FIRST EIGHTEEN YEARS of Jeremiah's prophetic career (roughly, 627–609 B.C.E.) are a subject of exuberant speculation. We know almost nothing about what he said or did in this so-called silent period, while a great deal is known about the dramatic events taking place internationally and in his own country.[33] On the world stage, the Assyrian empire was disintegrating with a speed that would have astonished even Isaiah, although he had predicted its demise. The collapse was all the more surprising because of the achievements of Ashurbanipal, the conqueror of Egypt and Iran, who not only projected Assyrian power further than any of his predecessors, but also assembled the finest library in the ancient world at his palace in Nineveh.[34] All this glory was undone before Jeremiah reached the age of forty. "Ashurbanipal controlled the greatest empire the world had known," writes one historian, "yet within two decades of his death the country was overrun, its cities destroyed, and Assyria as a significant political entity had disappeared forever."[35]

For a long time, the nations subjected to Assyrian rule had dreamed, fruitlessly, that the death of the emperor might also mean the end of his empire. The Judeans were hardly immune to such hopes, especially since a young man named Josiah, only a few years older than Jeremiah, was now their king. Josiah's grandfather, King Manasseh, had been a faithful (some said slavish) Assyrian vassal who imported a spectacular variety of Mesopotamian religious practices into Judah, ranging from the worship of the sun and stars, magic, and divination, to the placing of a statue of Asherah in the temple, accompanied by a house for her "sacred male prostitutes."[36] His son, who succeeded him around 642, was assassinated two years later by army officers who may have represented an anti-Assyrian party in the capital. According to the Bible, "the people of the land"—either a small group of influential landowners or a mass uprising of farmers— then executed the plotters and put the eight-year-old Josiah on the throne.[37]

By the time the young king came of age, the Assyrian empire was tottering. Led by the gifted Chaldean prince, Nabopolassar, Babylonian forces defeated the Assyrian army in a major battle, captured the city of Babylon, and began to extend their power throughout southern Mesopotamia. The Egyptians, who had refused to pay tribute even while Ashurbanipal lived, now mobilized their forces and began to reassert their old interests in Palestine and Syria. The Medes attacked Assyria's cities from the east, and the Scythians and Cimmerians swarmed down on her northern outposts.[38] Josiah took advantage of this period of imperial weakness to extend Judah's influence over the Hebrews still living in the former kingdom of Israel—he may actually have annexed several of the former Assyrian provinces[39]—and to make his own country virtually independent. Under his leadership, Judeans began to dream of a revived United Monarchy ruled, as in King David's time, from Jerusalem.

This nationalistic fervor was accompanied by a significant movement of religious purification and reform, apparently directed from the top down by the king and his chief supporters.[40] In the 620s, Josiah ordered the temple to be repaired and cleansed of all idolatrous objects. He purged the priesthood, smashed a furnace outside Jerusalem that had apparently been used for child sacrifice, and launched a national campaign to rid the nation of foreign religious cults and practices. "The official Assyrian religion being the very symbol of national humiliation," one historian notes, "any independence movement would naturally get rid of it and, having done so, would equally naturally go on to eliminate all religious features considered un-Israelite."[41] The nationalism in question, however, was not simply Hebrew but Judean, and not only Judean but Jerusalemite. Josiah went on to destroy the "high places" and local altars outside Jerusalem at which sacrifices had long been offered to YHVH, including those traditionally used by the Hebrews of the northern kingdom. His intention, quite clearly, was to make the Jerusalem Temple the indispensable center of Yahwist religious practice, just as the city itself would become the unified nation's political center.

Josiah's campaign of centralization was fueled by an astonishing (and still controversial) discovery. In 622, during the repair of the temple walls, a Book of the Law was found wedged into a cranny of an old wall and brought to the king's attention by the high priest. According to the biblical account, Josiah had the book read aloud to him and then tore his garments in grief, exclaiming, "Great indeed must be the anger of YHVH blazing out against us because our ancestors did not obey what this book says by practicing everything written in it."[42] The document seems to have been a version of the text now known as Deuteronomy, although scholars disagree about the extent to which it may have been written or rewritten in Josiah's time to support his religious reforms and political program.[43] After its authentication by the prophetess Huldah, Josiah read the book aloud to a great gathering at the temple, after which he and the people ceremonially renewed their covenant with YHVH. Finally, to memorialize the Hebrews' ancient liberation from Egyptian slavery and their receipt of the law on Mount Sinai, he ordered the first national celebration of Passover in Jerusalem.[44]

Among its other purposes, this celebration was very likely meant to express the king's determination to resist any return to Egyptian slavery—that is, to vassal status under the aggressive new pharaohs of Egypt's Twenty-sixth Dynasty. A decade after Ashurbanipal's death, the period of chaos in international relations was ending. The great powers contending for domination of the Middle Eastern world were effectively reduced to two: Babylon and Egypt. In Mesopotamia, the army of Babylonians and Medes led by King Nabopolassar and his son, the crown prince Nebuchadnezzar, went from victory to victory, taking the Assyrians' imperial capital, Nineveh, in 612, and their provisional capital at Haran in 610. Understanding that Babylon meant to succeed Assyria as ruler of the world, Egypt had already sent military forces to aid the Assyrians fighting with their backs to the Euphrates River.[45] Now, in 609, the young pharaoh, Necho II, marched north with a new army to prevent Nebuchadnezzar from smashing through the Assyrian lines.

Necho's hope, of course, was not only to stave off the Assyrian collapse, but to bring Palestine and Syria under his own sway. Josiah therefore went out with an army to confront him. The book of Kings says simply that he "intercepted" the pharaoh at Megiddo, in northern Israel, and that "Necho killed him at Megiddo in the first encounter."[46] Chronicles presents a much more elaborate scenario, in which Josiah insists on fighting Necho even though the pharaoh claims that he has no quarrel with Judah and that Egypt is fulfilling God's plan.[47] What is clear is that the reforming king, not yet forty years old, was mortally wounded by Egyptian bowmen at the pass of Megiddo and was taken back to Jerusalem, where he died amid great lamentation.[48] "Jeremiah composed a lament for Josiah which all the singers, male and female, still recite today when they lament for Josiah," says the Chronicler.[49]

Did Jeremiah admire Josiah and his religious policies? Was this the reason why we hear so little of him during the reign of the young reformer? Although the question has been much debated, the answer remains in doubt. Some aspects of Josiah's reign—in particular, the king's personal integrity and concern for "the poor and needy"—must have pleased him very much.[50] Very likely, the national campaign against idolatry and foreign religious practices also met with his approval.[51] By the time Josiah died, however, Jeremiah was clearly disenchanted with the failure of the reform movement to generate deeper changes in the behavior of the Judean ruling class and the attitudes of the people. In fact, he viewed the tendency to substitute ceremonial reforms for genuine spiritual transformation as a disaster for the faith.[52] All this became apparent when the prophet's silent period ended, and he made a shocking debut at the Temple of YHVH in Jerusalem.

Worshippers streaming to the temple on a cold morning in the winter of 609–608 were astonished to find a disheveled thirty-year-old man standing in the outer gate, preaching at the top of his lungs to a crowd that grew larger with each passing minute. It was not the sight of an unknown prophet ranting in the gate that made them stop instead of brushing past him to enter the inner courtyard; such performances had long been part of the environment of the Temple Mount. No—it was the content of the prophet's message, bordering on sacrilege and treason, that held them transfixed and brought the temple priests and prophets running from their offices to hear the stranger's compelling, inflammatory speech.

Jeremiah spoke in YHVH's name. We can imagine how much effort it must have taken for him to subdue his fear, for there was a new king in Judah, Jehoiakim by name, a bloody-minded fellow who had just executed a man for giving a speech very much like the one he now felt compelled to give. Jehoiakim had reason to worry about angry prophets and unruly crowds. After King Josiah's death, influential landowners had put his younger brother on the throne, but the pharaoh Necho had arrested the young king for plotting against Egypt, imprisoned him, and carted him off into exile.[53] Jehoiakim was Necho's creature, a fact that did not endear him to the Judeans loyal to Josiah's memory and the nationalist cause. When a wandering prophet named Uriah denounced his misdeeds, predicting the conquest of Judah and the destruction of Jerusalem as a result, Jehoiakim ordered him arrested, had him returned from Egypt, where he had fled, and executed him on the spot.

With Uriah's fate in mind, Jeremiah might have been tempted to soften his message at the temple gate. Little wonder that he had heard YHVH order him to "speak all of the words I have commanded you tell them; *do not omit one syllable.*"[54] Omitting nothing, the prophet's speech immediately captured the attention of the crowd.

"Put no trust in delusive words like these," he proclaimed caustically, "This is the sanctuary of YHVH, the sanctuary of YHVH, the sanctuary of YHVH!" Having silenced his audience, he proceeded more softly, offering them hope. "If you amend your behavior and your actions," he pleaded, "if you do not exploit the stranger, the orphan and the widow, if you do not shed innocent blood in this place, and if you do not follow alien gods to your own ruin, then here in this place I will stay with you, in the land that long ago I gave to your fathers for ever." A brief pause—and then he laced into them, his voice rising steadily in volume. "Yet here you are, trusting in delusive words, to no purpose. Would you steal, murder, commit adultery, perjure yourselves, burn incense to Baal, follow alien gods that you do not know?—and then come presenting yourselves in this Temple that bears my name, saying, 'Now we are safe—safe to go on committing all these abominations!'" Pointing dramatically toward the sanctuary, he shouted with real anger, "Do you take this Temple that bears my name for a robbers' den? I, at any rate, am not blind—it is YHVH who speaks!"

One imagines people in the crowd turning to one another and murmuring, "What? Did he call the temple a robber's den? Doesn't he know what happened to Uriah?" As if to confirm their worst suspicions, Jeremiah continued the attack, adding a new note of sorrowful solemnity: "And now, since you have committed all these sins—it is YHVH who speaks—and have refused to listen when I spoke so urgently, so persistently, or to answer when I called you, I will treat this Temple that bears my name, and in which you put your trust, and the city I have given to you and your ancestors, just as I treated Shiloh. I will drive you out of my sight, as I drove all your kinsmen, the entire brood of Israel."[55] "I will treat this Temple as I treated Shiloh, and make this city a curse for all the nations of the earth."[56]

There was no ambiguity here. As everyone knew, Shiloh was the original home of the Ark of the Covenant, the holy city that God had allowed the Philistines to destroy centuries earlier.[57] Driving "the brood of Israel" out of sight referred to the depopulation of the northern kingdom by the Assyrians. Quite clearly, Jeremiah was preaching the conquest of Judah and the destruction of Jerusalem by some foreign power, although at this point he had not yet identified the invader.

This was a novel and frightening doctrine—a dangerous heresy, in fact, to those who accepted as undoubted truth the idea that YHVH had promised to protect the capital, its rulers, and the temple against all enemies. Even Isaiah had never doubted the validity of that promise. Jeremiah's condemnation meant, in effect, that Judah had forfeited whatever claim it might have had to special treatment by YHVH—or at least that it would forfeit that claim if its rulers remained dishonest and unjust and its people lawless and idolatrous. What made the prophecy so disturbing was not only that it stripped away the long-accepted assumption of divinely guaranteed security, but that it threatened a terrible punishment for "ordinary" injustice, corruption, violence, and infidelity—the sort of behavior that many people considered business as usual. "What have we done to deserve such a terrifying judgment?" they must have wondered. But one defining characteristic of prophets like Isaiah and Jeremiah is their ability to recognize as radically evil those practices that self-interested parties dismiss as the unavoidable costs of managing an organization, government, or business.[58] Twenty-five hundred years later, those in the business of owning and trading Negro slaves would be asking themselves the same question: "What have we done to deserve such a terrifying judgment?"

In making the sentence of doom conditional on the Judeans' continued misbehavior, the prophet struck a note implicit in Isaiah's preaching, but not so clearly articulated and emphasized: There was still time to repent. A radical change of thinking and behavior among the nation's leaders and people could avert the divine decree.[59] Even more striking was his emphasis on an inner transformation—a change of heart—as the sine qua non for collective salvation. Bewailing the nation's failure to obey the law and heed the prophets, Jeremiah introduced a concept new to prophetic speech: sincerity. "Here is the nation that will not listen to the voice of YHVH its God, nor take correction," he thundered accusingly, pointing at the crowd. "Sincerity is no more, it has vanished from their mouths."[60] The prophet spoke out of deep disenchantment with the limitations of Josiah's reforms, which had changed the external forms of religious observance without altering the deep-rooted attitudes of the people. This failure also pointed to a structural problem that earlier prophets had not recognized. As he was later to write,

> The heart is more devious than any other thing,
> Perverse too: who can pierce its secrets?
> I, YHVH, search to the heart,
> I probe the loins,
> To give each man what his conduct
> And his actions deserve.[61]

The worshippers may have been glad to hear that they could avert YHVH's wrath by changing their attitudes and behavior, but this concession did not impress the temple priests and prophets, who were now plainly visible among the members of the crowd, listening carefully and murmuring to each other. Catching sight of them, Jeremiah spoke scathingly of the uselessness of ritual sacrifices without a change of heart. "YHVH of the Hosts, the God of Israel, says this: Add your burnt offerings to your sacrifices and eat all the meat! For when I brought your ancestors out of the land of Egypt, I said nothing to them, gave them no orders, about burnt offerings and sacrifices. These were my orders: Listen to my voice, then I will be your God and you shall be my people."[62] Then, after denouncing the persistence of pagan religious practices among rulers and people alike, he delivered another shock to the clerical establishment.[63]

> How dare you say: We are wise,
> and we possess the Law of YHVH?
> But look how it has been falsified
> by the lying pen of the scribes!"[64]

The temple scribes, liars? The accusation of official deception must have produced astonished gasps among his listeners. Jeremiah did not name the law book that had been falsified, but everyone understood his target was the written version of Deuteronomy whose appearance had amazed the country during the period of Josiah's reforms. In addition to teachings that seemed authentically ancient, that document contained certain passages which aroused suspicion: in particular, those requiring that sacrificial worship be centralized in "the place that YHVH will choose" (that is, the temple),[65] and those altering the traditional celebration of various religious festivals so as to put them under the control of the temple clergy.[66] The alleged lies of the scribes, who were part of the Jerusalem bureaucracy, had the effect of promoting the same ceremonial fetishism and spiritual complacency that the prophet identified as major obstacles to genuine repentance. And genuine repentance, he insisted, was all that stood between Judah and fiery destruction. "The Lord YHVH says this," he warned the horrified crowd. "My anger and my wrath shall be poured out on this place, over man and beast, trees of the countryside, fruits of the soil; it shall burn, and not be quenched."[67]

That was quite enough for the onlooking priests. In a moment, they seized Jeremiah bodily and were threatening him with execution for preaching the destruction of the temple and the city—that is, for prophesying falsely, a capital offense according to Mosaic Law.[68] According to the biblical account, "the people were all crowding around Jeremiah in the Temple of YHVH," a situation that prompted high officials to rush over from the royal palace to conduct a hearing on the spot.[69] Some in the crowd may have wanted to harm the prophet, but considering the role they played as jurors in the remarkable proceeding that followed, many probably sought to protect him.[70]

One can imagine the royal officials seated in high chairs on the steps leading up to the temple, with Jeremiah standing before them, flanked by the priests and the elders, and the people drawn up behind them in the temple square, crowding in close to hear the proceedings.[71] A high-ranking priest spoke first, addressing both the officials and the crowd.

"This man deserves to die," he said, "since he has prophesied against this city, as you have heard with your own ears."

Jeremiah then made a brief statement in his own defense. Yes, he had preached the destruction of Jerusalem. But if the Judeans changed their behavior, God would "relent and not bring down on you the disaster he has pronounced on you." He concluded by putting himself in the hands of the officials and the people. "Do whatever you please or think right with me. But be sure of this, that if you put me to death, you will be bringing innocent blood on yourselves, on this city and on its citizens, since YHVH has truly sent me to you to say all these words in your hearing."

This speech must have set the onlookers to murmuring among themselves. Perhaps the strange prophet was mistaken, but he was fearless—much braver, clearly, than the late Uriah—and he certainly seemed to believe that he was delivering God's message. Moreover, he was not prophesying an inevitable disaster, only a possible tragedy that might be averted, depending on how God's people behaved. At this point, one of the elders stepped forward, and the crowd quieted down. In King Hezekiah's time, he said, the prophet Micah had prophesied the destruction of the temple and had *not* been put to death; in fact, his words had persuaded the Judeans to pray for Jerusalem's salvation. Why not follow this precedent in the instant case?

So far as the officials and the people were concerned, that argument was the clincher. Turning to the assembled priests, the king's chief officer proclaimed, "This man does not deserve to die: he has spoken to us in the name of YHVH our God."[72] The crowd shouted its approval, and Jeremiah was released from custody, but the priests were not mollified. In the official view, to threaten the city and the temple with divine punishment was utterly impermissible. As primary interpreters of religious law, the clerics might still have insisted that Jeremiah be stoned to death for prophesying falsely, but they were prevented from doing so by Ahikam ben-Shaphan, a well-connected priest who, with his father, had been one of the leaders of the Josian reform.[73]

We do not know why Ahikam saved Jeremiah. He may have been unconvinced by the charge of false prophecy or impressed by the prophet's sincerity—or he may have felt that the reform movement was faltering under King Jehoiakim, and that zealots like Jeremiah were needed to keep the flame alive.[74] In any event, the beleaguered prophet emerged from this first confrontation with mixed feelings intensified. Clearly, if he continued to preach against Jerusalem's rulers, he was headed for continued persecution and ostracism—perhaps even outlawry. But YHVH had made good his promise of protection. Not even the temple elite had prevailed against him, and a few listeners, at least, believed he might be speaking God's word. Above all, his narrow escape at the temple left him enraged. Jehoiakim and his priests would rather sacrifice Judah than change their behavior; would rather murder authentic prophets than tolerate their disturbing visions. Jeremiah was grateful to Ahikam for sparing his life. He would soon make the rest of the elite regret deeply that he had been spared.

CHAPTER V

✳

"Deep Within Them I Will Plant My Law"
—JEREMIAH 31:33

W HILE JEREMIAH argued for his life at the temple, a war for world supremacy was taking place some four hundred miles north of Jerusalem. There, along the Euphrates River, the Babyonians under King Nabopolassar and his son, Nebuchadnezzar, fought to establish a bridgehead that would permit them to invade Syria and Palestine. King Necho's Egyptian army resisted them strongly, thwarting each Babylonian attempt to cross the river and making forays of its own into Nabopolassar's territory. For almost four years, the issue remained in doubt, with the Egyptians holding the apparent advantage.[1] In Jerusalem, sentiment among the king and his advisors was strongly pro-Egyptian; the pharaoh had acted cleverly in putting his nominee, Jehoiakim, on the throne. But one man, at least, was convinced that the king's policy was suicidal and said so: the incorrigible, "irresponsible" prophet from Anathoth.

How Jeremiah became convinced that Babylon would win the war is not entirely clear. It is possible that he went to the Euphrates himself to observe the situation on the ground. Many people in those days traveled widely, and the prophet tells one story that might provide evidence of such a journey.[2] But the hypothesis of a long trip to the north is unnecessary. As in Isaiah's case, symbols vouchsafed in visions combined with his own political insight and understanding of international relations to produce predictions not always accurate, but often remarkably prescient.

At least from the time that Egypt and Babylon crossed swords, Jeremiah understood that the world empire created by Assyria would survive under new leadership. Power would emanate from Mesopotamia, the great center of West Asian civilization, not from the played-out kingdom of the pharaohs. Babylon had long played the role of Athens to Assyria's Rome. The successor to ancient Sumer, she was as dominant culturally as Assyria was militarily. "Because of the firm cultural links between the two nations," notes one scholar, "Assyria could never treat its southern neighbor as it treated any other territory. Over the centuries various strategies were tried but they all foundered, and the irony was that in the end non-militaristic Babylonia conquered the great warrior nation."[3] Jeremiah put it neatly: "Babylon was a golden cup in YHVH's hand," he was later to write. "She made the whole world drunk. The nations drank her wine, and then went mad."[4]

From the very start of his prophetic career, Jeremiah had identified the better-developed North, not the South, as the chief source of danger to Judah. "The North is where disaster is boiling over for all who live in this land."[5] This vague threat was now replaced by one far more specific and, for a man of Jeremiah's preternatural sensitivity, horribly painful to imagine. The "disaster from the north" was Babylon, "the destroyer of nations," which he envisaged advancing on Judah "like the clouds, his chariots like a hurricane, his horses swifter than eagles."[6] Isaiah had described Assyria's advance in somewhat similar terms, but with a certain eloquent detachment.[7] Jeremiah's empathetic imagination literally made him ill:

> O my bowels, my bowels! I writhe with pain!
> Walls of my heart!

My heart is throbbing!
I cannot keep quiet,
for I have heard the trumpet call
and the cry of war.[8]

Pursued by excruciatingly vivid visions of a Babylonian conquest, he literally could not keep quiet. Speaking in marketplaces and on city streets, he warned the citizens of Jerusalem of what was to come, and gave voice at the same time to his own nightmares.

Yes, I hear screams like those of a woman in labor,
anguish like that of a woman giving birth to her first child;
they are the screams of the daughter of Zion, gasping,
hands outstretched,
"Ah, I despair! I am fainting away
with murderers surrounding me."[9]

As always, the prophet offered his listeners a way to avert these ghastly consequences: sincere repentance. At a potter's house, he had heard YHVH compare the House of Israel to "clay in the potter's hand" that could be molded this way or that, saved or sacrificed, according to the will of its creator and the quality of the material. Nothing was unalterably foreordained; the people themselves could influence their future by altering their thinking and behavior.[10] But few in Jerusalem took his warnings and entreaties seriously. Egypt was winning battles, not losing them, and in any case, YHVH had promised to protect the House of David.[11] So confident was King Jehoiakim of an Egyptian victory that he commissioned the construction of a new royal palace befitting a favored ally of the pharaoh. Jeremiah therefore resorted to extraordinary measures to make his message heard.

Once again, the symbol of the clay pot played an important role. Prompted by the divine voice, Jeremiah went to the temple and persuaded a few elders and priests to go with him to a city gate within sight of the Valley of ben-Hinnom, a place formerly used for pagan religious rites. With Josiah's reforms waning, some people were apparently returning to the old Baalist practices, including real or symbolic child sacrifices. Turning to his witnesses, the prophet predicted divine retaliation for this gross infidelity: a siege of Jerusalem in which children would truly be sacrificed. "I will make them eat the flesh of their own sons and daughters," he said, speaking of the Jerusalemites. "They shall eat each other during the siege, in the shortage to which their enemies, in their determination to kill them, will reduce them." Then he smashed an earthenware pot on the ground, saying, in YHVH's name, "I am going to break this people and this city just as one breaks a potter's pot, irreparably."[12]

Returning to the court of the temple, Jeremiah stood once more before the people who had earlier spared him from execution. Again, he prophesied the fall of Jerusalem to Babylon, since its people "have grown so stubborn and refuse to listen to my words."[13] This time, however, the authorities reacted without bothering to go through the formalities of a trial. The priest in charge of the temple police, a man called Pashur, seized him, had him beaten by policemen, and put him in the stocks at the temple gate for a full day and night in order to disgrace him publicly. He then barred him from returning to the temple precincts. When released the next day, Jeremiah flew into a rage, predicting that "the whole of Judah," as well as the treasures of its kings, would be carried off to Babylon. "As for you, Pashur, and your whole household," he told the official grimly, "you shall go into captivity; you shall go to Babylon; there you will die, and there be buried, you and all your friends to whom you have prophesied lies."[14]

A few years later, the prophet would endure worse physical punishment, but this episode of public humiliation brought him to the lowest psychological point of his career. Returning home,

he prayed to be revenged on his enemies, and then gave vent to
something approaching complete despair. "A curse on the day
when I was born," he moaned, "no blessing on the day my mother
bore me!"

> *A curse on the man who brought my father the news,*
> *"A son, a boy has been born to you . . ."*
> *Why ever did I come out of the womb*
> *to live in toil and sorrow*
> *and to end my days in shame!*[15]

Vindication of a sort, however, was just around the corner. Up
on the Euphrates, King Nabopolassar had fallen ill and returned
to Babylon, putting Nebuchadnezzar in charge of the army. The
Egyptians were encamped at Carchemish, a strongly defended
fortress city on the west bank of the river.[16] They had recently defeated the Babylonians in a serious battle fought several miles
south of the city, and were not expecting another fight so soon.[17]
Avoiding their outposts, Nebuchadnezzar crossed the river and
appeared suddenly with his army to the west of the city, cutting off
the Egyptian line of retreat.[18] The Egyptians, with their Greek
mercenary troops at their side, preferred a battle to a siege and had
every reason to think they would win it. But they had not faced
Nebuchadnezzar before. As Jeremiah himself reported it, casualties on both sides were heavy. There was, after all, a world to win.
Finally, outgeneraled and outfought, the Egyptians broke and ran.

> *What do I see?*
> *They are panic-stricken,*
> *in full retreat!*
> *Their heroes, beaten back,*
> *are fleeing headlong*
> *with not a look behind.*

Terror from every side!
—It is YHVH who speaks.
The fastest cannot escape,
nor the bravest save himself:
there in the north, there by the river Euphrates,
they have collapsed, have fallen.[19]

Driven south and west, the survivors fled into Syria, but when they fell back on the town of Hamath to make a last stand, they were exterminated. According to a Babylonian account, "not a single Egyptian returned home."[20] Nebuchadnezzar lost no time in continuing the invasion, marching his army across Syria to the Lebanese coast and then south to the Egyptian border.[21] There was virtually no resistance. As Jeremiah had predicted, the Babylonians were now masters of the entire region.

This was the prophet's moment. It was time to remind Jerusalem and the nation that his words had, from the beginning, been those of YHVH, and that Judah might still be saved from destruction if the government and the people heeded his message. Not long before the Battle of Carchemish, a scribe named Baruch ben-Neriah, a well-known official from a distinguished family, had become one of his few friends and followers.[22] Over the course of the next several months, Jeremiah collected samples of his poetry and prose, recollected other speeches and sermons, and dictated them all to Baruch, who transcribed the digest of his teachings on a long parchment scroll.[23] Since he was barred from speaking at the temple, he asked the scribe to read the scroll aloud for him "in the hearing of all the men of Judah who come in from the towns. Perhaps they will offer their prayers to YHVH and each one turn from his evil way, for great is the anger and wrath with which YHVH has threatened this people."[24]

The appropriate day came in December 604. Several months earlier, upon learning that his father had died in Babylon, Nebuchadnezzar had halted his campaign in the West and returned home to be crowned king. Now he was back in Philistia with a rested and reequipped army, demolishing the walls of Ashkelon, a city loyal to Egypt that had refused to submit to his rule. The Judean authorities (still Egyptian vassals themselves) declared a national day of fasting and summoned the people to the temple to pray for YHVH's protection. Baruch arrived on the appointed day with his scroll, took it to an open office belonging to an official he knew well, and read it out in a voice easily heard by the large crowd in the courtyard below.

The entire reading probably took almost two hours, but the people listened intently, as if frozen to the spot. Many of them knew the gist of Jeremiah's teachings. Even so, the cumulative effect of this recital, with its uncannily accurate predictions and heartrending visions of the disaster to come, was overwhelming. Another of Baruch's friends rushed immediately to the royal palace, where a meeting of top officials was being chaired by the secretary of state. After hearing a brief summary of the scroll, the group insisted on summoning Baruch to the palace, where they seated him in a chair and asked him to recite it. Again, the effect was instantaneous. If Jeremiah's views were as well founded as they seemed to be, Judah must abandon her Egyptian alliance and make peace with Nebuchadnezzar. "We must certainly inform the king of all this," said the secretary (a holdover from the reform administration of King Josiah). But first, it was necessary to confirm the scroll's authorship.

"Tell us," the official asked Baruch, "how you came to write all these words."

"Jeremiah dictated them to me, and I wrote them down in ink in this book."

"You and Jeremiah had better go into hiding; and do not tell anyone where you are," he replied.[25]

This was good advice. Later that day, another official read the scroll to Jehoiakim, who "was seated in his winter apartments—it was December—with a fire burning in a brazier in front of him."[26] Each time the official read three or four columns, "the king cut them off with a scribe's knife and threw them in the fire in the brazier until the whole of the scroll had been burned in the fire." Two of his administrators bravely objected to burning the scroll, but the king was adamant. How dare this troublemaker predict that Nebuchadnezzar would destroy his kingdom—and brand his regime an accomplice in its destruction? He ordered the arrest of Jeremiah and Baruch, but by this time, as the biblical account relates, "YHVH had hidden them."[27]

Jeremiah and Baruch were now outlaws. There was no longer any reason to avoid attacking the king by name. The prophet dictated another scroll to his scribe, adding new material condemning Jehoiakim in the most violent terms. Judah would certainly be conquered by the Babylonians, while, as for the king, YHVH "will have no one to sit on the throne of David, and his corpse will be tossed out to the heat of the day and the frost of the night."[28] It was probably at this point that he also added his denunciation of the ruler for building a lavish new royal palace using conscript labor. "Doom for the man who founds his palace on anything but integrity, his upstairs rooms on anything but honesty, who makes his fellow man work for nothing, without paying him his wages."[29] King Josiah had been a man of honesty and integrity, who cared for the poor and needy, but

> You on the other hand have eyes and heart for nothing
> But your own interests,
> For shedding innocent blood
> And perpetrating violence and oppression.[30]

After some time, the search for the fugitives was called off. Jehoiakim had more pressing matters to attend to. In 603, Nebuchadnezzar returned to Palestine to put down a rebellion on the Mediterranean coast, where Egyptian influence was still strong.[31] To avoid an attack on Jerusalem, the Judean king submitted to him, accepted vassal status, and paid a large tribute out of the temple treasures.[32] But this relationship did not last long. Less than two years later, the Babylonians fought a major battle against the Egyptian army in which, according to the Babylonian Chronicles, the combatants "inflicted a major defeat on each other," compelling Nebuchadnezzar to return home to retrain and re-equip his forces.[33] The pharaoh had forced a Babylonian retreat! Interpreting this as a sign of Nebuchadnezzar's weakness, Jehoiakim tore up his treaty with Babylon and declared Judah an independent ally of Egypt.

Jeremiah and his few allies were appalled at this misjudgment. Jerusalem was considered a great prize, and Nebuchadnezzar now had no reason to avoid taking it. First, the Babylonian king dispatched troops to the Arab territories of the southeast in order to protect his flanks and secure vital trade routes. Then he unleashed a devastating series of raids against Judah's rural districts by troops drawn from his own garrisons in Syria and from the neighboring nations of Syria, Moab, and Ammon.[34] In the midst of this debilitating campaign, King Jehoiakim died and was succeeded by his son, Jehoiachin, the "Coniah" of the Bible. One month later, Nebuchadnezzar took personal command of the Babylonian army, brought it into Judah, and put Jerusalem under siege.

This siege proved short and far less savage than that earlier predicted by Jeremiah. On March 16, 597, Jehoiachin yielded to the inevitable, surrendering his capital to the world conqueror. In view of the young king's cooperation, Nebuchadnezzar spared the city and most of its inhabitants. He looted the temple, of course, taking even "the golden furnishings that Solomon king of Israel had made for the sanctuary of YHVH." Then "he deported Jehoiachin to Babylon, as also the king's mother, his eunuchs, and the nobility of the country; he made them all leave Jerusalem for exile in Babylon. All the men of distinction, seven thousand of them, the blacksmiths and metalworkers, one thousand of them— all of them men capable of bearing arms—were led into exile in Babylon by the king of Babylon."[35] Finally, he put Jehoiachin's uncle, Zedekiah, on the throne of David, to rule the kingdom as a Babylonian vassal.

A national tragedy? Certainly. But it was now clear to Jeremiah, if it had not been clear before, that Nebuchadnezzar was a far more civilized conqueror than Tiglath-pileser and his Assyrian successors. Judah was not laid waste. The residents of Jerusalem were not slaughtered or tortured. The king was not replaced by a Babylonian governor, and it was quite clear that the purpose of the deportations was not to ruin the country but to disarm it, by removing top government officials, professional soldiers, and the "blacksmiths and metalworkers" capable of manufacturing weapons.[36] Equally important, the deported population was neither dispersed to destroy its ethnic identity, nor replaced by a motley collection of imported settlers. In accordance with Babylonian imperial policy, the Judean deportees were treated austerely but decently and permitted to live in roughly contiguous areas under the rule of their own elders.[37] Someday—it was not out of the question—they might even return to their own land.

The great issue, as Jeremiah now saw it, was to preserve the nation from obliteration by preventing any further rebellion against Nebuchadnezzar. It was time to return to the capital, where a king reigned who might, at long last, listen to him. If he would not listen, then all was truly lost. He and Baruch set out immediately for Jerusalem and the palace of King Zedekiah.

ZEDEKIAH SEEMS TO have been an earnest, well-intentioned man, not nearly as vainglorious or violent as Jeremiah's nemesis,

King Jehoiakim. The problem, as the prophet discovered upon his return, was that the contentious situation in Jerusalem demanded a powerful, ingenious ruler, someone at least as dedicated and ruthless as King Josiah—and Zedekiah was no Josiah. To begin with, his right to rule was questioned from the start. The Babylonians who had installed him in power called his exiled brother the king of Judah, and many of the nobles, administrators, and priests left to run the country in his absence were inclined to share that judgment.[38] Then, too, the conquerors had made off with the cream of the ruling class. Those left behind—a quarrelsome lot much given to plotting and political intrigue—Jeremiah called "bad figs, so bad as to be uneatable," in contrast to the "excellent figs" taken into exile.[39] Had Zedekiah been a politician of rare gifts, he might have overcome these difficulties, but he soon found himself trapped between bitterly opposed factions, unable either to resist their pressure or to resolve their conflict.

It is difficult to label these competing factions without reading modern political values back into the past. One might call them nationalists and collaborators, rebels and loyalists, or even holy warriors and pacifists, and in each case the effect would be misleading. On one side were those who believed, despite the overwhelming defeat and deportations of 598–597, that a rebellion against Babylon, backed by other nations in the region and supported by Egypt, might succeed—or else that it was worth attempting even though the chances of it succeeding were poor. We do not know the exact composition of this group, but it clearly included people of various classes strongly committed to the cause of Judean independence who were emboldened by priests and prophets predicting an imminent collapse of the Babylonian empire. Within a few years, they believed, Babylon would fall, and King Jehoiachin and the exiles would return with the treasures stolen by Nebuchadnezzar.[40] In the meantime, YHVH would protect Jerusalem from destruction, as Isaiah had promised.

It is common to brand the members of this group mad, fanatical, or at least wildly unrealistic. As one leading commentator puts it, rather kindly, "Judah's leaders, though no doubt brave enough men and sincerely patriotic, seemed totally unable to assess the realities of the situation."[41] But the situation at this point was not as clear as hindsight suggests. Despite his military prowess, Nebuchadnezzar had not succeeded in establishing firm control over the nations of Syria-Palestine and was forced to return every few years to suppress another uprising. More important, Egypt remained outside his control, and the Egyptian army that had held its own against him in 601 continued to rebuild under the leadership of aggressive new pharaohs. Even Jeremiah, although vehemently opposed to rebellion, estimated (quite accurately, as it turned out) that the Babylonian empire would not last long—no more than seventy years.[42] To many of his contemporaries, "it was still not clear whether Egypt or Babylonia would prevail in the long run."[43]

Jeremiah's opposition to the party of rebellion was, therefore, not based solely on a realistic estimate of Babylonian power, although he and his allies were convinced that a serious challenge to Nebuchadnezzar would end by extinguishing the Judean state. The theological dimensions of the loyalist position were revealed in 595, when an uprising in Babylon galvanized the rebel cause. The causes of this unusual disturbance remain obscure, but leading officials apparently participated in it, and it took Nebuchadnezzar a month to capture and execute the ringleaders.[44] Seeing this as a sign of serious internal weakness, perhaps the start of a major disruption of Babylonian society, the anti-Babylonian party convinced Zedekiah to invite the kings of neighboring nations to send envoys to Jerusalem to discuss possible joint action to regain their independence.[45]

The opening conference must have been held in a large hall, since Jeremiah reports that the priests and "all the people" (probably popular representatives) were present.[46] In a gesture that recalled Isaiah's dramatic appearance in Jerusalem wearing the garb of a prisoner of war, the prophet arrived at the meeting in costume. While the large crowd gaped, he paraded before them wearing an ox's wooden yoke. Then, ascending a platform, he spoke in YHVH's name:

> I by my great power and outstretched arm made the earth, man and the animals that are on earth. And I can give it to whom I please. For the present, I have handed all these countries over to Nebuchadnezzar King of Babylon, my servant; I have even put the wild animals at his service.[47]

What YHVH required, Jeremiah reported, was that all the monarchs represented there, including the king of Judah, "bend your necks to the yoke of the king of Babylon."[48] "Any nation or kingdom that will not submit to Nebuchadnezzar . . . I shall punish with sword, famine and plague—it is YHVH who speaks—until I have delivered it into his power."[49] As for the prophets who had predicted success for the independence movement, they were liars whose words must be disregarded. "Since I have not sent them—it is YHVH who speaks—they prophesy untruths in my name."[50]

"Nebuchadnezzar King of Babylon, my servant"—not a few people in the crowd must have found that phrase astonishing. Speaking through Isaiah, YHVH had called Tiglath-pileser "the rod of my anger," but "Nebuchadnezzar, my servant" took a step beyond that. Clearly, Jeremiah was not suggesting that the Babylonian king was some sort of Yahwist—he considered Babylon's religious practices barbarous—nor would he maintain even for a moment that "might makes right." But he was convinced that YHVH had cast Nebuchadnezzar in the role of conqueror for a specific purpose: to test and change his people. The Babylonian was not sent simply to punish them for their sins, but to give them the opportunity to break with the past, recognize their shortcomings, and transform their lives. Whether the Judean state remained independent or not was of no consequence compared with the enormous importance of this transformation. If Nebuchadnezzar's threat to Judah could produce such an effect, he would be functioning as YHVH's servant, indeed.

With these declarations, Jeremiah declared open war on the anti-Babylonian party, hoping to convince the king to stand fast against the forces of rebellion. Since Zedekiah was inclined to be impressed by prophetic declarations and gestures, the struggle at first took the form of a war of symbols. Shortly after Jeremiah appeared at the meeting of envoys, the independence party counterattacked. A temple prophet named Hananiah accosted him in the house of God, predicting in YHVH's name, with the crowd listening intently, that in two years' time the "yoke of Babylon" would be broken, and that the exiled king, the deportees, and the temple vessels would return to Jerusalem. Jeremiah responded with unusual mildness, "I hope so. May YHVH do so. May he fulfill the words that you have prophesied." But, he added, skeptically, "the prophet who prophesies peace can only be recognized as one truly sent by YHVH when his word comes true."[51] In other words, wait two years, then let's see what happens.

At this, Hananiah yanked the yoke from Jeremiah's neck and broke it, declaring that this was how God would soon deal with Babylonian power. For once speechless, Jeremiah left the temple, but he returned the next day wearing a new yoke, this one made of iron. "An iron yoke is what I now lay on the necks of all these nations to subject them to Nebuchadnezzar king of Babylon," he told Hananiah and the crowd. Then he threatened the nationalist prophet directly. "Listen carefully, Hananiah: YHVH has not sent you; and thanks to you this people are now relying on what is false. Hence—YHVH says this—I am going to throw you off the face of the earth." In recounting this dispute, Jeremiah (or

Baruch) adds, without further comment, "The prophet Hananiah died the same year, in the seventh month."[52]

Jeremiah had won that round, perhaps, but the internal conflict continued to intensify and to spread. Disagreements among
prophets were not unknown, of course, but for the first time on
record, the prophets of Israel divided into organized warring
camps, each camp accusing the other of false prophecy. Upon
hearing that some of the Judean exiles in Babylonia were also
being incited to rebel, Jeremiah sent a remarkable letter to that
community denouncing the prophets as liars and advising its
members to remain calm, build new lives for themselves in Babylon, and await liberation by YHVH. "Build houses," he wrote,
"settle down; plant gardens and eat what they produce; take wives
and have sons and daughters . . . you must increase there and not
decrease. Work for the good of the country to which I have exiled you; pray to YHVH on its behalf, since on its welfare yours
depends."[53]

Another scandalous innovation: Whoever had heard of pray-
ing for a pagan country? Then, referring to the exiles' inability to
worship at the Jerusalem Temple, he added, "When you seek me
you shall find me, when you seek me with all your heart, I will let
you find me—it is YHVH who speaks."[54] So much for the campaign to make the Jerusalem Temple essential to the practice of
Yahwism. Although God had promised to return the exiles in due
course to their homeland, the people's relationship with him did
not depend on the existence of a nation called Judah, a city called
Jerusalem, or a building called the temple. Synagogues, properly
so-called, were not yet in existence, yet the worship of YHVH
clearly continued in organized form outside the Hebrew state.[55]
Equally important, from Jeremiah's perspective, the conditions
for the heartfelt recognition of YHVH and his law might as well
be found outside the ancestral land as within it. The tie between
the people and the land was still strongly felt, but by reversing

priorities—by understanding that one's relationship to the law was not based on location—Jeremiah initiated the process that would make Judaism and its Christian and Muslim offspring world religions.

The prophet's influence at Zedekiah's court was not negligible, either. At crucial points during the crisis of the Judean state, Zedekiah turned to him for advice; but before long, it became obvious that his side of the debate was losing ground. Not long after receiving Jeremiah's letter to the Babylonian exiles, one of that community's leaders wrote to the high priest in Jerusalem demanding that the "madman who acts the prophet" be put in the stocks and punished for suggesting they should make their peace with the oppressor.[56] Although nothing came of this, the majority of Jerusalem's nobles, probably with considerable popular support, moved steadily toward open revolt. Frantically, Jeremiah denounced the nationalist prophets, accusing them of "adultery, persistent lying, and abetting of evil men," and ridiculing their visions of a Babylonian defeat and subsequent Pax Judaica. "I have heard what the prophets say who make their lying prophecies in my name" [says YHVH]. "'I have had a dream,' they say. 'I have had a dream!' How long will they retain this notion in their hearts, these prophets prophesying lies, who announce their private delusions as prophetic?"[57]

It was no use. Yielding to intense pressure, Zedekiah mobilized his army, reinforced the hill towns near Jerusalem as best he could, and stocked the city with supplies for a long siege. No doubt with Egyptian encouragement, the rulers of Tyre and Ammon made similar preparations. In 589, perhaps inspired by the fatal illness of the Egyptian pharaoh, Nebuchadnezzar made his move.[58] Under his command, the Babylonian army smashed through Samaria and into Judah, reducing the Judean strongpoints as it advanced. The last towns to fall were Azekah and Lachish. Excavations have turned up potsherds with messages written by the commander of a nearby outpost to the military governor of the region. "For the signal stations of Lachish we are watching," the last message says, "according to all the signs which my lord gives, because we do not see the signals of Azekah."[59] Azekah had fallen. Lachish would follow shortly, giving Nebuchadnezzar an unobstructed path to Jerusalem.

By January 588, the capital was under siege. Jeremiah's situation was increasingly dangerous, since preaching surrender to Nebuchadnezzar's forces could now be considered treasonous. Even so, when the king sent envoys to ask him directly whether YHVH would save the city, he replied that God himself was fighting against Jerusalem, and that Zedekiah would soon become a prisoner of war. To the people, he declared, "Those who stay in this city will die by sword, by famine, or by plague; but anyone who leaves it and surrenders to the Babylonians now besieging it will live; he will escape with his life." Unless the city were surrendered, he insisted, it would be burned to the ground by Nebuchadnezzar.[60] The prophet's enemies listened, recorded his words with care, and bided their time.[61]

A few months later, a combination of circumstances presented them with the perfect opportunity to strike. In the summer of 588, responding to a request by Judean envoys, the new Egyptian pharaoh, Apries, invaded Palestine to relieve Jerusalem.[62] Nebuchadnezzar marched his army south to meet this threat, temporarily lifting the siege, and King Zedekiah again asked Jeremiah to prophesy. Would the Egyptians triumph? Would Jerusalem be saved? The prophet answered with asperity. "Do not deceive yourselves and say: The Babylonians are leaving us for good. They are not leaving. Even if you cut to pieces the whole Babylonian army now fighting against you until there were only the wounded left, they would stand up again, each man in his tent, to burn this city down."[63]

Shortly after this, taking advantage of the respite in fighting,

Jeremiah attempted to leave Jerusalem for his nearby hometown, Anathoth, to participate in a division of property among members of his family.[64] This was a mistake. Spotted by a sentry at the Benjamin Gate, he was arrested, charged with desertion, and turned over to hostile officials, who imprisoned him in an underground cellar.[65] Even though he had advised others to escape the city, the charge of desertion to the enemy was almost certainly spurious. Jeremiah had little concern for his own safety and believed that God wanted him to continue his mission to the city.[66] Moreover, he was now preaching the fall of Babylon, predicting that, in due course, "the hammer of the whole world" would be destroyed, as it deserved to be, by the Medes.[67] Zedekiah understood all this, but was unable to release him for political reasons. He had, after all, incited others to abandon the city. Once again, the king sent for the prophet, asked his political advice, and received the same grim answer: "You will be handed over into the power of the king of Babylon."[68]

At this interview, Jeremiah made an urgent request to be removed from the cellar, whose dark recesses he found intolerable, and Zedekiah had him placed under house arrest at the Court of the Guard. This sign of royal favor infuriated the nobles who believed him to be a traitor. Storming into the palace, they demanded his life. "Let this man be put to death," they demanded. "He is unquestionably disheartening the remaining soldiers in the city, and all the people too, by talking like this. The fellow does not have the welfare of this people at heart so much as its ruin."[69]

Did Jeremiah continue to preach defeatism even while confined at the Court of the Guard? Considering what we know of his personality, this seems highly likely. In any event, Zedekiah found himself powerless against the nobles. He permitted them to lower the prisoner into an empty cistern, there to die of "natural causes" (an indication of their reluctance to end the life of one of YHVH's prophets by the usual methods of stabbing or stoning). As his legs sank into the mud at the bottom of the cistern, Jeremiah must have thought that God had finally abandoned him despite his promise of protection made sixty years earlier. As if by divine intervention, however, a savior suddenly appeared. An Ethiopian eunuch attached to the palace convinced the king that it would be a "wicked thing" to let the prophet die in the well. Extracted from the cistern, Jeremiah was returned to the Court of the Guard, where he lived until the city fell to the Babylonians one year later.

NEBUCHADNEZZAR disposed of the Egyptian army quickly. In a matter of weeks, his troops resumed the siege. Although Jerusalem was one of the most strongly fortified cities in the world, there could be little doubt of the eventual outcome. Little by little, over the course of months, the city's food supplies ran lower. Signs of famine appeared, and the numbers of those deserting to the Babylonians increased. It was probably at this time, when the day-to-day political struggle at Zedekiah's court was over and Jeremiah had time to contemplate the meaning of these events, that he made his greatest spiritual discovery.

One can imagine him, a white-bearded man in his seventies, sitting in his rooms at the Court of the Guard, talking quietly with visitors, or perhaps dictating fervently to Baruch. The question that returned constantly to his mind was this: Why had he failed? God had sent him "to tear up and knock down, to overthrow and destroy, to build and to plant," but only his negative prophecies had been fulfilled; nothing had been built or planted. Clearly, Jerusalem was doomed. Those who survived the siege would be deported, and the Judean state would cease to exist, at least for a time. Why, despite his dreadfully accurate predictions, did Judah's leaders and people not heed YHVH's word and repent? Why, even now, with the city starving, did they defend the doomed state against an overwhelming, God-sent force? And what would become of them—the people of the covenant—after Jerusalem fell and they were sent into exile?

He realized, when the answer came, that he had known it all along. Desperately desiring their repentance, he had preached to the Judeans as individuals, emphasizing the need for sincerity, for a change of heart as well as of external behavior. Each person, he had said again and again, must reject the counsels of his fearful, greedy heart and turn again to the God of personal morality and social justice. Since his countrymen trusted blindly that YHVH would protect them no matter what they thought and did, he had declared their hope for collective salvation a delusion, believing that events would teach them what words might not. But an openness to learning was not teachable. A conversion to new ways of thinking and acting could not be induced. The same un-opened, unconverted hearts that branded him a madman for preaching the fall of Jerusalem would interpret the disaster as they wished—as a defeat for YHVH, perhaps, or as a temporary setback to be nullified when Babylon collapsed and the exiles were restored to their homeland.

But if they did return to Judah with hearts and minds un-changed, what would save them, as world power shifted into the hands of a new empire, from repeating the same dreadful cycle of vassalage and rebellion, conquest and exile? No—this nightmare of repetition could not be their destiny. If YHVH's covenant with his people meant anything, it meant that he would save them, and that they would recognize him, permanently—and recognize him not just as some substitute for Baal or Marduk, but as the giver of a law embodying morality, justice, and peace. For this to occur, the repentance that Jeremiah had advocated must take place at the deepest personal level—the level he called the heart. But unless the whole community, not just a few individuals, changed in-wardly, the bureaucratic, power-driven state and its ritualistic temple elite would subvert whatever spiritual progress some of its members might make. The knotty question, then, was how an entire community—especially one as obtuse and stiff-necked as this one—could learn to change.

A new vision untied the knot. The imminent fall of Jerusalem was a sure sign that YHVH's original covenant with the Hebrews, made at the time of the exodus from Egypt, had been broken. But a new covenant would replace the old one in the days to come. In a voice now shaky with age, the old prophet dictated his insight to Baruch:

This is the covenant I will make with the House of Israel when those days arrive—it is YHVH who speaks. Deep within them I will plant my Law, writing it on their hearts. Then I will be their God and they shall be my people. There will be no further need for neighbor to try to teach neighbor, or brother to say to brother, "Learn to know YHVH." No, they will all know me, the least no less than the greatest—it is YHVH who speaks—since I will forgive their iniquity and never call their sin to mind.[70]

One can imagine Jeremiah's weathered face illuminated as Baruch read the message back to him. This was the answer to the problem of teachability. God would open the hearts of his people in a manner beyond the power of prophetic words or the force of events alone. This did not mean that the Hebrews would all become avatars of justice and morality, but that, in the course of their people's development, each one would develop a new capacity to learn the moral law. The command given to Isaiah to "make the heart of this people gross, its ears dull" had been rescinded. Henceforth, each generation could justly be held responsible for its own misdeeds. In the ancient days, YHVH told Jeremiah, children suffered for the sins of their fathers, but in the days to come, "each is to die for his own sin."[71] Under these circumstances, collective punishment would become an anachronism. With each person in a position to take the responsibility and consequences for his or her own actions, disasters like the destruction of Judah would no longer have any moral purpose or meaning.

One hears in this new doctrine a note of repentance emanating from YHVH himself—an implied admission that punishments administered to those incapable of responding to prophetic messages are unjust. After the fall of Jerusalem, as after the Flood, God repents, and, like a lover reuniting with his estranged beloved, promises a new beginning. "I have loved you with an everlasting love, so I am constant in my affection for you. I build you once more; you shall be rebuilt, virgin of Israel," he tells Jeremiah.[72] The promised restoration of the Hebrews to their home-lands thus takes on a new meaning, since the community of former exiles will be dedicated to righteousness, not power. "I will give them a different heart and different behavior. I will not cease in my efforts for their good, and I will put respect for me into their hearts, so that they turn from me no more."[73] Remarkably, it seems as if God has learned something from the disaster brought on a people incapable of understanding his word. Waiting in the Court of the Guard for the inevitable fall of Jerusalem, Jeremiah imagines a new type of society arising out of its holy ashes.

The end of Judah, when it came, was as ghastly as the prophet had foreseen. Shortly before the Babylonian army entered the capital, Zedekiah asked him, for the last time, to advise him on the subject of surrender. He must have anticipated the answer. Only by leaving Jerusalem and surrendering to Nebuchadnezzar could the king save his own life and prevent the city from being put to the torch. In a rare admission of fear, Zedekiah confessed that he was afraid that the Judeans who had already deserted to the enemy—evidently a sizeable number of people—would kill him if he appeared in their midst. Jeremiah assured him that they

would not harm him; he should trust in YHVH and throw himself on Nebuchadnezzar's mercy. Strongly tempted to follow the
prophet's advice, the king swore him to secrecy about their conversation and returned to his palace. But he remained there, par-
alyzed by indecision, with results fatal both for him and the city.

On July 18, 586, with famine raging in Jerusalem, Nebuchadnezzar's troops breached a city wall and poured through the gap.[74]
When Zedekiah saw that the capital was lost, he and his family
escaped and fled toward the trans-Jordanian territories, but the
Babylonians captured him near Jericho and brought him to Nebuchadnezzar's headquarters. There he was forced to witness the
execution of his own sons before being blinded and led in chains
to Babylon.[75] About one month later, the Babylonian king sent his
commander of the guard, one Nebuzaradan, to complete the destruction of the city. According to the book of Kings, the commander burned down the temple, the royal palace, Jerusalem's
houses, and the walls of the city. Then he "deported the remain-
der of the population left behind in the city, the deserters who
had gone over to the king of Babylon, and the rest of the common
people. The commander of the guard left some of the humbler
country people as vineyard workers and plowmen."[76]

The devastation was, if anything, worse than that reported by
the Bible. Archeological evidence confirms the destruction of
Jerusalem and of Judah's fortified towns.[77] The population was
reduced to a fraction of its former size by deportations, execu-
tions, famine, and disease, with the survivors eking out a living in
the countryside. Nebuchadnezzar made the territory a Babylonian province and appointed Gedaliah, an official friendly to Jeremiah, as governor.[78] The Babylonians offered the old prophet
passage to Babylon, but when he refused, they permitted him
to remain with Gedaliah at Mizpah, a town near the ruins of
Jerusalem that served as the province's administrative center.
There is no record of his activity there, but we can imagine him

counseling the new governor and advising his countrymen to remain calm, keep the peace, and await the eventual fall of Babylon and the return of the exiles.[79]

The story, however, was not quite over. In a matter of months, Gedaliah was assassinated by a fanatical nationalist of Davidic descent.[80] Fearing the Babylonians would believe them to be implicated in the crime, the governor's associates decided to leave the country for the safety of Egypt. Jeremiah, to whom they turned for advice, begged them to remain in the land that YHVH had promised to rebuild. He reminded them that during the height of the siege he had purchased a plot of land in Anathoth as a sign of faith that "people will buy fields and vineyards in this land again."[81] More clearly than before, the prophet emphasized the repentance of God. "I am sorry for the evil I have done you. Do not be afraid of the king of Babylon any longer; do not fear him—it is YHVH who speaks—for I am with you to save you and deliver you from his hands."[82] But even when he preached salvation rather than destruction, it was Jeremiah's fate to be disbelieved. Over his outraged protests, the band leaving for Egypt insisted on taking him with them, along with the ever-faithful Baruch.

At Tahpanes, just across the Egyptian border, the indomitable prophet lived out his final days. Uncompromising to the end, he denounced his fellow exiles for practicing idolatry and predicted the violent fall of their protector, the pharaoh.[83] One imagines that except for Baruch, they may finally have been glad to be rid of him, not recognizing that his rage was always the product of unextinguished faith and disappointed hope. If Jeremiah had not valued his people so highly, he would not have expected so much of them.

CHAPTER VI

✳

"I Will Make You the Light of the Nations"
—ISAIAH 49:6

LTHOUGH THE Babylonian empire fell at almost the exact time Jeremiah had predicted, nobody had anticipated the remarkable circumstances of its end.

Those who preached the empire's doom were few. Who, other than a handful of angry, perspicacious prophets, could have believed that the wise and mighty Nebuchadnezzar would prove to be the last great ruler of Babylon? What even Jeremiah expected, however, was a violent overthrow of the empire by some equally brutal and ambitious competitor. Considering what the Assyrians had done to their enemies and the Babylonians to theirs, it was only reasonable to expect the victors, whoever they might be, to continue the horrific cycle of imperial violence. Thus, near the end of his preaching career, Jeremiah foresaw a league of mighty nations that would come from the north to smash to pieces the "hammer of the whole world."[1] Babylon would be treated as she had treated others. Her idols would be shattered and disgraced, her towns and cities burned, her land turned into a desert.[2] The prophet clearly longed to see YHVH avenge the destruction of Jerusalem and his temple.[3] But even without this element of wish-fulfillment, a fiery end to Babylonian rule seemed likely.

That things did not work out this way at all struck many contemporaries, including the prophet known as Isaiah of Babylon, as a sign that God was working through history to effect a vast and novel change.

> *No need to recall the past,*
> *No need to think about what was done before.*
> *See, I am doing a new deed,*
> *Even now it comes to light; can you not see it?*[4]

We will return in a moment to the mysterious Second Isaiah, an exiled Jew whose remarkable work brought classical prophecy to its climax. But first, what was the great novelty that he found so inspiring? That story begins with the advent of one of the strangest figures ever to serve as king of Babylon: a man called Nabonidus.

The Jews had been exiles in Babylon for fifteen years when Nebuchadnezzar died with his rule unchallenged, his empire intact, and his reputation as a just king at its high point.[5] Two short-lived rulers succeeded him: a violent, incompetent son who was soon assassinated, and a general of the army who died in battle not long after seizing power. Nabonidus, who came to the throne in 556 with the support of the nobility and the army, was an influential official, possibly a son-in-law of Nebuchadnezzar, and a former governor of the city of Babylon.[6] For three or four years, he busied himself campaigning in Syria and Arabia, constructing buildings and irrigation works, rebuilding temples, and doing for the most part what one would expect of a Babylonian emperor. During the New Year's ceremony, which was considered crucial for the welfare of the city, the king "took the hand of Marduk," holding the god's statue by the hand as it was carried from its temple shrine in a grand procession to the Ishtar Gate.[7] But all this was to end in an entirely unexpected way.

In 552, to the wonderment of his subjects, Nabonidus abandoned his capital and his country. No longer would the New Year be celebrated in the manner required by the priests and followers of Marduk, nor would the world's most powerful conqueror lead his armies to new victories. Putting his son, Belshazzar, in temporary charge of the government, the king marched out of Babylon at the head of his personal troops. His destination was Taima, an oasis in the Arabian desert some eight hundred miles from Babylon. There he would remain, surrounded by soldiers, courtiers, and a small contingent of Babylonian settlers, for the next ten years.

Why Nabonidus left his homeland for the desert is still a disputed matter.[8] Some clues, however, may be found on two inscribed monoliths discovered in 1956 by an archeologist exploring the ruins of the Great Mosque in Haran, a city now located in southeastern Turkey. (The monoliths, their true purpose unknown, were being used as paving stones for the mosque.) Harran was Nabonidus's hometown; his mother, a devotee of the moon god, Sin, may have been high priestess there.[9] One monolith reads, in part,

> (This is) the great miracle of Sin that none of the (other) gods and goddesses knew (how to achieve).... Sin, the lord of all the gods and goddesses residing in heaven, has come down from heaven to (me) Nabonidus, king of Babylon! For me, Nabonidus, the lonely one who was nobody, in whose heart was no thought of kingship, the gods and goddesses prayed (to Sin) and Sin called me to kingship. At midnight he (Sin) made me have a dream and said (in the dream) as follows: "Rebuild speedily Ehulhul, the temple of Sin in Harran, and I will hand over to you all the countries."[10]

"The lonely one who was nobody"—that is, not a member of the royal family—credited the moon god with his sudden rise to world power. Like his mother, Nabonidus worshipped Sin as king of all the gods, a belief that the Babylonian priesthood considered not only idiosyncratic but dangerous. To them, as to most of their countrymen, the supreme figure in the pantheon was Marduk, the tutelary god of Babylon, whose glorification was considered necessary to maintain the city's supremacy and the health of the empire. The king, on the other hand, traced the growing problems of his subjects, including economic crises, plagues, and famine, to their disregard of Sin and their violent, immoral behavior. As he wrote on his monolith,

> The citizens . . . the administrators (and) the inhabitants of the urban centers of Babylonia, acted evil, careless, and even sinned against his great divine power, having not (yet) experienced the awfulness of the wrath of the Divine Crescent, the king of all gods; they disregarded his rites and there was much irreligious and disloyal talk. They devoured one another like dogs, caused disease and hunger to appear among them. He (Sin) decimated the inhabitants of the country, but he made me leave my city Babylon on the road to Taima. . . . For ten years I was moving around among these (Arabian cities) and did not enter my own city Babylon.[11]

One sees in this introspective monarch, passionately attached to his god, frustrated by the failure of religious reform, and demoralized by his people's disobedience, a rough, Babylonian version of Jeremiah. With problems in his homeland multiplying (many of them the results of an overstretched, increasingly costly empire), Nabonidus's physical and mental condition suffered to the point that he found the task of governing intolerable.[12] But how to escape without resigning the office granted him by the moon god? Perhaps Arabia, home of the lucrative spice trade, would provide an opportunity to increase the nation's wealth and an environment in which to recover his spiritual balance and health.[13] And so the king left Babylon—the worst possible time for such a retreat, as it turned out, since a new star was rising in the East that would soon put both his throne and empire in serious jeopardy.[14]

The name of this luminary was Cyrus, a magnetic young aristocrat shortly to be known as Cyrus the Great. Not long before the moody Nabonidus departed for Arabia, Cyrus became king of the Persians, a little-known Indo-European people occupying part of the southern Iranian plateau. The Persians' northern neighbors, the Medes, were one of the great powers of the ancient world, with vast possessions extending from northern Iran through the Caucasian region into central Anatolia. Somehow—the facts are disputed—war broke out between Cyrus and the Median king, Astyages.[15] The events of this first campaign established a pattern that would characterize Cyrus's activities ever after. Although his forces were greatly outnumbered by the Median army, the enemy troops rebelled, handed Astyages over to him in chains, and greeted him as their true ruler. Cyrus reciprocated by treating his former adversaries with generosity. After sparing Astyages's life, he named his new empire "the kingdom of the Medes and the Persians," paid homage to the Median gods, and incorporated their chief leaders into his administration as partners in empire.[16]

The year was 553 B.C.E. A mere fourteen years later, in a manner that seemed to many observers almost miraculous, the Persian king would find himself ruler of the largest and most diverse empire in world history. Today, if asked to name the greatest conqueror of ancient times, most people would probably select Alexander the Great. But Alexander merely reconquered the same territory, more or less, as that originally captured and administered two hundred years earlier by Cyrus of Persia. From the beginning, this shrewd, far-sighted ruler relied as much on political acumen as on military power to undermine his enemies' will to fight and win them to his banner. (The Medes' rebellion against their king was almost certainly prepared with Persian participation.) His revolutionary new policy, widely publicized, was to eschew deportation and other highly punitive measures, grant conquered nations a considerable degree of local autonomy, and treat local religions and cultural traditions with great respect. "Such respect," one historian notes, "must have been an amazing revelation for men who had grown accustomed to the governing techniques and attitudes of the Neo-Assyrian and Neo-Babylonian empires."[17] Indeed, it was this transformation in imperial practice that Isaiah of Babylon was shortly to celebrate as a "new deed" inspired by YHVH.

At the same time, of course, Cyrus remained a conqueror who had no compunction about using force to extend the boundaries of his growing empire. In the winter of 547, responding to an alleged incursion into his territory by the famously rich Lydian ruler Croesus, he quick-marched his army from its bases in eastern Anatolia across Turkey, captured Croesus's capital along with its fabled treasures, and seized the cities of the Ionian Greeks as well.[18] The next few years saw him campaigning in Central Asia, extending Persian power through eastern Iran into Afghanistan, Turkestan, and parts of India.[19] Finally, already master of much of the civilized world, he turned his attention to his prime target, Babylon.

Cyrus's remarkable victories roused Nabonidus from his Arabian slumber.[20] In 539 he celebrated the New Year's festival in Babylon for the first time in more than a decade, taking the hand of Marduk as tradition demanded—but the damage to his reputation could not so easily be undone. The king's long absence and his continued devotion to the moon god had opened the door to Persian political agents and local supporters, including the alienated priests of Marduk, who accused him of scandalous sacrileges, blamed him for the ills afflicting the country, and spoke of Cyrus as a god-sent liberator.[21] By fall, when the Persian army marched on Babylon, there were few in the country willing to defend his regime. Nabonidus concentrated his dwindling forces at the city of Opis on the Tigris River, directly in the path of Cyrus's advance, but the Persian army enveloped and crushed them. Sippar, north of the capital on the Euphrates, fell without resistance, and Nabonidus fled behind Babylon's walls. Two days later, to the world's astonishment, the Persians marched virtually unopposed into the city. Cyrus, who entered the capital two weeks later, was greeted as its savior and legitimate king.

The stunning capture of Babylon without a major battle was no doubt the result of Cyrus's reputation for leniency and justice, bolstered by the alienation of Marduk's priests and the subversive activities of his spies and local allies.[22] One can get some idea of the sources of the Persian emperor's popularity by reading his own words, written on the so-called Cyrus Cylinder shortly after his triumphant arrival in the city. "I am Cyrus, king of the world, great king, legitimate king, king of Babylon, king of Sumer and Akkad, king of the four rims (of the earth)," he proclaimed:

> When I entered Babylon as a friend and (when) I established the seat of the government in the palace of the ruler under jubilation and rejoicing, Marduk, the great lord, [induced] the magnanimous inhabitants of Babylon [to love me], and I was daily endeavoring to worship him. My numerous troops walked around in Babylon in peace, I did not allow anybody to terrorize (any place) of the [country].

As to the inhabitants of Babylon, he continued, "[I abolished] the corvee (forced labor) which was against their (social) standing. I brought relief to their dilapidated housing, putting (thus) an end to their (main) complaints. Marduk, the great lord, was well pleased with my deeds." While giving the local god credit for his victory and reforms—part of his usual modus operandi—Cyrus also returned the images of gods captured by the Babylonians to several Mesopotamian cities they had conquered. More important, from the perspective of the Judean exiles and other people deported by Nebuchadnezzar, he "gathered all their (former) inhabitants and returned (to them) their habitations."[23]

Not long after this, the Persian emperor extended the same treatment to the Judeans, whom we may now call Jews, since those exiled in Babylon were now referred to by that name.[24] Not only did Cyrus permit them to return to Judah, he encouraged them to do so, and returned the treasures taken from the Jerusalem Temple by Nebuchadnezzar as well. Later, his successors would help to finance the building of the Second Temple with state funds.[25] The biblical book of Ezra describes the king's proclamation in these terms:

> Thus speaks Cyrus king of Persia: "YHVH, the God of heaven, has given me all the kingdoms of the earth; he has ordered me to build him a Temple in Jerusalem, in Judah. Whoever there is among you of all his people, may his God be with him! Let him go up to Jerusalem in Judah to build the Temple of YHVH, the God of Israel—he is the God who is in Jerusalem. And let each survivor, wherever he lives, be helped by the people of that place with silver and gold, with goods and cattle, as well as voluntary offerings for the Temple of God which is in Jerusalem."[26]

A good many of the exiles (but far from all of them) accepted this invitation to return to their homeland, which now became Yehud: a province of the Persian empire.[27] In 515, after a period marked by economic hardship, civil strife, and considerable disillusionment, the Second Jerusalem Temple was dedicated, and a new chapter in Jewish history began. But well before Cyrus permitted the exiles' repatriation (probably around the time that he invaded the territory of the Lydian ruler, King Croesus), a new prophet living in Babylon had already declared him to be God's chosen instrument—a ruler whose destiny was not only to liberate the exiled Jews, but also to model the liberation of all the nations. This brilliant poet and theologian, whose identity remains a mystery, took the name Isaiah in memory of his illustrious predecessor, Isaiah of Jerusalem. We turn now to this unusual—and still controversial—figure.

AFTER MOSES LED the Hebrew slaves out of Egypt, the Bible tells us, they wandered for forty years in the desert before entering the land of Caanan. It is probably no coincidence that the captives deported from Judah had been living in Babylonia for the same period of time when a new prophet living among them was inspired to declare that their "term of service" had ended.[28]

> Comfort, oh comfort my people,
> says your God.
> Speak tenderly to Jerusalem
> and declare to her
> that her term of service is over,
> that her sin is atoned for,
> that she has received from the hand of YHVH
> double punishment for all her crimes.[29]

With these thrilling words of consolation and hope, Isaiah of Babylon announces his prophetic mission: to declare God's forgiveness of his people, the end of their Babylonian exile, and their return to the Promised Land. Earlier prophets had also predicted that YHVH would forgive the Jews and return them to their homeland, but this preaching strikes a dramatically new note.

The redemption that Isaiah foresees will not take place at some undetermined future time, but in a very few years—and it will not be limited to the Jewish exiles. The God who speaks through this prophet's lips is Lord of all the nations, not just of Israel. His promise of deliverance is extended to them as well. The new beginning that Isaiah proclaims amounts to nothing less than the dawn of a new period of world history, when all humanity will recognize YHVH as the God of integrity, freedom, and justice.[30]

Who was Isaiah of Babylon? The short answer is, nobody really knows. Ironically, considering that his writings are more unified and coherent than those of any other prophet, his personal life remains a mystery.[31] Some information, however, can be inferred from his writings. He is known to us as Isaiah because his preaching explores and extends many of the ideas associated with his eighth-century namesake, and because his writings were appended at some point to those of the earlier Isaiah.[32] It is fairly clear that he lived among the exiled Jews of Babylon.[33] Since he does not lament the destruction of Judah, but insists that a new era in history has begun for the Jews and for the world, it is reasonable to assume that he was taken to Babylon as a small child or that he was born in exile. His family's deportation and his own literary gifts suggest a middle-class or upper-class background. He seems to have been afflicted with a disfiguring childhood disease, and may have held a position, as some well-educated Jews did, in the Babylonian administration.[34]

At some point—the date is unknown—Isaiah began preaching in the cultic assemblies (an early version of the synagogue) that had replaced worship in the lost temple.[35] He had known for some time that he had prophetic gifts; like Jeremiah, he declared that "YHVH called me before I was born, from my mother's womb he pronounced my name."[36] But he also felt for some time that his talents were going to waste, that he had "toiled in vain" and "exhausted myself for nothing."[37] God "made my mouth a sharp sword," he complained, but "hid me in the shadow of his hand. He made me into a sharpened arrow, and concealed me in his quiver."[38] This frustrating anonymity may well have been a result of his disease, since disfigurement was thought to be a curse and might well have disqualified a would-be prophet, at least initially, from preaching in community assemblies.[39]

All this changed in the years after 550 B.C.E., when Cyrus of Persia began his march toward world power, and Isaiah felt called on to preach a startling new message.[40]

Two centuries earlier, the first Isaiah had described the conquering Assyrians as a weapon used by YHVH to punish a godless nation.[41] In the next century, Jeremiah went so far as to call Nebuchadnezzar, the destroyer of Jerusalem, YHVH's "servant."[42] But when it came to describing Cyrus, Isaiah of Babylon took a great leap further:

> *Thus says YHVH to his anointed, to Cyrus,*
> *whom he has taken by his right hand*
> *to subdue nations before him*
> *and strip the loins of kings,*
> *to force gateways before him*
> *that their gates be closed no more;*
>
> *I will go before you*
> *leveling the heights.*
> *I will shatter the bronze gateways,*
> *smash the iron bars.*
> *I will give you the hidden treasures,*
> *the secret hoards,*
> *that you may know that I am YHVH*
> *the God of Israel, who calls you by your name.*[43]

The pace and rhythm of this poetry is as swift and irresistible as an army on the march.[44] Even so, its content must have sent a shock throughout the exile community, for according to Isaiah, the conqueror who rides at the head of his victorious troops is not merely God's unknowing instrument; he is the "anointed one"— *mashiach*—a term that would eventually come into English as "messiah." The word was intended to startle, since it had previously been used only to describe Israelite and Judean kings, including the future ruler who would one day return the scattered Jewish people to their homeland.[45] But there was no mistaking Isaiah's meaning. In his poem, YHVH "takes the hand" of Cyrus, a reference to (and reversal of) the Babylonian practice by which the king "took the hand" of Marduk.[46] And he calls Cyrus "by name," another sign of his special favor toward the king, since this is also how he honors and adopts his chosen people:

> But now, thus says YHVH,
> who created you, Jacob,
> who formed you, Israel:
> do not be afraid, for I have redeemed you;
> I have called you by your name, you are mine.[47]

Quite clearly, Isaiah was announcing that the Persian conqueror, not some Davidic king, would be the long-sought liberator of the Hebrews. After conquering the rest of the civilized world, Cyrus would march on Babylon, and the period of exile would be over. "For your sake I send an army against Babylon," the prophet proclaimed in YHVH's name. "I will knock down the prison bars and the Babylonians will break into laments."[48] Although Isaiah was addressing the Jewish community, not the Babylonian populace, one can easily imagine Prince Belshazzar's police pricking up their ears at what must have seemed a typical example of dangerous pro-Persian propaganda. The notion that the authorities might consider them enemy agents may have alarmed the exiles as well, but what seems to have rankled them most was Isaiah's promotion of a pagan ruler to the position they had long believed would be filled by a descendant of the House of David.[49]

How could the Holy One of Israel possibly anoint a non-Jew—an unbeliever—to fulfill the promise of national redemption? Isaiah had two related answers, each of which pushed prophetic insight into new territory. One response derived God's ability to make great changes in history from his power as creator of the universe. The other redefined national redemption to provide the Jewish people with a new mission to the nations of the world.

First, the prophet insisted, YHVH can appoint Cyrus or anyone he pleases to be the Jews' liberator. He is not bound in the slightest by historical precedent, national loyalties, or even prior prophecies. His power and freedom to innovate are boundless and unquestionable, and he exercises this creativity continually.[50] "Now I am revealing new things to you," he says through Isaiah, "things hidden and unknown to you, created just now, this very moment."[51] These "new things" include a new type of empire and, like it or not, a Persian *mashiach*. Fortunately for the Jews, they also include a change of heart by YHVH—a renewed commitment to protect and cherish his people. "I did forsake you for a brief moment," he confesses in Isaiah's poem, "but with great love will I take you back." Now, he promises never again to abandon Israel:

> *For the mountains may depart*
> *the hills be shaken,*
> *but my love for you will never leave you*
> *and my covenant of peace with you will never be shaken,*
> *says YHVH who takes pity on you.*[52]

For the first time in the prophetic literature, YHVH is defined primarily as an innovator, and vast historical upheavals are seen not as a means of punishing the wicked, or as a threat to tradition, but as a fulfillment of his beneficent, saving will.[53] Isaiah derives God's power to innovate from his role as creator of the universe. In his vision, YHVH is the master craftsman who fashions the entire earth to suit his plan. "Who was it [that] measured the water of the sea in the hollow of his hand and calculated the dimensions of the heavens, gauged the whole earth to the bushel, weighed the mountains in the scales, the hills in a balance?"[54] But his creativity does not stop with the organization of the natural universe; it moves from ordering the stars to reconstructing human society.

> I it was who made the earth,
> and created man who is on it.
> I it was who spread out the heavens with my hands
> and now give orders to their whole array.
> I it was who roused him [Cyrus] to victory,
> I leveled the way for him.
> He will rebuild my city,
> will bring my exiles back
> without ransom or indemnity,
> so says YHVH of the Hosts.[55]

Mesopotamian literature may well have inspired this emphasis on the Creation. The Babylonians were famous for their creation myths, especially the Poem of Creation, which told a story of primeval chaos, the birth of several generations of quarrelsome gods, and the eventual triumph of the god Marduk over his rivals.[56] But Isaiah clearly distinguishes the Holy One of Israel from the heroic (and villainous) deities of the Babylonian epic. YHVH is no product of previous godly unions taking place in a period of uncreated chaos; he is "the first and the last," who "formed the earth and made it, who set it firm, created it no chaos, but a place to be lived in."[57] In a breathtaking act of imagination, the poet pictures God in space, looking down from a great distance on his handiwork:

> He lives above the circle of the earth
> its inhabitants look like grasshoppers.
> He has stretched out the heavens like a cloth,
> spread them like a tent for men to live in.

Then he delivers the punch line:

> He reduces princes to nothing,
> he annihilates the rulers of the world.[58]

No previous prophet had raised the Holy One of Israel to such stratospheric heights. In the work of the first Isaiah and Jeremiah, YHVH talks about what he will do, not about who he is. He does not say things like "I am YHVH unrivaled, I form the light and create the dark"; or "the heavens are as high above earth as my ways are above your ways, my thoughts above your thoughts."[59] Second Isaiah had a particular reason to emphasize God's absolute superiority to mankind. Cyrus of Persia was well on the way to becoming the most powerful ruler in world history. His empire would soon control an unheard-of expanse of territory, extending from Central Asia and India to Greece and North Africa. And the new, innovative methods that he adopted to rule this vast domain would enable him to return the Jews to Zion and to free other captive peoples.[60] This very greatness—a vast increase in historical scale—made it necessary to expand the cosmic scale that contained the Persian king and his works—in effect, to cut Cyrus "down to size." As his troops swept toward Babylon, many people, even among the Jews, would be tempted to equate might with right. Many would be inclined to consider the imperial liberator and his gods worthy of worship. All needed to understand that this dramatic change in history was the work of a supreme Creator who never merely ratifies power, but always judges it.[61]

Originally, Isaiah may have hoped that Cyrus would come to know YHVH and acknowledge his universal lordship.[62] According to some reports, the Persian king was no idolater but a follower of Zoroaster, a contemporary ethical prophet whose dualistic teachings, emphasizing the eternal conflict between good and evil, "Justice" and "the Lie," were far more advanced than those of earlier religions.[63] If he had hoped to win the enlightened monarch to Yahwism, however, the prophet would soon learn that Cyrus's policy was to "take the hand" of *all* his subjects' gods in order to win the loyalty of local elites, keep the nations divided, and maintain the stability of the empire.[64]

From Isaiah's perspective, this created a painful contradiction. Persian expansion was establishing an international framework in which the first Isaiah's vision of a diverse and peaceful world might conceivably be realized.[65] But unless the nations shared a common commitment to the transcendent values of social justice, personal morality, and peace—that is, unless they recognized that in some respects YHVH's law was superior to that of any national or imperial power—the great theo-political moment would pass. Without Persian tolerance, neither the Jews nor other captive peoples would be liberated and encouraged to practice their own religions. But if the result of this policy was merely to strengthen the old power-worshipping, injustice-sanctifying superstitions, history would revert to the ugly cycle of imperial aggression and anti-imperial revolt. To prevent this from happening, the ever-hopeful prophet announced another of God's "new things"—the potential conversion of all the nations to Yahwism.[66]

Isaiah was not initiating a missionary campaign in the modern sense. To begin with, he expected that the very liberation of the Jews would have a revolutionizing effect on world opinion. After all, the followers of YHVH were one of the few ancient peoples to survive destruction and deportation by the Assyrians and Babylonians and (with the exception of Israel's lost ten tribes) to have retained their religious identity.[67] If they regained their homeland as well, this would clearly be testimony to the power of their God. "YHVH bares his holy arm in the sight of all the nations, and all the ends of the earth shall see the salvation of our God."[68] Furthermore, while other nations trusted that their gods would give them victories, the Hebrew prophets had correctly predicted their own people's defeat, exile, and final liberation.[69] Emboldened by this record of prophetic success, Isaiah addressed the other "survivors of the nations" directly:

> *Who foretold this*
> *and revealed it in the past?*
> *Am I not YHVH?*
> *There is no other god besides me,*
> *a God of integrity and a savior;*
> *there is none apart from me.*
> *Turn to me and be saved*
> *all the ends of the earth,*
> *for I am God unrivaled.*[70]

This represented a remarkable turn in prophetic thinking. Jeremiah, too, was appointed as "a prophet to the nations," but spent his life attempting to convince his own people to repent.[71] By contrast, convinced that the Jews' sins had finally been atoned for, Isaiah of Babylon turned the full force of his oratory toward the outside world. "Pay attention to me, you peoples," he roared in YHVH's name, "listen to me, you nations. For from me comes the Law, and my justice shall be the light of the peoples."[72] Understanding that the One God implies the oneness of humanity, he opened the door of monotheistic faith to all, and in doing so redefined Israel's historic mission. The Jews would reestablish themselves in Palestine, but their destiny was not merely to be one nation-state among others. (In fact, they were unlikely to be more than a petty province of the Persian empire.) It was to witness YHVH to the world through their history, beliefs, and behavior.[73] "It is not enough for you to be my servant, to restore the tribes of Jacob and bring back the survivors of Israel. I will make you the light of the nations so that my salvation may reach to the ends of the earth."[74]

Rhetorically, Isaiah sometimes spoke as if the restored Israel would be a great imperial power—a "master of the nations" as well as "a witness to the peoples"—but it was clear that her authority would be spiritual and ethical rather than military or political. The earth's peoples would turn to YHVH spontaneously, out of the conviction that his teachings were just and true, not because they had been forced to accept them.[75] The idea of a voluntary spiritual consensus is the ultimate response of classical prophecy to the enterprise of empire-building. Implicitly, it annihilates the legitimacy of power-based imperial systems. For great empires generate goals and expectations that coercive methods cannot satisfy—hopes for human solidarity and world order, international standards of justice, national liberation, and the peaceful resolution of disputes. Isaiah's vision of a just, harmonious world was not some sort of religious supplement to existing imperial practices; it represented a frontal challenge to any system of governance that dashes these expectations by subordinating them to the preservation of violent, unjust authority.

> *Is not this the sort of fast that pleases me*
> *—it is the Lord YHVH who speaks—*
> *to break unjust fetters*
> *and undo the thongs of the yoke,*

to let the oppressed go free
and break every yoke .[76]

Magnificent words, then and now. But we should not be surprised to learn that the prophet of liberation soon found himself
under serious attack by the very rulers whose legitimacy he so de-
fiantly challenged.

ISAIAH HAD RUN some risk by praising Cyrus of Persia as a potential liberator of his people and according him the title *mashiach*.
As Jeremiah noted earlier in his letter to the Jews of Babylon, the
authorities there would not hesitate to roast prophets alive for
fomenting unrest among the exiles.[77] But the danger was limited,
initially, by the great distance separating Cyrus's army from Babylon, the weakness of Crown Prince Belshazzar's proxy government, and the alienation of the Babylonian priesthood from their
heterodox emperor, Nabonidus. (We have seen that the priests
of Marduk would soon welcome Cyrus as their own liberator
from imperial idolatry.) As the decade of the 540s wound down,
however, these protective conditions dissolved one by one. Triumphant in Central Asia, Cyrus turned his armies east, with
Babylon their obvious target. Nabonidus and his troops made
preparations for their return to the capital from Arabia. And Isaiah compounded his risks by turning the full force of his rhetoric
against his captors' gods, priests, and wise men.

What the Babylonians may have thought about Isaiah's assertion of YHVH's universal lordship is not clear, but they cannot
have been pleased by his vehement, satirical attacks on their own
religion. One can easily imagine the members of Isaiah's own
community warning him, threatening him, and finally, abusing
him physically to prevent him from exposing them all to official
retaliation. ("I offered my back to those who struck me," he

wrote, "my cheeks to those who tore at my beard; I did not cover my face against insult and spittle.")[78] Still, he could not hold his tongue. For a concomitant of his glowing vision of a peaceful, spiritually unified world was his need to expose YHVH's competitors (so to speak) as illusory, impotent no-gods, and their prophets and priests as charlatans.

Never before had a Jewish orator attacked the beliefs of others with such unbridled scorn. "Who ever fashioned a god or cast an image without hope of gain?" he asked. The wood carver selects a tree and "shapes it to human proportions, and gives it a human face, for it to live in a temple."

> For the common man [the tree] is so much fuel; he uses it to warm himself, he also burns it to bake his bread. But this fellow makes a god of it and worships it; he makes an idol of it and bows down before it. Half of it he burns in the fire, on the live embers he roasts meat, eats it and is replete. He warms himself too. "Ah!" says he, "I am warm; I have a fire here!" With the rest he makes his god, his idol; he bows down before it and worships it and prays to it. "Save me," he says, "because you are my god."[79]

This generalized ridicule was rough enough, but with Cyrus marching at last toward Babylon, Isaiah did not hesitate to predict the coming disgrace of the city's chief gods, Marduk (Bel) and Nebo.

> *Bel is crouching. Nebo cringing.*
> *Their idols are being loaded on animals, on beasts of burden,*
> *carried off like bundles on weary beasts.*
> *They are cringing and crouching together,*
> *powerless to save the ones who carry them,*
> *as they themselves go off into captivity.*[80]

To mock the Babylonian gods at a time of increasing danger for the city seemed almost certain to provoke some sort of retaliation by the authorities. But, to a militant monotheist like Isaiah, this was precisely the time to expose the state religion's pretensions, both to keep the Jews from straying and to win the idolaters to Yahwism. In Babylon, as elsewhere, the primary benefit promised by these pagan deities was security. They also promised military victories, civil stability, successful harvests, and protection against diseases and other natural disasters. With the empire crumbling from within and threatened from without, the uselessness of relying on such guardians seemed apparent. As for the city's priests, magicians, sages, and astrologers, an intelligentsia whose divinations and predictions filled thousands of clay tablets in her world-famous libraries, the prophet's criticism was merciless. "I am he who foils the omens of wizards and makes fools of diviners," he declared in YHVH's name, "he who makes the sages recant and shows the nonsense of their knowledge."[81] "Keep to your spells then, and all your sorceries," he advised "Lady Babylon." "Do you think they will help you? Do you think they will make anyone nervous?"

> You have spent weary hours with your many advisers.
> Let them come forward now
> and save you, these who analyze the heavens,
> who study the stars
> and announce month by month
> what will happen to you next.
>
> Oh, they will be like wisps of straw
> and the fire will burn them. . . .
> This is what your wizards will be for you,
> those men for whom you have worn yourself out since your youth.
> They will all go off, each his own way,
> powerless to save you.[82]

We cannot be entirely sure what happened next, but the fourth Servant Song, a poem probably written after Isaiah's death by one of his disciples, provides evidence of a violent official reaction.[83] We do not know the time of the prophet's arrest or the offense with which he was charged. Very likely, Nabonidus's return to the capital in 540 triggered a new campaign to stamp out pro-Persian sedition. If so, the priests of Marduk would surely not lift a finger to protect a blasphemous Jew who had ridiculed them and their beliefs, even if he had spoken only to assemblies of his own people. Isaiah had done nothing more than tell the truth as he saw it, but a legal defense was useless, since alien captives had no rights under Babylonian law.[84] Whatever the accusation leveled, its results were inevitable: imprisonment, torture, execution.

> By force and by law he was taken;
> would anyone plead his cause?
> Yes, he was torn away from the land of the living;
> for our faults struck down in death.
> They gave him a grave with the wicked,
> a tomb with the rich,
> though he had done no wrong
> and there had been no perjury in his mouth.[85]

Like Moses, who did not live to see the Promised Land, the prophet of the return would not return to Judah with his countrymen, nor would he witness the birth of the new monotheistic age that he had predicted. For his followers, the difficult question was how to interpret this tragedy. Why would YHVH, who had protected Jeremiah and his other messengers, sacrifice one whom he had called to serve him even before his birth? Had God abandoned his servant, perhaps because he was not a true prophet after all? If not, why would he let him be led like an animal to slaughter, executed, and—a great disgrace among Jews and other Middle Eastern peoples—buried among criminals and wrongdoers?

One answer, which seemed quite straightforward, was that by sacrificing Isaiah, YHVH was fulfilling his promise to save his people. The punishment suffered by the prophet might have fallen on the whole community—*would* have fallen on it, in fact, had its members been courageous or foolhardy enough to speak as he did. Most of them thrilled to Isaiah's prediction of imminent liberation and waited in hopeful anticipation of the Persian invasion. In their hearts, most were "disloyal" to Babylon, sympathizers with Cyrus, and scornful disbelievers in Marduk and Nebo. But they were not called on to prophesy the fall of Babylon and the old gods: Isaiah was. Recognizing (perhaps even welcoming) the danger of calling the idolaters to account, he substituted himself for the community, speaking aloud words that they were forbidden to utter, taking risks that he would never ask them to take, and accepting the punishment that might otherwise have fallen on them.

Considering the prophet's life as a whole suggested that this substitute punishment might also have a deeper meaning. Isaiah's sufferings had not begun with his arrest or even with the insults provoked by his preaching. As a child he had been disfigured by disease—smallpox, perhaps, or even leprosy—to the point that, to some in the community, "he seemed no longer human."

> *Like a sapling he grew up in front of us,*
> *like a root in arid ground.*
> *Without beauty, without majesty (we saw him),*
> *no looks to attract our eyes;*
> *a thing despised and rejected by men,*
> *a man of sorrows and familiar with suffering,*
> *a man to make people screen their faces;*
> *he was despised and we took no account of him.*[86]

People would avert their eyes from such a sufferer not just because he was unpleasant to behold, but because looking at an object of divine anger was considered an unlucky or dangerous act.[87] But Isaiah's life as a selfless man of God refuted the notion that he deserved his affliction. Innocent now, despite his punishment by Nabonidus, had he not been innocent then, despite his disease? And, if so, was his whole career from childhood onward not a way of standing in other people's places, of accepting punishment on behalf of the community, and thereby in some way atoning for its sins?

Isaiah's disciple thought so. "It was our sickness that he was bearing," he confessed, "our suffering that he endured."

> We accounted him plagued,
> smitten and afflicted by God;
> but he was wounded because of our sins,
> crushed because of our iniquities.
> He bore the chastisement that made us whole
> And by his bruises we were healed.[88]

In the disciple's thinking, Isaiah's disfigurement by disease presaged his torture by the Babylonian police. The insults he had borne then foretold the disgraceful death imposed on him later. And in both cases, he accepted a degrading penalty willingly, sacrificing himself silently for the benefit of others, "like a sheep that is dumb before its shearers, never opening its mouth."[89] Stricken with grief for their lost prophet and haunted by guilt for the way they had mistreated him, his survivors accepted moral responsibility for his death. "We had all gone astray like sheep, each taking his own way, and YHVH burdened him with the sins of all of us."[90] Yet, Isaiah had begun his prophetic career by announcing that Israel's time of servitude was over because her sins had been

forgiven. What sense did it make, then, to consider him, in his capacity as solitary sufferer, a stand-in for the Jewish community?

The figure immediately evoked by this question is Jeremiah,
whose empathy for his countrymen's suffering was so acute that
he became Israel, psychologically speaking, and stood in his people's place. Like Isaiah of Babylon, Jeremiah discovered his
prophetic vocation as a child, suffered insults, beatings, and imprisonment, declared the deities of other nations to be "no-gods,"
and ended his career in sorrow. Like Isaiah, too, he prophesied the
liberation of the Jewish captives by a loving God. But an aspect
of Isaiah's vision not yet present in Jeremiah is its global reach;
the prophet-in-exile foresees a worldwide liberation that will
unite all people in the recognition that they are YHVH's servants. Isaiah represents Israel just as Jeremiah did; but those for
whom he sacrifices, both as an individual and in his capacity as
"Israel," are the inhabitants of all nations.[91] This is what Isaiah's
disciple means by saying that God will grant the late prophet "the
many as his portion" and "the multitude as his spoil," that he will
have "long life," and that through him "YHVH's plans will prosper."[92] His universalistic vision will be realized, and his suffering—and that of the Jewish people—will be instrumental in
helping to realize it.

How will this vicarious suffering work? What is there about
the punishment endured by Isaiah or by the Jews that can atone
for other people's sins and free them from the necessity of undergoing the same torturous consequences? One can interpret this
mystically or even (as happened in the Middle Ages) economi-
cally, for example, by asserting that the sinner owes God a debt,
and that someone else's suffering pays the debt and squares one's
account with the Creator.[93] But there is a simpler interpretation
that is more consistent with the prophetic role played by Isaiah
and by Israel, as well as with what we know of human psychology.

Isaiah's suffering is vicarious in the sense that the prophet identifies with his people, sees the world through their eyes, experiences their catastrophes, understands their frustrations and yearnings, and feels the burden of their misdeeds weighing on his own soul. This radical empathy not only makes it possible for him to act with extraordinary selflessness, it also enables the group to identify with him—that is, to experience his empathetic thoughts and selfless actions as an example of what is possible for them. Through his words and his sacrifice, Isaiah tells the Jews that just as he represents all of them, they, in turn, represent all the other nations of the earth. By identifying their own painful experiences with those of other peoples, the Jews make it possible for the others to identify with them. This is how they will bless the nations and lead them in recognizing their oneness under the One God.

With this teaching, the prophetic tradition reaches its highest point. The vision of universal peace, with all nations governing their people and resolving their differences in accordance with YHVH's ethical laws, was first expressed by Isaiah of Jerusalem. It was the first Isaiah who discovered the spiritual implications of the new imperialism, and who turned the principle of universal lordship against the worshippers of global power. But Isaiah's residual nationalism—his belief that God would somehow protect Judah and the Davidides—limited his understanding of how that new order was to be constructed. Jeremiah took the next step by asserting the importance of the individual in the divine plan, and by witnessing in his own life the value of radical empathy with sufferers. Without a change of heart on the part of repentant individuals, a new covenant with YHVH—a new ethical consensus—would remain out of reach. Jeremiah's perspective, however, was focused on the shortcomings and needs of his own people and on the unparalleled disaster that had befallen them. Something more was needed to link his empathetic individualism with the global vision of the first Isaiah.

Isaiah of Babylon's life and death provided the missing element: a synthesis that pointed the way to eventual realization of his namesake's great dream. The key to the long-sought transformation was suffering—not suffering for its own sake (for pain in itself has no value), but suffering for others, as a way of affirming one's solidarity with them and bringing a new moral community into existence. The calamities visited on the Jews were not intended merely to qualify them for nationhood, but to make them and the nations understand the ultimate powerlessness of power, the ubiquity of suffering, and the need for universal liberation. "I have appointed you as a covenant of the people and light of the nations," YHVH says to Isaiah / Israel, "to open the eyes of the blind, to free captives from prison, and those who live in darkness from the dungeon."[94] Through radical empathy, both the Jews and their former enemies would undergo Jeremiah's change of heart, and with it a change of behavior. All nations would then be free to enter into a new covenant with one another and with the universal God. As a result, the door to a new age of righteousness, justice, and peace would finally swing open.

But what if this did not happen—at least, not right away? What if the returned exiles failed to identify their sufferings with those of other nations, and the nations failed to recognize the one God capable of uniting them as members of a single community? Under these circumstances, the old gods of power and privilege— the war gods—would retain their potency. The cycle of violent oppression and violent revolt would continue. Then the light of prophecy would grow dim for a while, to flash out again centuries later like an unexpected but long-awaited beacon.

CHAPTER VII

✴

"Now I Create New Heavens and a New Earth"
—ISAIAH 65:17

F OR THOSE LIVING in nations where Christianity is a strong cultural and religious force, it is virtually impossible to read the writings of Isaiah, Jeremiah, or Isaiah of Babylon without thinking of Jesus of Nazareth. This is because so many Christians from ancient times onward have interpreted Jesus's life and death as the fulfillment of Hebrew prophecy. One tradition, beginning with the gospel of Matthew, identifies him as the Immanuel of whom Isaiah spoke, the blessed child who would be called "Wonderful Counselor, Mighty God, Eternal Father, Prince of Peace."[1] Another, dating from the apostle Paul, asserts that Christ's death and resurrection inaugurated the "new covenant" with God preached by Jeremiah.[2] And a third, most recently dramatized in Mel Gibson's film *The Passion of the Christ,* views Jesus as the suffering servant of YHVH—the martyr Isaiah of Babylon described as giving his life in atonement for the sins of others.[3]

One Christian biblical authority puts the matter succinctly: "The writers of the Gospels saw even the details of Jesus' life on earth, his passion, his death and resurrection as the fulfillment of Old Testament predictions." He adds, however, that this interpretation of scripture "is conditioned by its own generation," and that "we can no longer concur in it."[4] Most contemporary schol-

ars would agree. Even those who see Christianity as the "theological terminus of the history of Israel" strongly question the idea
that the prophets' primary mission was to foretell the coming of
Jesus.[5] What remains relatively unexplored both by Christians
and Jews, however, is Jesus's relationship, and that of the religion
he inspired, to the tradition of classical prophecy.

Was Jesus of Nazareth a prophet of YHVH like Isaiah, Jeremiah, and Isaiah of Babylon? Answering the question is compli-
cated by one's preexisting religious beliefs. Most Christians would
probably answer, "Yes, but he was much more than that"—not
only a prophet, but also the Messiah whose coming the prophets
had foretold; and not just a mortal descendant of King David, but
God's only begotten Son. As a result, Christian thinkers have not
paid as much attention as one might expect to Jesus's prophetic
role.[6] Adherents of Islam, on the other hand, deny that Jesus was
either the Messiah or the second "person" of the Trinity, but af-
firm that he was a messenger of God.[7] Many Jews, finally, reject
the idea that he was a prophet of any sort, although some have
been involved in recent efforts to reassess this position.[8]

As one of these reassessors, I am convinced that Jesus was, indeed, a major prophet—a teacher and activist who made important contributions to the tradition dating back six centuries to the
two Isaiahs and Jeremiah. At the same time, though, his sayings
sometimes reflect a mode of thinking quite different from that of
the classical prophets. To understand both aspects of his prophetic
role—the classical and the apocalyptic—it will be useful to return briefly to the period just after the second Isaiah's martyr-
dom, when many Jewish exiles returned with high hopes to the
Holy Land.

POPULAR EXPECTATIONS ran high when Cyrus conquered Babylonia and permitted the exiles to return to Judah, just as the

prophets had foreseen.[9] But the years after their return dashed the people's hopes for a radically improved society and a great moral reform. Life in the impoverished province of Yehud was very hard. The community was rent by internal quarrels, and the spiritual resurgence that many had anticipated did not take place even after the temple was rebuilt.[10] Most disappointing, the transformation of world history predicted by Isaiah of Babylon failed to materialize. Although Jewish religious ideas gradually became more influential in the East, until "by Hellenistic times there [were] myriads of converts and 'fearers of God' among the nations," most nations did not recognize YHVH as God or adhere to Yahwistic ethics.[11] Nor did the Persian empire live up to Isaiah's glowing expectations. Despite the relatively enlightened policies of Cyrus the Great and his successors, the empire still remained a violent enterprise driven to expand and to maintain its conquests through force.

Serious disillusionment set in soon after the Persian king's death in 530, when it became clear that the old cycle of imperial aggression and violent revolt would continue. Cyrus's successor, Darius, seized the throne after a bloody power struggle and was then compelled to suppress rebellions in Babylon, Assyria, Egypt, and a dozen other nations.[12] He and his son, Xerxes, pushed the boundaries of the empire deeper into Asia and Europe, but found themselves trapped in an increasingly brutal struggle to maintain control over their restive, far-flung subjects. From the accession of Xerxes onward, Persian history was little more than "a holding operation in the face of challenges from rebellious subjects, ambitious satraps, and external enemies."[13] Finally, the empire's day was done. A series of defeats in Greece in the fifth century inaugurated a period of decline that culminated in the conquest of Persia and all its possessions by a new king of kings: Alexander the Great of Macedon. Two centuries after that, militant Jewish nationalists, the spiritual heirs of Elijah and Elisha, would launch an all-out guerrilla war to free Judea of domination by Greek imperialists and their local collaborators.

The impact of these disappointing events on prophecy was enormous. In a word, the tradition represented by the classical prophets fragmented. Isaiah and Jeremiah had been practical visionaries—influential political advisors as well as recipients of divine messages about history's inner meaning and direction. Now, practical politics and visionary prophecy parted company. While court officials and temple prophets advised rulers on matters of public policy and morality, a small contingent of ecstatic visionaries shared their vivid dreams of the Last Days with the community.[14] According to the pioneer sociologist Max Weber, this split occurred because "the priestly police power in the Jewish congregation" suppressed or marginalized the free-spirited prophets.[15] Others suggest that classical prophecy declined because scribal commentaries on sacred writings replaced new writings, or because idolatry, one of the earlier prophets' major targets, was no longer a threat to Judaism.[16] But another factor also seems crucial: the shattering of earlier hopes for the realization of YHVH's kingdom on earth.

From the time of Elijah onward, the prophets had often found themselves at odds with their nation's rulers. At great risk to themselves, they preached against the "royal consciousness" that implicitly sanctified power and justified oppressive social policies.[17] But Isaiah and Jeremiah were neither social revolutionaries inciting violent overthrow of the state nor utopian theorists advocating noble ideals that might or might not be realized in historical time. Their major interests and gifts lay in exploring the moral or theological meaning implicit in current events and projecting the consequences of people's behavior into the relatively near future. That future, to be sure, would be quite different from the present, but, in their view, it would represent a transformation of present trends, not simply a negation of them.

And the changes they foresaw were to take place through a combination of human and divine actions, not through God's action
alone. In the longed-for age of peace, YHVH would strengthen
people's capabilities to live justly and act empathetically; he would
not have to abolish human nature and society in order to re-
create them anew.

In the period of the Second Temple, all these fundamental
assumptions were challenged. Isaiah's vision of a new age of international harmony and equality of peoples had not material-
ized. Neither had Jeremiah's new covenant with YHVH, nor
Isaiah of Babylon's universal moral consensus. There seemed only
two possibilities: to admit that these goals were utopian and give
them up, or to idealize them. The strategy adopted by those who
did not wish to surrender them was to remove them from the
stream of real-world historical developments and redefine them
as ideals to be realized through divine intervention at the end of
history. In the last centuries before the modern era, Jewish
prophecy therefore became increasingly eschatological—that is,
focused on the violent sequence of events leading to a Day of
YHVH, when God would judge the nations and establish his
kingdom on earth.[18] The visions reported by seers like Joel,
Zecharaiah, and Daniel were of a new sort: vivid, lengthy, and
luridly dramatic, with the elaborate symbolic content of complex
dreams.[19] Unlike the straightforward commands, condemnations,
and predictions offered by earlier prophets, they resembled
coded messages that, once deciphered, promised to unlock the secrets of the end times.

The new style of prophecy became increasingly popular in the
centuries after the collapse of Persian power.[20] So different was
it from classical prophecy that some scholars have questioned
whether it ought to be called by the same name at all.[21] In the older
tradition, YHVH's messages had always been open and public,
not secret or occult. Expressed in plain language, they were trans-

mitted to the prophet for immediate publication, so that people might act on them immediately. This was why Isaiah of Babylon had contrasted YHVH with pagan gods who "speak in secret in some corner of a darkened land." "I YHVH, speak with directness; I express myself with clarity," he declared.[22] By contrast, "Apocalypse means 'revelation.' It proposes in esoteric language to unlock the secrets and set forth the program of the last events, which are thought to be imminently impending."[23] The prophet who receives such knowledge, of course, is no mere spokesman for YHVH, but an initiate—a diviner—who must decode the message for the uninitiated, if he decides to share it at all.

More important, the classical prophets had never predicted an unalterable future. In their view, human beings always had the power, through their own action, to avert YHVH's wrath.[24] But in apocalyptic prophecy, "the epochs of world history are predetermined" and history moves toward a great destruction, followed by a sensational intervention and the advent of God's eternal rule.[25] The notion that some sort of great destruction would precede the coming of the kingdom of God is equally foreign to classical prophecy. For Isaiah and Jeremiah, peace would arrive when "the nations voluntarily [attach] themselves to a God whose significance for them they have come to appreciate."[26] Moreover, although the older prophets frequently predicted the violent overthrow of empires, they rarely envisioned YHVH taking revenge on Israel's enemies. By contrast, apocalyptic thinking consistently associates divine intervention with a violent "justice"—indeed, a bloodbath of cosmic proportions—that is hard to distinguish from revenge.

Overall, the new prophetic style initiated a split between the human and divine realms that the classical prophets would have found disturbing, if not downright un-Jewish. Well before Christian theologians developed their doctrine of the Fall, Jewish sectarians pictured the material world as fallen, and redeemable only after a final apocalyptic battle between the forces of light and darkness.[27] While Isaiah of Jerusalem and Jeremiah had interrogated history to discover the choices God had laid before his people, the new prophecy reeled off scenes unalterably scripted by the divine director. While Isaiah of Babylon had preached YHVH's ability to create "new things" in history, the apocalyptic prophets relegated history itself to the category of an "old thing." Giving up on man's potential to partner with God in creating a new world society, they eagerly anticipated the moment when history itself would roll up like a scroll, and, amid scenes of unexampled violence, a triumphant YHVH would take possession of his kingdom.[28]

Jesus of Nazareth inherited and made use of both prophetic traditions, classical and apocalyptic. His conception of how the kingdom of God was to be inaugurated was strongly influenced by the literature of apocalypse. But his imperishable contribution—or so it seems to me—was made on the terrain of ethical creativity originally cultivated by Isaiah, Jeremiah, and Isaiah of Babylon. We can understand this more fully by situating him in his own time.

THE INTERNATIONAL situation facing Judea in Jesus's time was similar in many ways to that confronted by earlier prophets. In 65 B.C.E., the independent state created by the Jews after liberating themselves from Greek domination became a vassal of the Roman empire. Like Assyria and Babylonia, Rome was an aggressive superpower combining overwhelming military superiority with administrative ingenuity, economic rapacity, and its own brand of "high culture."[29] Judea's ruling elite—the Herodian dynasty, the temple hierarchy, and elements of the aristocracy—maintained order on behalf of the Romans to secure their own privileges and a certain degree of local autonomy. But while Judah had negotiated relatively loose vassal arrangements with Assyria and Babylon, Judea's relationship to Rome was intimate (if not suffocating), and intensely fractious. The Jewish population had exploded, with perhaps one million people living in Palestine at the time of Jesus's birth, and another five million or so living elsewhere in the empire.[30] Factional fights within the Jewish ruling classes were bitterly divisive, and there was great turbulence among the common people, especially those driven to the wall by Rome's economic exactions and those of local landowners and traders.

Even before Jesus's time, there were plentiful signs of the violent anti-Roman agitation that would later erupt in the massive rebellions known as the Jewish-Roman Wars. In 6 B.C.E., the Romans were compelled to put Judea under the direct custody of a procurator, and two years later (very likely, the year of Jesus's birth), a serious revolt in Galilee resulted in the burning of several towns, the enslavement of rebel sympathizers, and the crucifixion of some 2,000 Jews.[31] Jesus's response to this volatile situation initially resembled that of the classical prophets. Like Isaiah and Jeremiah, he detested the empire and its local collaborators but refused to sanction active rebellion against it.[32] Again like them, he reframed an imperial conception—the Augustan Peace or Pax Romana—in terms drawn from his own tradition, and turned it against both the Romans and the Judean elite.

Rome's ambition to place the world under a single rulership and to establish a universal peace no doubt inspired Jesus (as Assyria had inspired Isaiah) to envisage the universal, peaceable, righteous kingdom of God.[33] Of course, the Galilean prophet understood that this new order could not come into existence under Roman rule, or, indeed, under the aegis of any empire driven to expand and maintain its own power by the use of state terror. How, then, to realize God's kingdom in practice? Since Roman power was irresistible, and apocalyptic thinking prevalent—and since Jesus could feel the approach of a catastrophic war in Judea—he accepted the perspective of eschatological prophecy. In his prevision of the coming end times, he seemed to anticipate a Roman attack on Israel—"Jerusalem surrounded by armies" and "*the disastrous abomination,* of which the prophet Daniel spoke, set up in the Holy Place."[34] According to the disciple Luke, he also warned that the Jews would be deported en masse and Jerusalem "trampled down by the pagans until the age of the pagans is completely over."[35] Then, all heaven would break loose:

> Immediately after the distress of those days, the sun will be darkened, the moon will lose its brightness, the stars will fall from the sky and the powers of heaven will be shaken. And then the sign of the Son of Man will appear in heaven; then too all the peoples of the earth will beat their breasts; and they will see the Son of Man coming on the clouds of heaven with power and great glory. And he will send his angels with a loud trumpet to gather his chosen from the four winds, from one end of heaven to the other.[36]

"Jesus saw himself as God's last messenger before the establishment of the kingdom," says a leading New Testament scholar. "He looked for a new order, created by a mighty act of God."[37] On the other hand, he also stated, in answer to a question from the Pharisees, that God's kingdom was already present. "The coming of the kingdom of God does not admit of observation and there will be no one to say, 'Look here! Look there!' For, you must know, the kingdom of God is among you."[38] Even this much-debated passage resists interpretation in classical prophetic terms. If the kingdom (a word Jesus used in many different senses) was already present even though Augustus Caesar was still in power, it must be a spiritual empire somehow existing outside the tissue of temporal events that we normally call history.[39] Again, one sees that the effect of eschatological thinking is to separate the historical world from the realm of eternal spirit. In the hands of thinkers like Saint Augustine, this dichotomy was to become very important in the development of Christian thought, but it has little to do with the ideas and sensibility of the prophets.

All this being said, it is clear that Jesus spent little time describing the end times or the manner in which God would eventually rule his kingdom. His ministry was devoted to teaching people how to define the righteous society and how to live in the present, despite the oppressive weight of imperial violence and local injustice. It is when he develops the themes of justice, repentance, and compassion originally elaborated by Isaiah, Jeremiah, and Isaiah of Babylon, and extends these teachings into new ethical territory, that the Nazarene occupies the terrain of classical prophecy.

Like the first Isaiah, Jesus insists that a society is judged not by its wealth, power, or formal religious observances, but by the way it cares for the poor and the unprotected members of the community.[40] But he broadens the application of Isaian justice to include new and controversial categories of people requiring care and protection. In addition to widows, orphans, and strangers—that is, people outside the protection of the clan system—these protégés are now to include groups tabooed or denigrated by current social norms, including diseased people, lunatics, social outcasts, sinners, criminals—even tax collectors and Roman soldiers.[41] Jesus's own practice was to extend respectful care to "the least among you": women, children, slaves, and all those deprived of recognition and dignity by their anonymity and powerlessness.[42] The inclusion of new categories of worthy outcasts, furthermore, implied an expanded moral duty toward them—not just to give alms, but to provide loving care. Jesus's cures, exorcisms, and revivifying acts (reminiscent of those performed by Elijah and Elisha) demonstrated that those customarily considered accursed or abandoned by God were also YHVH's children, and were therefore curable through the power of his love.

Second, very much like Jeremiah, Jesus appeared at the Jerusalem Temple at great risk to himself. Calling it, as the older prophet did, a "robbers' den," he denounced the institutionalized corruption to be found there and outraged the authorities by predicting the destruction of the city.[43] Again like the "weeping prophet," he preached the need for inward repentance and a new moral sensibility, and experienced in his own psyche the suffering of others. Once again, however, Jesus took a step beyond his predecessor, this time by expanding Jeremiah's practice of compassion to require forgiveness on a level not previously imagined. "Love your enemies, do good to those who hate you, bless those who curse you, pray for those who treat you badly."[44] And, "Be compassionate as your Father is compassionate. Do not judge, and you will not be judged yourselves; do not condemn, and you will not be condemned; grant pardon, and you will be pardoned."[45] This emphasis on the healing power of forgiveness provided an answer to the question that tortured Jeremiah—how to induce repentance in those whose hearts seemed impermeable to change.[46] It has since inspired modern prophets like Mohandas Gandhi, Martin Luther King, Jr., and Nelson Mandela to attempt to transform the thinking of heartless rulers through the practice of nonviolent resistance.

Finally, developing the emphasis on direct action illustrated by Jeremiah and Isaiah of Babylon, Jesus required his disciples and other followers to act immediately on these principles without waiting for the authorities or society at large to accept them. Although it is not clear that he identified himself consciously with Isaiah's "servant of YHVH," he let himself "be taken for a criminal," underwent torture, and was crucified "as a ransom for many."[47] Not only did Jesus preach forgiveness, he forgave his executioners. Not only did he heal the ill, feed the poor, and work with sinners, he affirmed that others had the capacity and responsibility to do the same.[48] "You know that among the pagans their so-called rulers lord it over them, and their great men make their authority felt," he said. "This is not to happen among you. No; anyone who wants to become great among you must be your servant, and anyone who wants to be first among you must be slave to all."[49]

This advocacy of direct, sacrificial action in support of new ethical norms represented another attempt to resolve the contradiction between the prophetic ideal of the peaceable, just kingdom, and the reality of power-ridden institutions like the Roman empire and the Jewish temple-state. Perhaps, if people acted as Jesus and his disciples did, exemplifying the kingdom in their own lives, they would prepare the ground for its flowering like sowers of seeds.[50] In one sense, hindsight tells us, this strategy worked. Through the spread of Christianity, the ethical ideals of the Jewish prophets became the heritage of the nations.[51] In another sense, however, it failed tragically. Christianity's very success as an organized religious movement positioned its leaders to become members of the Roman elite. When, three centuries after Jesus's crucifixion, the new faith became the state religion of the Roman empire, it embraced the very hierarchy of power, the very callousness toward the weak, the very injustice, inhumanity, and violence that the prophets had condemned.[52]

To some extent, the eschatological trend in Judeo-Christian thought can be held intellectually responsible for this reversal. To assert that the kingdom could be realized only at the end of history (or, in some mystic sense, alongside history) divided human existence into a time-bound, corrupt, historical world "beneath," and an eternal, shining world "above." If the kingdom had come as quickly as Jesus and others thought it might, the effect of this split might not have been disastrous for prophecy.[53] But its nonappearance nullified the most fundamental principle of prophetic thought—YHVH's immanent presence in historical events—and encouraged believers to adopt a resigned determination to wait history out. Some day, the book of Revelation promised, the pagan world would go up in flames, a cosmic war would destroy much of humanity, space and time would end, and God would create the world anew.[54] In the meantime, one could work to make the empire a bit more civilized, but there was little one could do about the realities of power. It would take a miracle—literally—to realize the just and peaceful world society envisioned by the prophets.

Criticizing this sort of thinking is easy, but solving the problem that produced it is hard. For if the social and personal visions of the great prophets were, by nature, unrealizable in historical time, what sense did it make to consider them true prophets? Despite their involvement in current events and their attempts to make sense of human history and personality, were they not, in the end, as otherworldly and utopian as the later preachers of the apocalypse? And if their visions were somehow to be fulfilled in this world rather than a posthistorical future, how and when would this happen? These important questions would carry over into the next millennium, occupying religious and political thinkers from the time of Jesus to the present day.

"Until when, Lord?"[55] Almost three millennia after Isaiah's appearance at the court of King Ahaz, the world still awaits the great transformation that the prophets of Israel envisioned. Some may conclude that the prophetic goals of social justice, self-respect, compassion, and peace are unrealistic ideals that can never be fully realized in history. Others, following the eschatological line, expect them to be realized, but not by human means in historical time. I want to make another argument entirely, one which ends this study of prophecy with some prophetic good news. It seems to me that we have entered a new era of human development that, for the first time in history, makes the realization of these goals possible. Whether we will have the will and the wit to realize them, of course, is not predetermined. But I have no doubt that they are genuine possibilities, not empty dreams, and that if we do *not* make them real, the consequences will be as disastrous for us as they were for our ancestors.

Recall that prophets tended to appear, even in ancient days, not when the Jews were most impoverished and miserable, but when times were relatively good. It was when the nation's power and wealth were increasing, its trade and territory expanding, and its international connections multiplying that freelance prophets arose to call attention to glaring injustices and immorality at home and growing military dangers abroad. (This is one reason their messages seemed so out of tune and unwelcome to many of their countrymen.) Even in Jesus's Palestine, where some sectors of the rural population groaned under the Roman yoke, many in the cities prospered.[56] This sort of rapid, uneven social change was particularly likely to evoke prophetic protest. If large landowners and merchants prospered while peasants went hungry, if kings built new palaces and cities using conscript labor, or if priests conducted elaborate rites while their congregants continued to cheat and exploit one another, one could expect to hear from these men of God.[57]

The prophets' responses to these contradictions always combined anger with hope. Anger, because they saw injustice and immorality clearly where others saw only the inevitable costs of maintaining power or doing business. Hope, because profound changes in society stimulated them to envision a further transformation. Trade was burgeoning; why not use the nation's new wealth to eliminate poverty and rebuild communities instead of simply aggrandizing the rich? The state bureaucracy was expanding; why not use government to settle disputes fairly instead of selling justice for money? The temple was drawing enormous crowds; why not use it to launch a spiritual renewal rather than merely maintaining it as a ceremonial arena and a sinecure for priests? It is notable that men like Isaiah and Jeremiah did not denounce trade, government, or ritualized worship per se. Their interest was not in turning back the clock to some primitive golden age before commerce, state development, or organized religion, but rather, in liberating human development from the perverse values that were deforming it and the fixations holding it back.

Even so, the evils that most aggrieved them—deepening social divisions, unjust and callous government, perpetual warfare, routinized religion, and popular immorality—worsened even as their nation's wealth and military might increased. It seemed that those addicted to wielding coercive power and pursuing selfish pleasures could no more break their habits than (to quote Jeremiah) a leopard could change his spots.[58] For this reason, the prophets saw the revolution in international affairs that defined their era as an opportunity—a God-sent revelation—as well as a danger. The rise of the great empires demonstrated that the Hebrew peoples had been living in a fool's paradise. What they had thought was military strength was the illusion of strength. What they had defined as internal stability was institutionalized disorder. The wealth and privileges of the upper classes—even their right to live in their own country—could be taken away in an instant. The state's political independence was not worth a fig. And the people's belief that "their" God would save them no matter what sins they committed could now be exposed as arrogant complacency.

In fact, they concluded, YHVH had commissioned the empires, as he had commissioned the prophets, to teach his people lessons that had to be taught. In crucial ways, these teachings seem more relevant today than ever.

One lesson, first imparted by Isaiah, emphasized *the hidden con-*

nection between local injustice and global catastrophe. The consequences of corrupt, callous, and shortsighted government policies may not seem serious, so long as their primary victims are poor and voiceless people, but these evils put the whole society at risk. Isaiah recognized that unjust government dissolves and demoralizes communities, leaving them unprotected against foreign and domestic dangers. By favoring some groups and disfavoring others, it inflames civil conflicts rather than resolving them. By becoming hostage to a few passionately self-interested constituents, it blinds itself to problems threatening the whole. In the United States, for example, the results of Hurricane Katrina in 2005 made it clear that the effects of natural disasters are worsened a hundredfold by unjust, uncaring rulers and a social system that neglects and penalizes the poor. Americans had a harder time recognizing the connection between terrorist attacks against their country and a U.S. foreign policy conducted largely in the interests of energy companies, armaments manufacturers, and a few other extravagantly influential government clients. When people are under attack, as the prophets well knew, it is hard for them to see that their misfortune has internal as well as external sources.

A second prophetic lesson, associated particularly with Jeremiah, spelled out *the disastrous consequences of spiritual deadness:* an unrepentant state in which people refuse to change their customary lifestyles even to prevent avoidable suffering. Once again, the prophet's listeners were tempted to tune him out, or worse. Who wants to be scolded for such commonplace sins when life will go on in any case much as it did before? But the prophet is the person who sees the uncommon results of apparently mundane evils. As Martin Buber says, he or she is the one "who has been set up against his own natural instincts that bind him to the community, and who likewise sets himself up against the will of the people to live as they have always lived, which, naturally, for the people, is identical with the will to live."[59]

Consider chattel slavery, an institution that flourished in the United States for more than 250 years because it was profitable, and because most people wanted to live as they had always lived. Prophets like Frederick Douglass and William Lloyd Garrison arose to condemn the spiritual deadness that permitted commerce in human beings, but it took a national catastrophe—a civil war—to liberate the slaves. Generations later, we look back and ask, "How could our ancestors have tolerated such an obvious moral outrage for so long?" But a modern Jeremiah might note that every year Americans kill more than 40,000 of their own people and seriously injure a million more on the nation's highways. Traffic accidents are the number one cause of death for Americans aged three to thirty-three.[60]

Why tolerate a disaster equivalent to a major war each year? Because we can't imagine living without the freedom to drive private vehicles where and when we please? Because so much money has been invested in the automotive/highway construction/ petroleum products system that safe, efficient public transportation is a rarity? Because this carnage has simply become invisible, or acceptable to us as collateral damage? One may as well ask why the world's richest and most powerful nation tolerates the highest rate of child poverty in the industrialized world, violent and impoverished urban communities, politicians bought and paid for by the highest bidder, grotesquely segregated and underfunded public schools, "deindustrialized" wastelands, prisons bursting at the seams, needless abortions, environmental devastation, and other evils accepted by millions as unavoidable costs of living in a modern society. Surely, one day, our descendants will ask, as we ask about our slave-holding forebears, "How could they have tolerated these outrages for so long?"

Finally, it is not hard to imagine how the prophets of old would respond to claims that our nation's security, world order, and the progress of civilization itself depend on the United States

remaining the world's sole superpower, with military bases in
more than sixty other countries, an unmatchable technological
lead over any possible competitor, and a willingness to punish or
occupy any nation whose leaders refuse to bow to our wishes.
People today who criticize these claims and practices are often
said to hate America. Especially in wartime, they are accused of
failing to "support the troops." If only their accusers would read
the Bible. "Let this man be put to death," Jeremiah's enemies advised the king. "He is unquestionably disheartening the remaining soldiers in the city, and all the people too, by talking like this.
The fellow does not have the welfare of this people at heart so
much as its ruin."[61]

Jeremiah did not hate his nation; he loved it enough to preach
against its militarization even when Jerusalem was under attack.
The lesson that he and the other prophets never ceased to emphasize was *the uselessness and evanescence of imperial power.* Every empire claims that its monopoly of power must be maintained and
expanded to bring order, civilization, and peace to an anarchic
world. But imperial violence brutalizes both the conquerors and
the conquered, reducing everyone to the same barbaric level. The
predecessors of America's high-tech invasion forces were Assyria's iron-clad legions, with their "chariot wheels like torna-
does."[62] ("Shock and awe" tactics, indeed!) The predecessors of
today's suicide bombers were the Israelites who preferred death
or mass deportation to Assyrian rule, and the Judeans who fomented two hopeless revolts against Rome.[63] The prophets understood quite clearly that in this sort of contest there could be no
moral winners. Whichever deity either side claimed to follow,
their true god was the insatiable god of war.

By bringing diverse nations under their rule, the ancient empires created a crude simulacrum of a world community that their
elitist, power-driven policies could never realize. What Isaiah of
Babylon recognized was that only a worldwide spiritual and

political awakening could unite the peoples of the earth on the basis of their common membership in a single human community. As wildly unrealistic as it may sound, it is precisely this alternative, which one might call globalization from below, that gives us cause to hope that the prophetic vision may finally, over the course of the next few centuries, be realized.

Were the prophets' dreams of a just and peaceful kingdom utopian? One has to admit that in many ways they were. Modern students of social conflict and conflict resolution have recognized that to do away with violent abuses of power, bloody revolts, and common forms of self-destructive behavior, certain basic material and psychological needs shared by all people must be satisfied. Among these are needs for adequate food, clothing, living space, medical care, and social services; identity, recognition, and human bonding; physical security; cognitive and moral meaning; and opportunities for personal growth and development.[64] Under the conditions prevailing in ancient societies and, for that matter, in modern societies until fairly recently, powerful elites maintained their position (or tried to) by satisfying their own needs and denying the same satisfaction to others. But we now have the technical and cultural potential to make these blessings universal, and so to eliminate the false need for coercive power over others.

The key to unlocking this potential is globalization. Globalization itself—not simply the globalization of capital, but the enormous expansion and multiplication of transnational contacts, communications, and human transactions of all sorts—is creating the basis for the nonviolent construction of a world community. We inhabitants of earth are beginning to live on a global scale as the prophets once lived in Judah. We talk to one another, travel to one another's communities, buy one another's products, contract one another's diseases, marry one another's

sons and daughters, and sing one another's songs. The great historical movement of our time is the transformation into neighbors of those who were formerly strangers. The process is fraught
with difficulties. It often produces violence, as groups formerly
isolated but now in contact struggle to defend their values and
identities against new threats and temptations. But the cure, as
the prophets would have said, is not to go backward toward cultural chauvinism, but forward, toward ethical globalization.

The great question is: How, as former strangers, are we now
to relate to one another as neighbors? The next step in our
progress toward the prophetic kingdom may be that indicated by
Isaiah of Babylon and practiced by Jesus of Nazareth (within the
constraints imposed by their own societies): the development of
a global ethical consensus. Even though religion plays a disturbing role in inspiring or justifying some modern conflicts, there are
signs of ethical convergence, as members of various faiths (including secular rationalists) come to agreement on many of the
basic principles that should govern a decent society.[65] Some of
these principles, like the definition of social justice, are drawn directly from prophetic sources. Others are derived from modern
ideas about the causes and cures of violent conflict. But what
drives this movement is a new recognition, based on the reality
of globalization, that the stakes of succeeding or failing to reach
some agreement across existing lines of culture, nationality, and
religion are enormous.

One does not have to look far for indications of what may
happen if the search for a new global morality fails. What some
scholars call the "clash of civilizations" does not begin to describe
the dangers suggested, in a horrifying but relatively limited way,
by the attacks on America of September 11, 2001.[66] We have been
warned. Around the world, huge populations long subjected
to domination by powerful, neoimperial elites are dreaming of

liberation, unification—and revenge. The Hebrew prophets and our own experience teach us there is no security in coercive power—that only justice and righteousness, radical empathy and self-sacrifice will protect us. We will either abandon the fictive superiority that alienates us from our brothers and sisters around the globe, or pay a terrible price.

Baal or YHVH. Coercion or justice. Domination from above or globalization from below. Now, as ever, the choice is ours.

ACKNOWLEDGMENTS

✳

I AM GRATEFUL TO George Mason University and its Institute for Conflict Analysis and Resolution for providing me with the intellectual, moral, and financial support necessary to complete this book. Special thanks are owed to Sara Cobb, director of ICAR; graduate research assistants Daniel Stillwagon and Karen Grattan; faculty colleagues Kevin Avruch, Marc Gopin, Jamie Price, Dean Pruitt, and Daniel Rothbard; and the students of ICAR for helping me introduce many of the ideas fleshed out in *Thus Saith the Lord*. As always, Maureen Connors of George Mason's Fenwick Library provided extremely helpful bibliographical assistance. Thanks, too, to President Alan Merton and Provost Peter Stearns for their continued support, which (inter alia) permitted me to spend the spring of 2004 doing research at the British Library and the British Museum.

In writing a book outside one's own academic specialty, conversations with those more expert than the author are indispensable. Among those who generously consulted with me about various issues discussed here—but who are not to be saddled with any of my errors or peculiarities of interpretation—are Ronald C. Clements, professor emeritus of biblical history at Cambridge University; William C. Flanders of Washington, D.C.; Susan Gresinger Flanders, rector of St. John's Episcopal Church in Chevy Chase, Maryland; David Ford, regius professor of theology at Cambridge University; Roger Greaves, dean of Clare College at Cambridge University; Rev. Bob Tucker, director of the Foundation for Contemporary Theology in Houston, Texas; Dr. Anthony Buzzard, president of the Atlanta Bible College in

Atlanta, Georgia; and Dr. Charles Twombly of the Wesley Theological Seminary. Rabbi Bruce Aft of Congregation Adat Reyim
in Springfield, Virginia, read through the entire manuscript and
made a number of astute and useful suggestions.

My personal support group was particularly strong and active
in helping me to bring this project to conclusion. Thank you for
being so helpful and understanding, and for keeping me pointed
toward the finish line. I think especially of Kevin and Sheila
Avruch, Joe Tarantolo and Elissa Feldman, Jonathan Macy, Chris
and Lois Mitchell, Buzz and Alice Palmer, Jamie Ryerson, Jill Ryerson, Ellen and Michael Schwartz, daughters Hannah and Shana
Rubenstein, sons Alec and Matt, Deann Rubenstein, and, of
course, Emma and Eli. Thanks, too, to dear Tatiana for being such
a good listener.

Finally:

To my literary agent Gail Ross, and to Jenna Johnson and
David Hough of Harcourt, thank you for putting so much creative energy into this project.

To Jane Isay, my extraordinary editor, you are simply the best
reader in the world. I can't imagine writing a book without you.
Well, I can—but it wouldn't be nearly as good or as much fun to
write. Thank you again, my friend.

To Susan Ryerson: Your love is the rock on which I build.

ENDNOTES

✳

CHAPTER I: *"If YHVH Is God, Follow Him!"*

1 On threshing in ancient Israel, see B. S. J. Isserlin (2001), 155. For Israelite agriculture in general, see ibid., 149–59.

2 *Nevi'im* is the plural of the Hebrew *navi*. The word is sometimes rendered *nabi*. "The species of man that bears the word from above downwards and from below upwards is called *nabi*, announcer." Buber (1949), 57.

3 The territory occupied by modern Syria was then known as Aram, but for ease of understanding, I have replaced "Aram" with "Syria," and "Aramean" with "Syrian" throughout.

4 YHVH, the name of the Hebrews' God, is sometimes rendered as "Yahweh" or "Jehovah," and sometimes (following the Jewish custom of replacing the not-to-be spoken holy name with a more conventional title) as "the Lord." I follow Martin Buber's (1949) usage. The God of the Bible has a name, but we do not know how it was pronounced.

5 To give Jehosophat rather than Ahab the credit for making this request is consistent with an alleged pro-Judean bias in the book of Kings. According to some commentators, Kings was compiled by Judeans eager to dramatize their countryman's exemplary piety and to paint the Israelite ruling house as a den of religious backsliders and villains. See, e.g., Gottwald (1964), 58–59; Finkelstein and Silberman (2001), 194–95.

6 T. C. Mitchell, "Israel and Judah Until the Revolt of Jehu (931–841 B.C.)" (1982), 455. See also Herbert B. Huffman, "The Expansion of Prophecy in the Mari Archives: New Texts, New Readings, New Information," in Gitay (1997), 7–22. According to Oates (1986), 178, "Divination was undoubtedly the most important of the disciplines that a Mesopotamian would have

characterized as 'scientific,' and should be viewed not as some primitive magical or occult activity but as one of the most basic features of Babylonian life."

7 Newsome (1984), 5–9. The Jerusalem Bible (JB) calls the prophetic bands "brotherhoods" (e.g., II Kings 2:3, 5). The King James Version (KJV) says "sons of the prophets," and the Jewish Publication Society's Jewish Study Bible (JPS) has "disciples of the prophets." Compare Amos 7:14: "I was no prophet, neither did I belong to any of the brotherhoods of prophets." With regard to female prophets, see, e.g., Isaiah 8:3: "I went to the prophetess [JPS: "I was intimate with the prophetess"] and she conceived and gave birth to a son." See also II Kings 22:14–20 (the prophetess Huldah authenticates the Book of the Law found by Hilkiah).

8 Deut. 18:9–12.

9 I Kings 22:15.

10 I Kings 22:11.

11 Controversy continues about the existence (or not) of a Davidic-Solomonic empire. The so-called biblical minimalists, represented by Davies (1994), believe that the archeological evidence does not support (and, by implication, refutes) the existence of a United Monarchy as mighty or prosperous as that described in the Bible. See also Finkelstein and Silberman (2004), 128–45, arguing that while there is no reason to doubt the historicity of David and Solomon, "It is hard to see any evidence of a unified culture or centrally administered state" (at 142). Davies and others argue that the story of a prosperous United Monarchy is a myth constructed by post-exilic Jews for political purposes of their own. Dever (2002) and others strongly disagree, arguing that the evidence does support the existence of such a culture and state, although the extent of its wealth and territory can be debated.

12 The great difficulties of dating biblical events accurately are discussed in some detail in Gottwald (2001), 53–57. I generally adhere to the chronology established by Mordechai Cogan, "Chronology, Hebrew Bible," in *The Anchor Bible Dictionary* (1992), Vol. I, 1005–11.

13 See Isserlin (2001), 95–96, passim. Population estimates for the eighth century put Israel's population at about 350,000 and Judah's at about 110,000.

14 T. C. Mitchell, op. cit., 467. See also 1 Kings 16:27 for a mention of Omri's "valor."

15 Two biblical passages, II Kings 18:18 and II Chronicles 21:6, refer to Athaliah as Ahab's daughter, while two more, II Kings 8:26 and II Chronicles 22:2, refer to her as Omri's daughter (i.e., Ahab's sister). Chronological considerations favor the former denomination. See T. C. Mitchell, "Israel and Judah from Jehu Until the Period of Assyrian Domination (841–c.750 B.C.)" (1982), 488, citing H. J. Katzenstein, "Who Were the Parents of Athaliah?" 5 *Israel Exploration Journal* 194 (1955).

16 The battle of Qarqar (853 B.C.E.) pitted the allied forces of Israel, Damascus, Hamath, and a small Egyptian contingent against the Assyrian army led by Shalmaneser III. T. C. Mitchell believes that the figure of 2,000 chariots for Ahab's contribution is too large and may reflect a scribal error. See "Israel and Judah Until the Revolt of Jehu (931–841 B.C.)" (1982), 478–79. Other scholars consider it accurate. See Gottwald (2001), 308, n. 78.

17 The battle is described in Herzog and Gichon (1997), 159–65. Despite its importance, it is not mentioned in the Bible, presumably because of the animus of the authors of the books of Kings and Chronicles toward Israelite kings generally, and Ahab in particular. Shalmaneser III claimed victory (see ANET, 278–79), but as Gottwald (2001) points out, "This is belied by the fact that he retreated following the battle, and in his subsequent three campaigns into northern Syria did not penetrate beyond Qarqar" (193).

18 These wars are reported in I Kings 20. A modern version may be found in Herzog and Gichon (2002), 152–59, who state that ben-Hadad formed and led a coalition to resist the growing power of Israel.

19 I Kings 20:29.

20 I Kings 20:30–32.

21 I Kings 20:42–43.

22 I Kings 20:23, 28.

23 For holy war as a contest between gods, see, e.g., Judges 5:23, the Song of Deborah, where they are cursed who "never came to YHVH's aid, / to YHVH's aid among the warriors."

24 See, e.g., Deuteronomy 7:1–2, 16; 20:10–18. Gottwald (2001) remarks that while "the motif of obligatory ritual murder of captives recurs in the laws and narratives of Deuteronomy through Kings," "it appears that the obligation to destroy all captives and booty was honored more in the breach than in the observance" (at 62). See also the commentaries in JPS, 382–83; 412–13.

25 According to the JPS commentators (at 382), various internal factors "suggest that the law of the ban is an anachronistic literary formulation. It first arose centuries after the settlement; it was never implemented because there was no population extant against whom it could be implemented. Its polemic is directed at internal issues in 6th century Judah."

26 Herzog and Gichon (2002), 166.

27 I Kings 22:8.

28 I Kings 22:15–17.

29 An associated meaning is that YHVH, Israel's "shepherd" (as in Psalms 23:1), would not fulfill the role of its protector at the battle.

30 I Kings 22:19–23.

31 See Armstrong (1993) and Bloom (2005) for extended discussions of YHVH's irascible, sometimes capricious personality.

32 I Kings 22:27.

33 I Kings 22:28.

34 I Kings 20:43. The reference is to Ahab's mood when the anonymous prophet doomed him earlier for sparing the captured King ben-Hadad.

35 I Kings 21:20, 18:18.

36 I Kings 17:1.

37 According to Armstrong (1993), 27, "The story of Elijah contains the last mythical account of the past in the Jewish scriptures."

38 The beginning of the Elijah cycle of tales (I Kings 17:1 et seq.) is famously abrupt. Buber (1949) believes that his story was originally a book whose beginning has been lost (at 77). See also Blenkinsopp (1996), 58.

39 The usual interpretation of Elijah 17:1 is suggested by the JB's headnote, "Elijah foretells the drought." To the same effect, see Podhoretz (2002), 92, and Blenkinsopp (1996), 59.

40 A severe drought at this time is attested to by some ancient historians; see T. C. Mitchell, "Israel and Judah Until the Revolt of Jehu (931–841 B.C.)," (1982), 473.

41 These lines of Isaiah (7:23–28) envision the results of an Assyrian invasion, but they are identical to the results of an extended drought.

42 For intercession as a prophetic function, see Barton (1986), 102 et seq. This was one way in which the prophet's calling resembles that of the priest. See Sigmund Mowinckel, "Cult and Prophecy," in Petersen (1987), 74–91.

43 The miracles attributed to Elijah include supplying the hungry with miraculous food (I Kings 17:13–16), raising the dead (17:17–24), calling lightning down on his enemies (II Kings 1:9–13), and dividing the waters of the river Jordan (II Kings 2:8–9). His life ends, of course, with the miracle of his ascension to heaven in a fiery chariot—an exception to the normal process of dying (II Kings 2:11–12).

44 Isserlin (2001), 234–35. See also Buber's (1949) enlightening discussion of "YHVH and the Baal" (at 70–80).

45 I Kings 18:10. This procedure may imply that Israel had treaties with neighboring states providing for the extradition of fugitives. See Gottwald (1964), 62. It also suggests Israel's "mini-empire" status under the Omrids.

46 In I Kings 18:14–15, Ahab's majordomo, Obadiah, tells Elijah how he sheltered one hundred prophets of YHVH whom Jezebel was attempting to "butcher." The possibility of Yahwist attacks on the Baalists is implied by Elijah's treatment of them at Mount Carmel, and, some time later, by the massacre perpetrated by Jehu at the Temple of Baal (II Kings 10:19–27). See Kaufmann (1960), 140.

47 I Kings 18:1.

48 I Kings 18:17–19.

49 I Kings 16:31–33; 18:4; 19:10, 14. The Biblical text accuses Ahab of "serving" and "worshipping" Baal. I agree with those who consider this an exaggeration of his actual policy, which was to permit

Jezebel to worship her own gods in Samaria. See esp. Gottwald (1964), 58–59: "There is no evidence that Baal worship was introduced anywhere else in Israel than at the capital. . . . It is also apparent that Ahab did not intend to replace Yahwism with Baalism." Similarly, "there is no reason to believe that Jezebel launched a purge of all Yahweh prophets in Israel. Her wrath seems to have been confined to those court prophets who directly opposed her adherence to the Baal cult." (Ibid.)

50 Blenkinsopp (1996), 59.

51 I Kings 18:19. The KJV and JPS refer to 450 prophets of Baal and 400 of Asherah (or "of the groves"), while JB simply has "the four hundred prophets of Baal."

52 I Kings 18:21. The JB translates this as, "How long do you mean to hobble first on one leg then on the other?" The JPS version is, "How long will you keep hopping between two opinions?" and the KJV has it, "How long halt ye between two opinions?"

53 I Kings 18:22: "But the people never said a word."

54 Bright (1972), 125; Gottwald (1964), 59 et seq.

55 For lower classes, the system may not have been so beneficial. See Gottwald (1993), 139–64.

56 Phoenician products, including works of ivory, metal, glass, seashell, pottery, sculptured figurines, etc., have been found throughout the area by archeologists. See, e.g., Isserlin (2001), 195–96.

57 See Isserlin (2001), 181–91; Finkelstein and Silberman (2001), 193.

58 See Gottwald (1993), 139–73. The Naboth story (infra at pp. 21–24) reflects this development, which becomes a major topic of criticism for prophets of the eighth century.

59 These practices, and Elijah's challenge to them, are insightfully described by Buber (1949), 70–80. On the other hand, Kaufmann (1960) vigorously denies that there was significant Baal worship at this time among the Israelite population, arguing that it "was limited to court circles" (at 273; see also 138–42). In his view, which emphasizes Israel's consistent monotheism, Elijah's audience on Mount Carmel "is assumed to have a monotheistic, not a

syncretistic outlook" (at 142). I agree with Gottwald (1993) that Kaufmann "undertakes contorted explanations to convince us of Israel's ignorance of living polytheism and of Israel's absolute imperviousness to ideas and influences from these cults. . . . Few close readers of the Bible have been able to believe that the pagan religions were such a dead issue for Yahwists, or so uncomprehended by them, nor have they been able to conceive the monotheism of biblical Israel as a single intuition and system of belief that underwent no development through the centuries" (at 195).

60 See Finkelstein and Silberman (2001), 151: "In expanding from the original hill country domain of the northern kingdom of Israel to the heart of former Canaanite territory . . . the Omrides fulfilled the centuries-old dream of the rulers of the hill country of establishing a vast and diverse territorial state controlling rich agricultural lands and bustling international trade routes. It was also—of necessity—a multiethnic society."

61 Blenkinsopp (1996), 58. Davies (1994), 68, refers to an additional jar circa 800 B.C.E. found in the Negev referring to "YHVH of Teman and his Asherah." See also Gottwald (2001), 191, and compare Buber (1949), 75: "Whoever Baalizes YHVH introduces Astarte into the sanctuary."

62 See, e.g., Isserlin (2001), 247–48.

63 According to James (1960), 124–25, this sort of "syncretic" development may have taken place much earlier, when the Israelites first settled in Canaan and the desert god of Sinai took on many of the characteristics of Baal. "Since both [YHVH] and Baal were Storm-gods, the givers of rain and fertility, and sky-beings, their assimilation was inevitable, even though in origin Yahweh was not a typical vegetation deity."

64 Finkelstein and Silberman (2001), 192. Since each emerging nation tended to look to one of its gods, in particular, as its principal deity and war leader, this may have intensified competition between adherents of the "Great Baal" and of YHVH.

65 Buber (1949), 75: "The Canaanite soil cultivation is linked with apparently unbreakable bonds of tradition to sexual myths and rites; whereas YHVH by His uncompromising nature is

altogether above sex, and cannot tolerate it that sex, which like all natural life needs hallowing by Him, should seem to be declared holy by its own natural power."

66　See I Kings 14:24: "There were even men in the country who were sacred prostitutes." Although this is one of the pagan practices said to have been engaged in during the reign of Rehoboam in Judah (931–913 B.C.E.), biblical and extra-biblical evidence suggests that it continued for a long time. See, e.g., II Kings 23:7, and the discussion in Buber (1949), 74–80. Heschel (1962), 452, speaks of "the alcoholic and sexual orgiasm of the Baal cult."

67　In the time of Elijah's disciple Elisha, the king of Moab sacrificed his eldest son and heir on the wall of his capital, upon which the horrified (or impressed) Israelite army lifted its siege and withdrew: II Kings 3:27. A century later, King Ahaz of Judah "caused his son to pass through fire, copying the shameful practices of the nations which Yahweh had dispossesed for the sons of Israel": II Kings 16:3. (The JPS reads "consigned his son to the fire.") See also Jeremiah 7:31.

68　I Kings 18:27.

69　I Kings 18:28. Self-mutilation in the course of achieving a prophetic ecstasy seems to have been a common custom, perhaps even among Hebrew prophets. Zechariah 13:6 implies as much when he prophesizes the elimination of false prophets. The false prophet, he says, will renounce his profession, "and if anyone asks him, 'Then what are these wounds on your body?' he will reply, 'These I received in the house of my friends.'"

70　I Kings 18:37. The JPS has it, "for You have turned their hearts backward."

71　I Kings 18:38.

72　I Kings 18:40. The KJV says that Elijah "slew" the prophets, but the Hebrew verb is the same as that used to describe the slaughter of animals.

73　I Kings 18:44 relates that Elijah "bowed down to the earth and put his face between his knees." The KJV says that "he cast himself down upon the earth and put his face between his knees," and JPS says that he "crouched on the ground and put his face between his knees." The JPS commentary notes that "the fetal position is not known to have been adopted for prayer," but does not comment on the prophetic penchant for symbolic gestures.

74 Running before the king's chariot was also a customary method of honoring a monarch. Elijah may have believed that the demonstration on Mount Carmel had saved the king for Yahwism. See the discussion *infra* at pp. 27–28.

75 The description that follows is drawn from those furnished by Herzog and Gichon (1997) of King Solomon's chariot force (at 117–18), King Ahab's army at Qarqar (at 163–64), and the forces attacking Ramoth-gilead (at 166–67).

76 Naboth answers Ahab, "YHVH forbid that I should give you the inheritance of my ancestors": II Kings 21:3. See also Blenkinsopp (1996), 60.

77 II Kings 21:7.

78 Of course, we do not know what Ahab was thinking on the road to Ramoth-gilead, but the thoughts imagined here are consistent with the Biblical story, which I have not altered.

79 For the requirement of two eyewitnesses, see Goldin (1952). Blasphemy was punishable by death, and the story suggests that sedition was as well. Some modern commentators believe that the story's tendency to cast primary responsibility on Jezebel for the crime against Naboth represents a misogynous stereotype, one which in this case attempts to establish a connection between immorality and idolatry. See, e.g., II Kings 21:25–26 and the JPS commentary on these verses.

80 II Kings 21:16.

81 The exchange between Elijah and Ahab is described in II Kings 21:19–24. Because the JPS translation of these verses is more vivid and revealing than that of the JB, I have combined the two translations.

82 II Kings 21:29.

83 Cf. I Kings 18:37.

84 The search for Ahab is described at II Kings 22:31–33.

85 II Kings 22:34. JB translates this instruction, "Get me out of the battle," and KJV has it, "Carry me out of the host." The JPS version quoted above seems closer to the meaning of the literal Hebrew, "Get me outside the camp."

86 The Biblical account (I Kings 22:34) emphasizes that Ahab was struck by chance, demonstrating, according to JPS, "the role of Providence in the fall of an arrow." It would not be unreasonable to speculate, however, that a Syrian bowman recognized the king despite his disguise, or even that some Israelite enemy pointed him out to the Syrians.

87 II Kings 22:37.

88 II Kings 22:38. This bathing apparently fulfilled a part of Elijah's curse, although the prophecy as stated in 21:19 speaks only of the dogs licking his blood.

89 See Blenkinsopp (1996), 60–61: "We have the impression, above all, of a *solitary* figure. The impression may, however, be misleading. Both [Elijah] and his disciple Elisha are addressed as 'father'... the title implying leadership of the prophetic coenobia that Elijah visited for the last time shortly before his mysterious disappearance from the scene." Cf. Gottwald (2001), 215: "Fierce fighting between advocates of Yahweh and advocates of Baal over which should be the state deity are reported in the prophetic traditions about Elijah"; Kaufmann (1960), 140: "In all likelihood it was the prophets who roused the people to rebellion, and it was the people who eventually slaughtered the Baal prophets." Kaufmann's position is consistent with his overall insistence (at 138–48) that the people were devoted to YHVH and that the Baal cult was a foreign excrescence of limited significance.

90 Compare his condemnation of Ahab's son, Ahaziah, which apparently took place after a violent encounter with Ahaziah's soldiers. II Kings 1:1–16.

91 Some historians believe that the revolt led by Elisha was, in effect, a "peasants' rebellion" against "the rich and powerful": See, e.g., Newsome (1984), 15. Gottwald (2001, 235) opines that "the bands of prophets around Elisha appear to be drawn from the lower levels of society." Similarly, Kaufmann (1960) states that "the people demolish the temple and its altars, and turn the site into an outhouse," but II Kings 10:27 attributes this act to the "guards and squires," i.e., to Jehu's men, not "the people." There is virtually no independent evidence that the rebellion of Jehu had a class-based content or program.

92   See, e.g., II Kings 2:15; 4:1; 4:38–41; 6:1–2. In the last passage, "The brotherhood of prophets said to Elisha, 'Look, the place where we live side by side with you is too confined for us. Let us go to the Jordan, then, and each of us cut a beam there, and we will make our living quarters there.'"

93   See, e.g., II Kings 6:5–7, 9–10, 17–19; II Kings 7:6–7. Even the prophet's corpse was said to have healing powers (II Kings 13:20–21). Von Rad (1965), 27, remarks that "nowhere in the Old Testament are so many miracles crowded into so small a space, and nowhere is such open pleasure taken in the miraculous, or such sheer delight shown at the repeated and astonishing proofs of the prophet's *charisma.*" Elisha also used methods of inducing an "ecstatic" state—for example, listening to music—that were common among the brothers, although not employed by Elijah. See II Kings 3:15–16.

94   II Kings 2:23–25.

95   II Kings 2:11–12.

96   II Kings 2:9. Elisha asks Elijah for "a double share of your spirit," referring to the double share of an estate owed to the eldest son.

97   II Kings 2:10.

98   II Kings 2:14–15. Elisha's vision here may be a version of the "call vision" of later prophets like Isaiah and Jeremiah. See, e.g., Isaiah 6; Jeremiah 1. An odd feature of the story is the brothers' insistence on searching for Elijah's body, since "the spirit of YHVH may have taken him up and thrown him down on a mountain or into a valley": II Kings 2:16. Could they have suspected that the ultramilitant disciple might have done away with his more moderate master? The search, undertaken over Elisha's objection, was fruitless, of course—another validation of his vision.

99   I Kings 19:12. This "gentle breeze" (JB) is the "still small voice" of the KJV and the "soft murmuring sound" of the JPS.

100   I Kings 19:10, 14.

101   I Kings 19:18. According to Gottwald (1964), 61, the "seven thousand" to be saved apparently refers to "the Yahweh zealots under Elisha who were ready to fight until Baal was removed."

102   Not surprisingly, a number of modern commentators believe that the story was concocted after Elijah's death, to legitimize the

two-pronged attack on the Omrid regime that Elisha incited or approved. Kaufmann (1960), 281, believes that the prophecy may be dated "around 840" on the basis of internal evidence, i.e., well after the death of Elijah. Gottwald (1964), 61, terms it "an inept attempt to justify the later extremism of Elisha in uprooting Ahab's house by claiming that such extremism had been endorsed by his master Elijah when in fact it had *not.*" A more agnostic statement to the same effect may be found in Blenkinsopp (1996), 63.

103 For the story of Elisha's healing of a Syrian general, Naaman, who had leprosy, see II Kings 5. In II Kings 6:15–23, Elisha captures a band of Syrian raiders and prevails on the king to release them.

104 The Assyrian inscription is on a statue of Shalmaneser from Ashur; see T. C. Mitchell, "Israel and Judah Until the Revolt of Jehu (931–841 B.C.)," (1982), 485. According to Gottwald (2001), 88, "There is no close parallel to this overt intervention of an Israelite prophet in the affairs of a foreign state."

105 The meeting of Elisha and Hazael is described in II Kings 8:10–15. I have slightly altered the JB's "What is your servant? How could this dog achieve anything so great?" for ease of understanding.

106 II Kings 9:14 states that Jehoram of Israel was "defending Ramoth-gilead against Hazael," implying prior Israelite control of the city, but most modern commentators believe that Jehoram was besieging the (Syrian-controlled) city. See, e.g., T. C. Mitchell, "Israel and Judah Until the Revolt of Jehu (931–841 B.C.)," (1982), 445–46; Herzog and Gichon (1997), 203. It may also be that the city changed hands in the battle.

107 II Kings 9:14–15; 10:32–33; 12:17–18; 13:3, 7. See also Herzog and Gichon (1997), 173–75; Finkelstein and Silberman (2001), 202–3.

108 Finkelstein and Silberman, ibid.

109 Finkelstein and Silberman (2001), 129, 201; see also Isserlin (2001), 85. I follow the custom of scholars who place words missing from the actual inscription in brackets.

110 II Kings 9:1–13.

111 II Kings 9:17–25. The reference to Naboth of Jezreel is intended

to demonstrate that Elijah's prophecy condemning the House of Ahab was being fulfilled.

112 II Kings 9:30–37.

113 Isserlin (2001) remarks, "Syrian support for Jehu's rebellion, whom Haezel regarded as his instrument, may be referred to. If so, relations between Damascus and various factions in Israel may have been more complex than the biblical narration suggests" (at 85).

114 II Kings 10:6–11.

115 II Kings 10:12–14, 17.

116 II Kings 10:18–27.

117 Von Rad (1965), 28.

118 The king referred to was Manasseh (687–642). See II Kings 21.

119 Buber (1949), 95. Buber spells the divine name JHVH.

120 Gottwald (1964), 80. See also Isserlin (2001), 85–86.

121 For the wars between Israel and Judah, see II Kings 14:8–14; Isaiah 7:1.

122 II Kings 13:7.

123 Reade (1998), 63–64; illustrations, 23, 62–63. See also T. C. Mitchell, "Israel and Judah from Jehu Until the Period of Assyrian Domination (841–c. 750 B.C.)," (1982), 489–90; Finkelstein and Silberman (2001), 206.

124 Reade (1998), 63.

CHAPTER II: *"What Are Your Endless Sacrifices to Me?"*

1 Isaiah 7:3. On the scholarly consensus with regard to the site of the king's meeting with Isaiah and his inspection of the water supply, see Irvine (1990), 147–48 and fn. 51.

2 II Kings 15:19–20: "In [Menahem's] times, Pul king of Assyria invaded the country. Menahem gave Pul a thousand talents of silver in return for his support in strengthening his hold on the royal power. Menahem levied this sum from Israel, from all the men of rank, at the rate of fifty shekels a head, to be given to the king of Assyria, who then withdrew, and did not stay in the country." Scholars disagree about the year in which Menahem paid tribute.

T. C. Mitchell, "Israel and Judah from the Coming of Assyrian Domination until the Fall of Samaria and the Struggle for Independence in Judah (c. 750–700 B.C.)" (1991), 326, text and fn. 19, argues for the year 743 or 742. A.K. Grayson, "Assyria: Tiglath-pileser III to Sargon II (744–705 B.C.)" (1991), 77, and certain other scholars favor the year 738. Assyrian documents suggest that the event took place late in Menahem's reign, probably in 738. See Gottwald (1964), 121; Irvine (1990), 25. In quantity, the tribute probably amounted to between twenty and thirty tons of silver, an indication of Israel's great wealth in the mid-eighth century. See Finkelstein and Silberman (2001), 206–8.

3 Isaiah 5:28–30. See Machinist (1983) for an impressive series of parallels between Isaiah's descriptions of the Assyrian army and Tiglath-pileser's inscriptions.

4 There is considerable disagreement about the role of King Jotham, son of Uzziah, in the Syro-Israelite crisis, as well as the relevant dates. Gottwald (1964), 149–50, asserts that Jotham led an anti-Assyrian party and wished to join the coalition, but there seems little support for this idea in the biblical text (II Kings 15:37) or in other documents. Irvine (1990), 105–6, believes that the effort to form the anti-Assyrian coalition began in the 740s, and that Jotham resisted participating because he did not wish to return Judah to the status of a vassal of Israel.

5 The candidate was the "son of Tabeel" mentioned in Isaiah 7:6. Some scholars speculate that this putative king was another son of Jotham, perhaps by a Phoenician princess. See, e.g., Gottwald (1964), 150–51, and fn. 72. Irvine (1990), 154–55, citing L. D. Levine, suggests that the candidate was a "Tubailide," a prince of the Tyrian royal house, who might have been supported by a populace fed up with Davidic rule.

6 II Kings 15:37–8.

7 This view of Irvine's (1990), 298–99, seems plausible, given the general anti-Assyrian mood of the region. To the same effect, see Gottwald (1964), 151, referring to a possible suspicion of parricide against Ahaz, and concluding that "the purpose of terrifying Judah was to encourage defection from Ahaz's already wavering ranks."

8 II Chronicles 28:5–8. The numbers of Judean soldiers allegedly killed (120,000) and civilians captured (200,000) in this campaign appear to be wildly exaggerated.

9 II Kings 16:3–4 accuses Ahaz of various forms of idolatry, including "causing his son to pass through fire." Some scholars (e.g., Irvine, 1990) consider this chapter tendentious and aimed at picturing Ahaz, regardless of the evidence, as a prototypical "bad king." Buber (1949), 134, suggests that the siege may be the occasion on which Ahaz committed this act, which could be done symbolically rather than by literal child-killing, remarking that this is "what West Semitic kings used to do in such circumstances." (Cf. II Kings 3:27, where the besieged king of Moab sacrifices his eldest son on the city wall.)

10 For a report of cannibalism during the Syrian siege of Samaria, see II Kings 7:26–29.

11 II Kings 14:13–14.

12 It is not certain where Isaiah preached or to whom. Considering the importance of the "throne vision" (Isaiah 6) in his personal history (see discussion infra, pp. 60–62), and considering also that there is no indication that he was excluded from the temple, shunned, or persecuted as were Amos and Jeremiah, it seems likely that Jerusalem's greatest prophet would have spoken in the temple as well as to his friends and disciples.

13 Although we know little of Isaiah's background other than his father's name (Amoz), Bright's (1972) assessment of his social position is generally accepted: "Judging by the ease with which he approached the king, he was of good family, if not a member of the court itself" (at 288). See also Blenkinsopp (1996), 106, describing him as "a well-known public figure with access to leading members of the court and to the king, at least in times of national crisis."

14 See, e.g., II Samuel 12.

15 The dates of the speeches cited are uncertain. One of the great problems of interpreting the book of Isaiah, often noted by commentators, is that the book is not compiled in chronological order—it is an edited and reedited patchwork that often gives little indication of when a particular prophecy was made. Cf. Kaufmann (1960), 379: "The book of Isaiah is generally regarded

as the most composite and disordered of the prophetic books."
See also Seitz (1993), 4–18; Irvine (1990), 113–32. Thus, many
speeches and oracles refer to the invasion and spoliation of Judah
without making it clear whether the invasion in question is the
Syro-Israelite campaign of 734–732 or the Assyrian campaign
conducted by Sennacherib more than thirty years later. While
consulting the leading interpreters, I have been compelled (as
they were) to make my own sense of the texts.

16 Isaiah 1:7–9. The JB editors believe that "the occasion of this
prophecy is probably the siege of Jerusalem, 735" (at p. 971). Others (e.g., Seitz, 1993, 23, 32) ascribe it to the siege of 701 by the
Assyrians.

17 Isaiah 1:4.

18 Isaiah 1:29–31; 3:16–24; 5:11–12, 21–22.

19 Isaiah 1:17, 23; 3:14–15.

20 Isaiah 5:8–10.

21 Isaiah 1:23.

22 See, e.g., the "Persian Verse Account" in which Cyrus the Great
explains his defeat of Nabonidus of Babylon based on the latter's
sacrilegious actions during the New Year's festival: Pritchard
(1969) (ANET), 314; Oates (1986), 135.

23 Isaiah 1:11, 13, 15–17.

24 Isaiah 1:19–20.

25 Isaiah 11:5.

26 The Hebrew term *shub* means both to return (to God) and to repent. Buber (1949), 134, believes that bringing Shear-yashub also
represented "in bodily form the divine protest against the sacrifice of the first born [i.e., Ahaz's son], and at the same time the
divine warning: Now the decision begins, who is of the remnant,
who will return to Me, and whom I shall preserve."

27 Buber (1949), 135, prefers "keep still" and Heschel (1962), 80,
prefers "be quiet" to the JB's "stay calm." The JPS translation says
"be calm." Calmness, in my view, suggests a state of mind that
quietness alone does not.

28 Isaiah 7:4–5. I have altered the JB's language slightly for ease of
understanding. Irvine (1990), 141–147, summarizes the strong
scholarly disagreements over the meaning of Shear-yashub's

name and Isaiah's purpose in taking him to the meeting with Ahaz. Irvine's conclusion, which seems to me judicious, is that "With the symbolic name of his son, Isaiah affirmed that Ahaz and the Davidic dynasty would survive the crisis, if they would retain their confidence in YHVH's promise to safeguard Jerusalem and his anointed" (at 147).

29 Isaiah 7:7–9b. For purposes of clarity, I have replaced "Aram" with "Syria," "Ephraim" with "Israel," and "the son of Remaliah" with "Pekah." (To refer to a person as "the son of" someone else, without using his own name, was a deliberate insult; I have omitted the nuance here.) The JB's "six or five years" is translated by other sources (e.g., JPS) as "sixty-five years," probably the more accurate translation, but one which has produced considerable discussion of the reason for this erroneous prediction of how long it would take Israel to fall, especially in light of the more accurate prediction made in the "Immanuel" passage, Isaiah 7:16. Clements (1980), 85, thinks that v. 8b was inserted later, but Seitz (1993), 77–78, disagrees.

30 Some scholars (e.g., the JPS) translate *im lo ta'aminu* as "If you will not believe." Irvine (1990), 156–59, summarizes the disagreements and makes a strong argument that the phrase is best translated "be firm, stand still, or hold steady." The controversy is significant, since interpreters like von Rad believe that Isaiah is advising Ahaz to abandon all defense measures, whereas Thompson (1982), 27–29, and others believe that he is not advocating any position other than to act on the basis of faith. Considering Jerusalem's very strong defensive position, I believe that Isaiah is advising the king to defend his city against the siege without joining either the Syro-Israelite coalition or calling on the Assyrians for aid.

31 Isaiah 7:10–16. I have used the JB translation of the "Immanuel passage," adding the translation of Immanuel (God is With Us), and replacing the JB's "maiden" (cf. the KJV's "virgin") with the "young woman" preferred by the JPS and, now, by virtually all scholars. I have also replaced the JB's "refuse evil and choose good" with the JPS's "reject the bad and choose the good"—see fn. 55, infra. The scholarly controversies about the Immanuel

passage are well summarized and commented on by Irvine (1990), 159–71. Irvine and many others have pointed out that a "sign," in the prophetic lexicon, is not necessarily a miracle, but can be a natural event (cf. Isaiah 37:30) or even a deliberate act, such as Isaiah's decision to go about the streets "naked and barefoot" like a prisoner of war (Isaiah 20:1–5). Although the Greek-language Septuagint translated the Hebrew word used in v. 14 as "virgin," an error passed on through the KJV and other sources, the actual word used is *almah*—"young woman"—and not *b'tulah*—"virgin." The JB's "maiden" is an unhelpful compromise, since, as the JPS commentary points out (at 798–99), "All modern scholars . . . agree that the Hebrew merely denotes a young woman of marriageable age, whether married or unmarried, whether a virgin or not."

32 Interpreters disagree about whether the "young woman" of the prophecy was a wife of Ahaz, of Isaiah, or of an unnamed person. The interpretation that seems to make the most contextual sense is that the woman was one of Ahaz's wives and the child "none other than Hezekiah, son and heir to Ahaz, an identification that has been widely accepted": Blenkinsopp (1996), 101, and see fn. 68 at 262 explaining that Hezekiah would then be 18 or 19 years of age when he became king. To the same effect, see Seitz (1993), 79; Irvine (1990), 168–69. On the interpretation of "reject the bad" and "choose the good," also a topic of much disagreement, see Irvine, op. cit., 170–71.

33 Kaufmann (1960), 379, lists the errors in prediction made by Isaiah, remarking that "for Isaiah in particular, the rift between prophecy and reality . . . is in evidence throughout." See also the discussion of "true and false prophecy" in David Noel Freedman, "Between God and Man: Prophets in Ancient Israel," Gitay (1997), 63–67.

34 Isaiah 7:18–19. Irvine (1990), 172–73, feels that Isaiah's threatening words here "are aimed against the many Judeans who were supportive of Rezin and Pekah," but this interpretation does not seem to be supported by other evidence.

35 Isaiah 8:7–8. The phrase "flooding it up to the neck" is generally held to mean that, even in case of an Assyrian invasion, Jerusalem

and the Davidides would be spared. See, e.g., JPS commentary at 800.

36 Isaiah 7:20. The threat of shaving even "the hairs of the feet" (i.e., the pubic hair) was one of emasculation.

37 Isaiah 7:23–25.

38 II Kings 16:7–8. The basic premise of Irvine's impressive study (1990) is that this passage is tendentious. According to him, Ahaz did not ally himself with Assyria until after Tiglath-pileser attacked Damascus. Therefore, there was no real break between Isaiah and Ahaz on this issue; their major disagreement was about whether or not Judah should join the Syro-Israelite alliance. In my view, the evidence, although well presented, does not justify relegating the passage in Kings to the realm of fiction, especially since the appeal to Tiglath-pileser helps one to make sense of a number of Isaiah's speeches, as well as Hosea 5:13: "Judah has appealed to the Great King."

39 Isaiah 6:3. I have replaced the JB's "Sabaoth" with the more understandable equivalent, "of the Hosts."

40 See, e.g., Exodus 33:20, where YHVH warns Moses, "You cannot see my face, for man cannot see me and live." See also Genesis 32:31, Judges 13:22. Buber (1949), 127, points out that Isaiah "sees" YHVH as the elders on Sinai "saw the God of Israel" (Exodus 24:10); that is, he sees only God's gown overflowing in the temple.

41 Isaiah 6:5–7. Buber argues that "unclean lips" is a parallel reference to King Uzziah, who was dying of leprosy at the time. "Isaiah identifies himself and his rebellious, faithless people with the rebellious, faithless king; as the king is unclean, so is Israel, and so too is Israel's son Isaiah" (at 130).

42 Isaiah 6:9–13. I have replaced the JB's "gross" with the KJV's and RSV's more vivid and direct "fat."

43 For interpretations of this vision, see, for example, Buber (1949), 126–34; Heschel (1962), 113–14; Carroll (1979), 134–35; Seitz (1993), 54–60. Davies (2000), 141–44, 173–99, offers a useful compendium of interpretations and his own theological resolution of the problem.

44 See the text supra at 8–9.

45 On this point, the JPS commentary is illuminating: "Shockingly,

the prophet is not supposed to help the people understand the danger to which their sinfulness exposes them. . . . God no longer desires repentance; rather, God wants to vent divine anger on the nation. Some rabbinic commentators, unable to imagine such an interpretation, argue that the imperative verbs must be taken as future-tense verbs. Hence God does not order Isaiah to cause the people to misunderstand; rather, God predicts that they will not achieve understanding in spite of Isaiah's speeches, because the people do not want to acknowledge the truth" (at 797). Other interpretations (inter alia) are that YHVH is having one of the fits of irascibility of which he often repents; that he is speaking ironically, since Isaiah obviously wants to save his people (see Clements, 1980, 72–76); and that his unfathomable purposes and absolute freedom transcend ethical standards as humans understand them. Cf. Davies, 2000, 191–99: "It is absolutely essential for Isaiah's theology that Yahweh is non-ethical" (at 193).

46 II Kings 15:10, 13–14.

47 A. K. Grayson, "Assyria: Tiglath-pileser III to Sargon II," 73–74.

48 Aberbach (1993), 8–10, vividly describes these weapons and their impact on "the poetry of the prophets."

49 See, e.g., illustrations in Reade (1998), 65–71, 80–88; Herzog and Gichon (1997), 160–61, 164–65, 194–95, 208–9, 222–23; Kramer (1967), 63–67. See also A. K. Grayson, "Assyrian Civilization" (1991), 220. On ancient siege craft and defenses, see Herzog and Gichon (1997), 221–23.

50 The numbers of soldiers participating in battles are rarely given by ancient records. Roux (1992), 348, estimates that "the king of Assyria was in a position to mobilize an army of 400,000 to 500,000 men, reserves excluded." Grayson, "Assyrian Civilization" (1991), 217, agrees, but adds that a call-up of troops this large was "extremely rare." Cf. Herzog and Gichon (1997), 159: "The strength of the Assyrian war machine can only be guessed, but it was undoubtedly the most sophisticated and complex the ancient world had known to date."

51 The Bible is filled with stories of successful, albeit painful defenses against sieges by Israelites, Judeans, Moabites, and other peoples. For example: II Kings 3:24–27 (Israelite siege of

Kir-hareseth in Moab); II Kings 6:24 ff. (Syrian siege of Samaria); II Chronicles 32:9–23; Isaiah 36:1–37:37 (Assyrian siege of Jerusalem).

52 As Gottwald (2001), 135, points out, the policy of incorporation was originally used as a punitive response to vassal kings who withheld tribute or rebelled in other ways, but "at the height of empire, virtually the entire Assyrian domain had been given provincial status, with only a few peripheral regions exempted, Judah being one."

53 See, for example, "The Vassal-Treaties of Esarhaddon," in Pritchard (1975), 53 (ANET, 534–41). "(This is) the treaty of Esarhaddon, king of the world, king of Assyria, son of Sennacherib, likewise king of the world."

54 For lists of those submitting to the Assyrians, see T. C. Mitchell (1991), 325–26. The duties of an Assyrian vassal were onerous; they included garrisoning and feeding the emperor's troops, permitting his officers to conscript local men as soldiers and workers, granting his countrymen trade privileges, and paying him exorbitant sums by way of taxes and tribute. See Gottwald (2001), 135, 223–24.

55 Finkelstein and Silberman (2001), 206–9.

56 This policy of mass deportation may be the first known instance in history of what scholars now call "ethnocide" or "cultural genocide." See, e.g., Stuart D. Stein, "Ethnocide" (2003).

57 For details of Assyrian deportation policies, see Oded (1979). See also II Kings 17:5–6.

58 See, e.g., II Kings 17:24–34.

59 Roux (1992), 307–8.

60 Roux (1992), 307. See also T. C. Mitchell (1991), 341–42.

61 On identity as a nonnegotiable basic human need whose denial can produce violent, self-destructive behavior, see John W. Burton, *Conflict: Resolution and Provention* (Macmillan, 1990).

62 In a well-documented article, Machinist (1983), 727, notes a series of close parallels between the Assyrian kings' descriptions of their glory and achievements and Isaiah's descriptions of the Assyrians. He does not, however, make the connection between the Great King and YHVH discussed here.

63 See, e.g., Reade (1998), 37–38. The illustrations on these pages do not do justice to the great profusion of winged spirits to be viewed in the Assyrian collections of the British Museum and in New York's Metropolitan Museum of Art.

64 John S. Holladay Jr., "Assyrian Statecraft and the Prophets of Israel," in Petersen (1987), 123.

65 Ibid.

66 Ibid., 126–31. The author concludes, "Once indicated, the parallels between the role of the prophet in eighth-century Israel and the role of the royal herald in Neo-Assyrian statecraft are unmistakable" (at 130).

67 Cf. Holladay (1987), 134: "The institution of the suzerain, or 'great king,' as it classically flourished in the ancient Near East, furnished an ideal theological model for Israel's understanding both of the sovereignty of God and of her peculiar relationship to them."

68 See Isaiah 8:9–10; 10:5–19; 14:24–27.

69 Isaiah 1:27–28.

70 On Israel, see Isaiah 9:8–9, passim; 10:1–2. On Assyria (inter alia), see Isaiah 10:5, 13–19.

71 Isaiah 11:1–9.

CHAPTER III: "BLESSED BE MY PEOPLE EGYPT"

1 Isaiah 3:12–15.

2 Isaiah 3:5–6.

3 Isaiah 2:6–8; 3:16–24; 5:8–10, 11–12, 20, 21–22.

4 For a useful summary of the scholarly controversy about the dates of formation of the anti-Assyrian alliance and of the Syro-Israelite war against Judea, see Irvine (1990), 104–7, 298–99. According to T. C. Mitchell (1991), 331 ff., "How the Philistian campaign of Tiglath-pileser fits in with the Syro-Israelite attack on Ahaz in Jerusalem is uncertain." See also A. K. Grayson (1991), 77. Other scholars believe that the rebellion of Gaza and Ashkelon was part of the same region-wide revolt that involved Israel and Syria, and that the Assyrians decided to attack Philis-

tia first, to prevent the Egyptians from interfering. See Irvine (1990), 70–71. This view seems convincing, among other reasons, because it makes sense of the Philistine attack on Judah reported in II Kings 28:18. Irvine also argues (at 104–7) that the attack against Judah by Israel and Syria in 734 took place before the Assyrian attack on Philistia, at the end of a long period in which Syria led in the formation of the anti-Assyrian coalition.

5 See II Kings 15:29. The sequence of conquests by Tiglath-pileser cannot be precisely dated. For the campaigns of 733–732, see T. C. Mitchell, "Israel and Judah from the Coming of Assyrian Domination Until the Fall of Samaria" (1991), 333–36; Finkelstein and Silberman (2001), 215–17. Gottwald's (1964), 122, brief reconstruction of the events seems reasonable.

6 II Kings 17:1. For the view that Hoshea's revolt was encouraged by Assyria, see Gottwald (1964), 122.

7 II Kings 17:10–18. The scholarly controversy about the meaning of this "cultic reform" is well summarized by Irvine (1990), 79–83. Bright (1972), 275, maintains that the new altar reflected Ahaz's "recognition of the overlord's gods." See also Heschel (1962), 81–82. But Cogan (1974), 42–60, points out that it was not Assyrian policy to insist on this type of recognition. Irvine argues, correctly in my view, that no disapproval of the new altar was registered by the high priest or expressed in the book of Kings, and that the only connection between the "cultic reform" and Ahaz's homage to Tiglath-pileser was the elimination of the dais for his own throne from the temple "in deference to the King of Assyria" (II Kings 16:18).

8 Finkelstein and Silberman (2001), 43 ff.

9 Isaiah 8:16–17.

10 The details of the fall of Samaria are sketchy. See T. C. Mitchell, "Israel and Judah from the Coming of Assyrian Domination" (1991), 338–44. See also II Kings 17:1–6; 18:9–12. II Kings 17:4 seems to say that Shalmaneser imprisoned Hoshea in chains before the capture of the city. Bright (1976), 273–74, speculates that the king might have been imprisoned during an attempt to make peace with the invader, but the biblical account is not entirely coherent.

11 II Kings 17:24.

12 Whether Sargon II was Shalmaneser's son or a usurper is a matter of some doubt. See A. K. Grayson, "Assyria: Tiglath-pileser III to Sargon II" (1991), 87–88.

13 Quoted in Finkelstein and Silberman, ibid., 219–220. See also Pritchard (1958), 195–96 (ANET, 284–87). The reference to "gods, in which they trusted" is considered by some commentators (e.g., T. C. Mitchell, 1991, 333–34) to be evidence of continuing idolatry among the Israelites.

14 There may have been some continuing contact between the deportees. T. C. Mitchell, op. cit., 341, cites the postbiblical book of Tobit, which "purports to describe the adventures of a Jew deported from Israel by Shalmaneser . . . to Nineveh where had trading relations with other Jews in Media."

15 Finkelstein and Silberman (2001), 221.

16 II Kings 17:33–34.

17 Finkelstein and Silberman (2001), 243.

18 Ibid., 245.

19 II Chronicles 30:1 ff.

20 Isiaiah 27:4, 2–3.

21 Isaiah 5:1–4.

22 This is one possible meaning of Isaiah's prophecy that the Assyrian flood would cover Judah "up to the neck."

23 Isaiah 28:17.

24 See the account of Sargon II's campaigns in Grayson, "Assyria: Tiglath-pileser III to Sargon II (744–705 B.C.)" (1991), 88–100.

25 The Chaldean's real name was Marduk-apaliddina (Marduk being the name of the Babylonians' chief god, and apaliddina meaning "provides an heir"). He is called Merodach-baladan in II Kings 20:12 and Isaiah 39:1.

26 Both sides claimed victory in the Battle of Der, but the Elamites seem clearly to have won it. See Grayson, "Assyria: Tiglath-pileser III to Sargon II (744–705 B.C.)" (1991), 97–98. See also Bright (1972), 278.

27 Grayson, ibid., 88–89; Gottwald (1964), 162–63.

28 The pharaoh in question was either Py or Shabako; the chronol-

ogy of Egyptian rule and activities in this period is in some doubt. See T. G. H. James, "Egypt: The Twenty-fifth and Twenty-sixth Dynasties," in Boardman et al. (1991), 692–93.

29 Isaiah 20:2. It is generally understood that the prophet probably went about clad only in a loincloth.

30 Isaiah 20:3–5. I have replaced the biblical "Cush" (the JPS's "Nubia") with "Ethiopia."

31 Isaiah 18. For interpretation, see JPS commentary at 819–20; Gottwald (1964), 163; Seitz (1993), 143–45; Heschel (1962), 85–86.

32 Grayson, op. cit., 89. There are differing versions of Sargon's campaigns in the West, depending upon how one dates this campaign or that. Compare Grayson, ibid., 88–90, with T. C. Mitchell (1991), 345–46, and Bright (1972), 278–80.

33 The most complete description of these reforms is that in II Chronicles 29–31. See also II Kings 18:1–8, a much shorter version which contains the fascinating detail that Hezekiah "smashed the bronze serpent that Moses had made; for up to that time the Israelites had offered sacrifice to it; it was called Nehushtan." The implication that the king wished to centralize worship in Jerusalem is on the basis that he "abolished the high places" and the altars at which some Hebrews had long worshiped YHVH. See also Borowski (1995), who argues that centralization was also intended to lay the groundwork for an independence revolt.

34 Many commentators speculate that Isaiah approved of Hezekiah's reforms, although there is no evidence at all bearing on this issue. Recognizing that Isaiah would not have approved unless there were also ethical reforms, Bright (1972), 282, states, "Though we lack direct information, Hezekiah's reform undoubtedly had social aspects as well," but later admits, "What measures Hezekiah may have taken we do not know." More judiciously, Gottwald (1964), 166–67, states that Isaiah's approval was "probable," but that his main interest was "to gain a hearing with the king and especially to influence the domestic and foreign policies of Judah."

35 Some commentators, e.g., Gottwald (1964), 166, and Kaufmann (1960), 389, believe that Isaiah 9:1–7 is a coronation hymn for

Hezekiah, while others believe that it refers to a future messianic ruler. See also the nuanced discussion in Seitz (1993), 84–87. I have used the JB translation, with two exceptions: (a) Instead of "dominion is laid on his shoulders," I use the JPS's "authority has settled on his shoulders," which has a clearer meaning to modern readers. (b) Instead of the titles, "Wonder Counselor, Mighty God" (familiar to readers of the RSV and listeners to Handel's *Messiah*), I use the JPS's "The Mighty God is Planning Grace." The JPS commentary (at 802) explains, "This long sentence is the throne name of the royal child. Semitic names often consist of sentences that describe God; thus the name Isaiah in Hebrew means 'The Lord Saves.'" I have, however, replaced the JPS's "a peaceable ruler" with the more familiar "Prince of Peace." Buber (1949), 140, also insists that the king's title or "secret name" "is composed of three parts rather than four, which he translates as "counselor of the valiant God," "father of the spoil" (i.e., those delivered from Assyrian domination), and "prince of peace."

36 II Kings 18:8.

37 T. C. Mitchell (1991), 350–52, 360.

38 Gottwald (1964), 169–73, speculates that Isaiah's somewhat mysterious verbal attacks on Shebna, Hezekiah's chief steward, and his successor, Eliakim (22:15–25) were part of this political campaign. "We may conjecture that the actual sin of Shebna which incurred Isaiah's wrath was his vigorous leadership of the insurrectionist faction in Hezekiah's court" (at 171–72).

39 II Chronicles 32; T. C. Mitchell (1991), 356–59.

40 Isaiah 39:6. See also T. C. Mitchell, ibid., 353; Gottwald (1964), 177–78.

41 Isaiah 30:1–3.

42 Isaiah 31:1, 3.

43 For descriptions of this campaign, see T. C. Mitchell (1991), 359–66; A. K. Grayson, "Assyria: Sennacherib and Esarhaddon (704–669 B.C.)," in Boardman, et al. (1991), 110–11; Bright (1972), 283–84; Finkelstein and Silberman (2001), 259–63. In "Hezekiah's Reforms and the Revolt against Assyria," Borowski (1995) argues that the reforms were intended (inter alia) to make the revolt possible by centralizing the king's control over local re-

sources, and that the battles for more than forty cities imply a high degree of popular support for the rebellion.

44 See text and illustrations in Reade (1998), 65–70. Reade notes that the costumes worn by some prisoners reappear in later sculptures showing members of Sennacherib's bodyguard, suggesting that some of the deportees became soldiers in his army (at 70–71).

45 Bright (1972), 284.

46 Pritchard (1958), 200 (ANET 288).

47 Ibid.

48 There is considerable scholarly debate about whether there were two sieges of Jerusalem, one in 701 and the other in the 680s, or only one. Some historians (e.g., Grayson, "Assyria: Sennacherib and Esarhaddon (704–669 B.C.)," op. cit., 109–11) believe that there were two, while others (e.g., T. C. Mitchell, "Israel and Judah," 1991, 361–68) follow the biblical account suggesting that there was one. Bright (1972), 284–85, argues that the hypothesis of a second invasion and siege is "plausible."

49 Some scholars have argued that the bribe offered by Hezekiah, together with the loss of significant territory to Sennacherib, convinced the Assyrian king to abandon the siege of Jerusalem, since these measures "would sufficiently insure against Hezekiah's rebellion in the future" (Gottwald, 1964, 186). In this case, the report of the siege and its denouement would either be legendary or referable to a second siege (see, Bright, op. cit., 285).

50 II Kings 18:19–25. I have abridged the cup-bearer's speech without using ellipses for ease of reading.

51 II Kings 18:29–35.

52 Isaiah 37:6–7. Sennacherib was, in fact, assassinated in 681 and succeeded by his son, Esarhaddon. "The identity of the murderer or murderers is not certain, and the circumstances of the assassination remain one of the great mysteries of ancient history" (Grayson, "Assyria: Tiglath-pileser III to Sargon II (744–705 B.C.)," in Boardman et al., 1991, 119 ff.).

53 Isaiah 10:5–7.

54 Isaiah 10:13–14. I have replaced the JB's "pushed back" the frontiers with the JPS's "erased."

55 Isaiah 10:15, 16. See also Isaiah 37:26, 29: "Your part was to bring down in heaps of ruins fortified cities. . . . Because you have raved against me and your insolence has come to my ears, I will put my ring through your nostrils, my bit between your lips, to make you return by the road on which you came."

56 Isaiah 37:34–35: "It is YHVH who speaks: I will protect this city and save it for my own sake and for sake of my servant David."

57 See, for example, M. R. Smallman-Raynor and A. D. Cliff, *War Epidemics: An Historical Geography of Infectious Diseases in Military Conflict and Civil Strife, 1850–2000* (Oxford: 2004).

58 The idea, popular at one time, that under pressure Isaiah became a Judean nationalist is convincingly refuted by Gottwald (1964), 193–96. See also Kaufmann (1960), 392–95: "The future Davidide will not dominate other nations; he will impose on the world no *Pax Israelitica;* he will be rather 'an ensign of peoples, whom nations shall seek'" (at 394).

59 See especially the oracles on foreign nations in Isaiah 13–23, and the discussions in Seitz (1993), 115–201.

60 Isaiah 19:23–25.

61 Isaiah 2:2, 4. Gottwald's interpretation of the "adjudication" passage (1964), 199–203, which I find convincing, is that nations recognizing the authority of Yahwistic ethics "will submit their disputes to a jointly accepted arbitration. The arbitration is to be reached by *torah* and *debar Yahweh,* which means precisely the deliberation of prophets. . . . Now the prophets are to be the regular and trusted spokesmen to the nations." The interpretation is supported by 2:3: "The Law will go out from Zion, and the oracle of YHVH from Jerusalem."

62 See, for example, Kaufmann (1960), 386–87, which terms the passage "the beginning of prophetic eschatology." Reading chapter 2 as a unit, Kaufmann describes it as "a vision of the universal doomsday of YHVH in which the idolatry that has dominated men will be crushed before the supreme majesty of YHVH 'when he comes to judge the earth'" (at 387). This reading seems to me to read the assumptions of later apocalyptic literature back into Isaiah. Cf. HC, which states flatly, "As in later apocalyptic literature the description of the city's restoration is here accom-

panied by cosmic changes "in the latter days" (v. 2) (at 498). Gottwald's (1964), 202, interpretation seems preferable: "The limiting phrase 'in the latter days' (*beaharith hay-yamim*) does not mean the end of history but rather an important turning point in history." See also the discussion of eschatology *infra* at 162–64.

63 Cf. Gottwald (1964), 202–3: "The expectation of the prophet in this regard does not seem to be particularly idealistic. He does not hold that the eradication of war will bring about an eradication of evil in human nature, or vice versa, that the elimination of armed conflict requires first the complete removal of evil from the human heart."

64 Isaiah 9:7. That Isaiah also envisioned a "peace of the animals," when "the wolf lives with the lamb, the panther lies down with the kid, calf and lion cub feed together with a little boy to lead them" (11:6) has led some commentators to conclude that his vision of the kingdom must be posthistorical. But this is to read modern distinctions between social and natural history back into an eighth-century B.C.E. mind. Considering the possibilities of social transformation that history was already demonstrating, ancient thinkers like Isaiah could reasonably envision an equivalent natural transformation (in effect, a speeded-up evolutionary process) taking place in historical time.

65 This experience is well documented, but I owe my own knowledge of it to interviews with Ludwig and Edith Libman, survivors of Auschwitz, conducted in Chicago, Illinois, over the course of the years 1974–1975.

66 II Kings 19:35–37, repeated in Isaiah 37:36–38. Both accounts give the figure of 185,000 corpses, which may be exaggerated by a factor of ten or one hundred.

67 See discussion of this theory and citations in T. C. Mitchell (1991), 367.

68 See, e.g., Grayson, "Assyria: Sennacherib and Esarhaddon (704–669 B.C.)," op. cit. at 111.

69 Prichard (1958), 201 (ANET 288). See also Reade (1998), 65–69, with excellent illustrations.

70 Grayson, op. cit., 119–21.

71 J. Oates, "The Fall of Assyria (635–609 B.C.)," in Boardman et al. (1991), 162–93.

72 II Kings 21:3–4 ff. For a pro-Manasseh version of this king's reign, see Finkelstein and Silberman (2001), 264–67.

73 II Kings 21:16.

74 Isaiah 22:1–14. Seitz (1993), 159–62, associates this speech with the salvation of Jerusalem from Sennacherib, but also discusses difficult questions about its dating.

CHAPTER IV: *"The Heart Is More Devious Than Any Other Thing"*

1 Bright in AB (1965), lxi, "To understand the books of the prophets as books in the modern sense is to misunderstand them. They are, rather, collections of collections—anthologies if you wish—which were brought together by many hands over a considerable period of time." Kaufmann (1960), 412–15, takes issue with this emphasis on editorial "revision, glossing, and expansion," arguing that "the rift between prophecy and reality that manifests itself throughout the book" suggests that much of the work is authentically Jeremiah's.

2 Jeremiah 8:23. I have substituted the AB translation of the last line for the JB's somewhat obscure "for all the dead out of the daughter of my people." See Bright in AB (1965), 63.

3 Jeremiah 12:1.

4 Jeremiah 20:7. I have replaced the JB's "butt" with the word "fool."

5 Von Rad (1965), 193.

6 The last two lines are from Jeremiah 17:14, 18.

7 Jeremiah was intensely interested in Babylonian affairs, and some Babylonian writings display an emotional, confessional individualism similar to his. See, e.g., the discussion of Nabonidus infra at 132–35. Debate among scholars continues about the extent to which the book of Jeremiah may have been composed or edited in Babylon during the exilic period or even later. See the summary of the controversy in Stulman (1998), 168–72.

8 Buber (1949), 181. See also von Rad (1965), 202–3, emphasizing

the conflict between Jeremiah the prophet and Jeremiah the man, and Stulman (1998), 137–58, analyzing Jeremiah's prophetic persona.

9 See, e.g., Jeremiah 3:12, 4:1, 25:5, 35:15.

10 Cf. Jeremiah 7:24: "But they did not listen, they did not pay attention; they followed the dictates of their own evil hearts, refused to face me and turned their backs on me."

11 The date of Jeremiah's birth is uncertain. Bright in AB (1965), lxxxxvii, believes that he was probably born in the 640s and was therefore about eighteen when he experienced his call. Others date the call as early as his infancy (see JPS commentary at 921) or as late as 616 B.C.E. (see Gottwald, 1964, 244). I assume that he had not yet left his family home in Anathoth.

12 Buber, op. cit., 163; see also Bright (1965), lxxxxvii–lxxxxviii.

13 Compare the JPS's "I am still a boy," and the RSV's "I am only a youth." The JB's "child" has the advantage of emphasizing Jeremiah's resistance to the call.

14 Jeremiah 1:4–10.

15 Isaiah 6. And see discussion supra at pp. 52–55.

16 Jeremiah 1:11–16.

17 Jeremiah 1:17–19.

18 There is no mention of Jeremiah appearing in Jerusalem until the Temple Sermon (609) reported in Jeremiah 7, 8:1–3. Kaufmann (1960), 410, concludes imaginatively that "during Josiah's reign he was an obscure rustic visionary, an object of reviling and abuse by his neighbors."

19 Jeremiah 20:8–9. Bright in AB (1965), 129, prefers "Outrage! Robbery!" to "Violence and ruin!" He suggests that this was a cry uttered by people attacked by robbers (at 48). I have replaced the JB's rather pallid "it wearied me" with "it exhausted me."

20 E.g., Jeremiah 4:19:

> I am in anguish! I writhe with pain!
> Walls of my heart!
> My heart is throbbing!
> I cannot keep quiet,
> for I have heard the trumpet call
> and the cry of war.

21 See the classic discussion of "Cult and Prophecy" by Sigmund Mowinckel in Petersen, ed. (1987), 74–98.

22 Jeremiah 6:13.

23 See Jeremiah 11:18–20.

24 This theme is explored in relation to the youth revolts of the 1960s in Erik H. Erikson, *Identity, Youth, and Crisis* (W. W. Norton, 1968); Kenneth Keniston, *Young Radicals: Notes on Committed Youth* (Harcourt, Brace, 1968); and Hannah Arendt, *On Violence* (Harvest Books, 1970).

25 E.g., Jeremiah 3:9–10: "[Israel's] faithless sister Judah . . . went and played the whore. So shameless was her whoring that at last she polluted the country; she committed adultery with lumps of stone and pieces of wood."

26 Jeremiah 13:26–27. See also 2:20, 24–25; 3:1–10; 4:30.

27 Jeremiah 16:2.

28 Jeremiah 16:3–4.

29 For comparable behavior patterns in other innovative rebels, see Erik H. Erikson, *Young Man Luther: A Study in Psychoanalysis and History* (W. W. Norton, 1993), and *Gandhi's Truth: On the Origins of Militant Nonviolence* (W. W. Norton, 1993).

30 Jeremiah 20:9.

31 Jeremiah 20:7. The Hebrew *patah* describes human seduction. See the JPS's "enticed" and commentary at 966. The commentator's suggestion that "you have overpowered me" suggests a rape seems to me to obscure the volitional component in Jeremiah's decision.

32 Jeremiah 15:18–19.

33 On his silent period, which may not have been so silent, see Gottwald (1964), 239–45; Bright in AB (1965), xc–xcvi.

34 See A. K. Grayson, "Assyria, 668–635 B.C.: The Reign of Ashurbanipal," in Boardman et al. (1991), 142–54.

35 J. Oates, "The Fall of Assyria (635–609 B.C.)," in Boardman, et al. (1991), 183.

36 See the slightly conflicting accounts in II Kings 21:1–9 and II Chronicles 33:1–10. II Chronicles 33:11–17 reports a "conversion" of Manasseh to Yahwism that II Kings does not mention. Josiah removed "the house of the sacred male prostitutes" as part of his reform: II Kings 23:7.

37 II Kings 21:19–24; II Chronicles 33:21–25. And see the discussion of these events in T. C. Mitchell, "Judah Until the Fall of Jerusalem (c. 700–586 B.C.)," in Boardman et al. (1991), 373–83. Some scholars believe that anti-Assyrian activists perpetrated the assassination of Amon, and that Ashurbanipal's return "prompted the counter-coup." See, e.g., Bright (1972), 315. Mitchell disagrees on the basis of chronological considerations (op. cit. at 182).

38 See J. Oates, "The Fall of Assyria," in Boardman et al. (1991), 162–82.

39 T. C. Mitchell, ibid. at 386–87; Isserlin (1998), 90; Bright (1972), 316.

40 II Kings 22:2 states that Josiah "did what is pleasing to YHVH, and in every respect followed the example of his ancestor David, not deviating from it to right or left." The Josian reforms are summarized in II Kings 22, 23, and (in somewhat greater detail) in II Chronicles 34, 35. See also Finkelstein and Silberman (2001), 275–92; Kaufmann (1960), 287–90, 405–9; Bright (1972), 318–23.

41 Bright (1972), 318. Bright states that "the reform was quite obviously a facet of resurgent nationalism," but adds that a return to tradition prompted by "a premonition of doom and a gnawing insecurity, together with a nostalgic longing for the better days of long ago," was common throughout the region in this period (at 319).

42 II Kings 22:13; II Chronicles 34:21.

43 Davies (1994), 39, declares that both the discovery of the book and the Josianic reform itself "ought to be approached as a pious legend: possible, but extremely improbable." Others do not go as far, but assert that certain parts of the book, in particular those dealing with the centralization of worship in Jerusalem, "must be considered a product of the age in which it first appears as a historical factor, the age of Hezekiah and Josiah" (Kaufmann, 1960, 174). According to Bright (1972), 320, the book was "re-edited in the generation preceding the reform," but "this was no new law, still less the 'pious fraud' it has sometimes been called, but rather a homiletical collection of ancient laws that derived ultimately from the legal tradition of earliest Israel." A number of scholars

have noted that the literary form of Deuteronomy, which describes a covenant or treaty between YHVH and the Hebrews, is similar to that of contemporaneous Assyrian vassal treaties. See T. C. Mitchell, "Judah Until the Fall of Jerusalem (c. 700–586 B.C.)," in Boardman et al. (1991), 388, n. 140; Finkelstein and Silberman, op. cit. at 281. Finkelstein and Silberman also note that much of the "Deuteronomistic History" of Kings and Chronicles also appears to date from the time of Josiah, when there was a rapid spread of literacy in Judah (at 284).

44 II Kings 23:23. II Chronicles 35:1–18 describes the celebration in more detail.

45 T. G. H. James, "Egypt: The Twenty-fifth and Twenty-sixth Dynasties," in Boardman et al. (1991), 714–15.

46 II Kings 23:29.

47 There is some disagreement about the accuracy of the account in Chronicles, with certain scholars (e.g., Finkelstein and Silberman, 2001, 290–91) arguing that it is unlikely that Josiah had an army large enough to challenge the Egyptians; others (e.g., Herzog and Gichon, 1997, 256–57) contending that the armies were well enough matched, especially considering Josiah's strategic position; and still others (see Finkelstein and Silberman, op. cit., 291, citing Nadiv Naaman) suggesting that Josiah might have been summoned to pay homage to Necho at Megiddo and executed there.

48 II Chronicles 35:19–24.

49 II Chronicles 35:25. I have replaced the JB's "singing men and singing women" with the JPS's "singers, male and female."

50 See Jeremiah 22:15, comparing Josiah's son Jehoiakim invidiously with his father.

51 Bright in AB (1965), xci, argues that "it is almost unthinkable that Jeremiah could have opposed Josiah's effort to rid the land of the very paganism against which he had preached with such vehemence," noting also that Jeremiah had probably been nurtured on the Mosaic covenant outlined in Deuteronomy, and that "the men of the reform and their sons" later "stood up for Jeremiah and saved his life" (at xcii). See also Kaufmann (1960), 415–17. Gottwald (1964), 239–43, on the other hand, questions these

hypotheses. For Buber's subtle discussion of Jeremiah's possible attitude toward centralization of the cult, see (1949), 168–70.

52 See, e.g., Jeremiah 3:16; 4:4; 6:20; 7:4–7, 21–23; 8:8; 9:25–26.

53 II Kings 23:33–34; II Chronicles 36:1–4. The biblical account does not give a motive for the removal of Jehoiakim's brother, but it is hard to imagine any other motive, particularly if Jehoahaz was the favorite of the "country people," as reported in II Kings 23:30. See also T. C. Mitchell, "Judah Until the Fall of Jerusalem (c. 700–586 B.C.)," in Boardman et al. (1991), 392–93.

54 Jeremiah 26:2. Emphasis added.

55 Jeremiah 7:13, 14–15. In place of the JB's "the place I have given to you," I have substituted "the city I have given to you," following 26:9, which makes the meaning of "place" clear: "This Temple will be like Shiloh, and this city will be desolate and uninhabited." In place of the JB's "the entire race of Ephraim," for the sake of clarity, I have substituted "the entire brood of Israel." ("Brood" is used by the JPS instead of "race.")

56 Jeremiah 26:6. This is a repeated or "doubled" version of Jeremiah's Temple Sermon.

57 The destruction of Shiloh referred to by Jeremiah (and also in Psalms 78:60) is not narrated in the Bible, although it is assumed to have happened during the Israelites' wars with the Philistines at the time of Samuel. See JPS commentary on Samuel 5:1–12, at 570.

58 See Buber's discussion of prophetic "unconditionality" in Biemann (2002), 119–23.

59 Jeremiah 26:4–6. This point is made even more explicitly in the shorter version of Jeremiah's temple speech summarized in 26:1–6, in which YHVH tells Jeremiah, "Perhaps they will listen and each turn from his evil way; if so, I shall relent and not bring the disaster on them which I intended for their misdeeds" (at 26:3).

60 Jeremiah 7:28.

61 Jeremiah 17:9–10. Cf. 4:4: "Circumcise yourselves for YHVH; off with the foreskins of your hearts."

62 Jeremiah 7:22–23. I have used the JPS's "burnt offerings" instead of the JB's "holocausts."

63 The practices denounced by Jeremiah include the cult of Ishtar (the Queen of Heaven) (7:17–19), child sacrifice (7:31–32), and worship of the sun, moon, and stars (8:1–2), all of which are associated with Babylonia and Assyria.

64 Jeremiah 8:8. This passage has produced wildly differing translations and interpretations. Bright (1965), 63, points out that the last two lines read literally, "Truly, behold, it is to *seqer* it has wrought, the *seqer* pen of the scribes," with *seqer* meaning false or falsely, a deceit or delusion. The JPS (without commentary) effectively bowdlerizes the passage by writing "Assuredly, for naught has the pen labored, / For naught the scribes!" This follows the KJV's similar "Lo, certainly in vain made he it; the pen of the scribes is in vain." The RSV, closer to the JB's version, but even more pointed, has "But, behold, the false pen of the scribes / has made it into a lie." Buber (1949), 168, agrees that Jeremiah was protesting against "the lying style of the scribes."

65 Deut. 12:11, 13–14.

66 Deut. 16:1–17. Buber (1949), 168–69, speculates that "in the priests' house at Anathoth there was preserved in an oral tradition" an ancient version of Deuteronomy that was inconsistent with "the sections later disseminated among the people and apparently influenced by the special views and needs of the Jerusalem priesthood." In any event, says this commentator, "The fact that vain confidence is the enemy of faith appeared to Jeremiah as the problematics of the reform, the vain confidence of those who say they have the sanctuary and the vain confidence of those who say they have the book."

67 Jeremiah 7:20.

68 Deut. 18:20.

69 Jeremiah 26:9.

70 Most commentators incline to the view that the crowd was a potential lynch mob. Bright in AB (1965) speaks of a possible "lynching" (at 170), and the JPS commentary (at 979) states that "the people react by calling for Jeremiah's death." The JPS, like the KJV, has Jeremiah being seized by "the priests and the prophets and all the people," while the JB translation has him seized only by "the priests and prophets." The AB translation is

consistent with the JB, with Bright in AB (1965), 169–70, noting that while the Hebrew adds "and all the people," these words seem to be drawn from an earlier verse and are not to be taken literally: They mean, at most, "various of the people." It is likely that Jeremiah's speech angered some of the people, but the idea that the crowd intended to lynch him in the temple seems improbable, particularly in view of the story's denouement. For the complete account of the trial, see Jeremiah 26:11–24.

71 For an artist's reconstruction of the temple, see Isserlin (2001), 249.

72 Jeremiah 26:16 states that these words were uttered by "the officials and all the people" to "the priests and the prophets." I assume they were uttered by an official with the demonstrated approval of the people.

73 Jeremiah 26:24: "But Jeremiah had a protector in Ahikam son of Shaphan, so he was not handed over to the people to be put to death." Bright in AB (1965), xcviii, notes that Ahikam may have been a son of the king's secretary of state, and comments (at 170), "One gains the impression that but for Ahikam not even the support of the princes would have sufficed to save Jeremiah from the crowd." But this latter interpretation seems mistaken. In the first place, the crowd had approved Jeremiah's acquittal. Second, handing a condemned person over to the people to be put to death was not an indication that the crowd wanted him executed. As Isserlin (2001), 108, points out, "There was no publicly appointed executioner" in ancient Israel. Stoning was the usual method of capital punishment, with the witnesses for conviction casting the first stones, followed by the whole community. "In judicial matters the pursuit of justice thus remained to a remarkable extent vested in the community," Isserlin remarks.

74 Cf. Bright in AB (1965), xcvii: "Under Jehoiakim the reform, already wearing thin, may be said to have lapsed."

CHAPTER V: *"Deep Within Them I Will Plant My Law"*

1 The Egyptians won several battles during this period, including a battle against the Babylonian garrison at Quramati in early 605.

See T. C. Mitchell, "Judah Until the Fall of Jerusalem (c. 700–568 B.C.)," in Boardman et al. (1991), 394.

2 This is the story of the buried waistcloth, representing Judah's pride, which YHVH commanded Jeremiah to bury near the Euphrates and then dig up: Jeremiah 13:1–11. Bright in AB (1965), 95–96, and other scholars believe that such a journey was unlikely, and that Jeremiah may have gone to nearby Parah, whose spelling in Hebrew would be identical to "to the Euphrates."

3 A. K. Grayson, "Assyria 668–635 B.C.: The Reign of Ashurbanipal," in Boardman et al. (1991), 161.

4 Jeremiah 51:7.

5 Jeremiah 1:13.

6 Jeremiah 4:6–7, 13.

7 Isaiah 5:26–30.

8 Jeremiah 4:19. I have replaced the JB's "I am in anguish!" with the AB's more literal and expressive "O my bowels, my bowels!" See Bright in AB (1965), 30. Bright points out, quite correctly, that "none of this material can be dated with precision," noting that some might suppose that these verses were composed while the Babylonian invasion was in progress, but that this is not necessarily true, since "the prophet had long been haunted by a premonition of disaster, and his imagination was exceedingly vivid" (at 34). To the same effect, Gottwald (1964), 248–49, believes that Jeremiah's vision of the Battle of Carchemish was also a pre-vision. With the latter view, Bright in AB (1965), 308, disagrees.

9 Jeremiah 4:31.

10 Jeremiah 18:1–12.

11 Gottwald (1964), 248, remarks that Jeremiah's warnings about a Babylonian victory must have been disbelieved, since "the Egyptians seemed always to get the better of the neo-Babylonians when the latter had not the help of the Medes," and the Medes were busy extending their own empire into Anatolia.

12 Jeremiah 19:9–10.

13 Jeremiah 19:15.

14 Jeremiah 20:6.

15 Jeremiah 20:14–15, 18.

16 The site of Carchemish is in what is now southern Turkey, near the Syrian border.

17 See T. G. H. James, "Egypt: The Twenty-fifth and Twenty-sixth Dynasties," in Boardman et al. (1991), 716.

18 So D. J. Wiseman, "Babylonia 605–539 B.C." in Boardman et al. (1991), 230. Cf. Saggs (2000), 164.

19 Jeremiah 46:3–6. V. 2 makes it clear that this is a description of the Battle of Carchemish.

20 In "The Fall of Assyria (635–609 B.C.)," 183, Oates notes that this statement is probably exaggerated. For the other events of the fall, see Oates, 162–93; Bright in AB (1965), xxxiv–xxxviii; Roux (1992), 372–77.

21 Roux (1992), 38. Roux quotes the Babylonian Chronicles: "As for the rest of the Egyptian army which had escaped from the defeat (so quickly that) no weapon had reached them, in the district of Hama the Babylonian troops overtook and defeated them so that not a single man escaped to his own country."

22 On Baruch's background (as noted by Josephus), see T. C. Mitchell, "Judah Until the Fall of Jerusalem," in Boardman et al. (1991), 395–96.

23 The episode of the scroll is contained in Jeremiah 35:1–32. The exact contents of the scroll are not known, but various scholarly reconstructions have been attempted. See Gottwald (1964), 250, n. 74. Gottwald believes that it probably contained "the political, social, and religious indictments of Judah and the threats of a northern invader," as well as the Temple Sermon, condemnations of kings Jehoahaz and Jehoiakim, attacks on false prophets, and the account of the Battle of Carchemish (at 251).

24 Jeremiah 36:7.

25 Jeremiah 36:17–19. The biblical account has "the officials" speaking to Baruch, but I assume that the secretary, Shaphan, did most of the talking. "Shaphan the secretary" is mentioned in II Kings 22:12 as one of Josiah's high officials associated with the reform. It was his son, Ahikam, who saved Jeremiah from a death sentence after his Temple Sermon.

26 Jeremiah 36:23. The Bible says "the ninth month," which by our reckoning was December.

27 Jeremiah 36:23–30.

28 Jeremiah 36:30.

29 Jeremiah 22:13.

30 Jeremiah 22:17.

31 Nebuchadnezzar's exact target on this campaign is not known. See D. J. Wiseman, "Babylonia 605–539 B.C.," op. cit., 231; T. C. Mitchell, "Judah Until the Fall of Jerusalem," op. cit., 397.

32 II Kings 24:1 states that Jehoiakim became Nebuchadnezzar's vassal for three years. II Chronicles 36:6 has the king being carried off to Babylon "in chains," which is either an invention or a reference to his being compelled to come to Babylon to witness Nebuchadnezzar's victory celebration. See the JPS commentary at 1823–24.

33 Wiseman, op. cit., 233.

34 II Kings 24:2. See also Wiseman, 232; Mitchell, 398–99.

35 II Kings 24:13–16. The JPS suggests that the numbers of people deported may be exaggerated (at 777).

36 See the JPS commentary at 776.

37 See T. C. Mitchell, "The Babylonian Exile and the Restoration of the Jews in Palestine (586–c. 500 B.C.)," in Boardman et al. (1991), 418–19, 421–22; M. A. Dandamaev, "Neo-Babylonian Society and Economy," ibid., 257.

38 Babylonian tablets designate Jehoiachin "king of Judah" and describe him being treated relatively well, at least until the disaster of 586. See T. C. Mitchell, "The Babylonian Exile," 418. See also Gottwald (1964), 258, stating that Zedekiah was regarded as "a temporary appointee looking after the king's affairs in his absence."

39 Jeremiah 24 relates the vision of the two baskets of figs.

40 Jeremiah 28:1–4.

41 Bright in AB (1965), civ.

42 Jeremiah 29:10.

43 Isserlin (2001), 90.

44 D. J. Wiseman, "Babylonia 605–539 B.C.," op. cit., 233. Gottwald (1964), 257, characterizes the revolt as "a serious army uprising" that "had to be crushed with heavy loss of life among the rebels."

45 Bright in AB (1965), cv, suggests that Zedekiah organized this meeting, which seems possible, although he would probably not

have done it on his own initiative. To the same effect, JPS commentary at 981. Mitchell, op. cit., 401–2, believes that the emissaries came to enlist Zedekiah's participation in a rebellion, and that they may have been in communication with the instigators of the uprising in Babylon.

46 Jeremiah 27:16.

47 Jeremiah 27:5–6.

48 Jeremiah 27:12.

49 Jeremiah 27:8.

50 Jeremiah 27:15; 16–21.

51 Jeremiah 28:9.

52 Jeremiah's dispute with Hananiah is recounted in Jeremiah 28.

53 Jeremiah 29:6–7.

54 Jeremiah 29:13. Bright in AB (1965), 211, points out that "for a command to Jews to pray for the hated heathen power is otherwise unexampled in literature of the period."

55 According to T. C. Mitchell, "The Babylonian Exile," 425, "It can only be speculation that this beginning [i.e., the construction of synagogue buildings] took place in the Babylonia of the Exile." Kaufmann (1960), 451, puts the matter well: "So long as Israel refused to sing YHVH's song on foreign soil, it was impossible for their religion to become in reality the religion of other peoples. The idea of the unique sanctity of the holy land was not done away with. . . . But life in exile necessarily gave birth to a radically new type of cult, a cult without sacrifice or priesthood: the worship of the synagogue."

56 Jeremiah 29:26–27. It is unclear from the text whether the prophet, speaking for YHVH, is predicting their capture, threatening to expose them, or celebrating their capture and predicting their execution.

57 Jeremiah 23:14, 25–26.

58 On the timing of Nebuchadnezzar's invasion, see T. G. H. James, "Egypt: The Twenty-fifth and Twenty-sixth Dynasties," in Boardman et al. (1991), 718.

59 Herzog and Gichon (1997), 259–61.

60 Jeremiah 21:5–6, 9–10. I have replaced the JB's "Chaldeans" with "Babylonians."

61 This is probably the context for the plot against Jeremiah recorded in 18:18. "'Come on,' they said, 'let us concoct a plot against Jeremiah. . . . Come on, let us hit at him with his own tongue; let us listen carefully to every word he says.'" Bright in AB (1965), 126, dates the plot to Jehoiakim's reign, but it seems more pertinent to the time of the siege.

62 Jeremiah 37:5. For the events described here, see also Gottwald (1964), 274–79.

63 Jeremiah 38:10.

64 Jeremiah 38:12. Gottwald (1964), 276, opines that Jeremiah's father may have died, making it necessary to divide his property among several sons.

65 The episode of Jeremiah's "desertion" and punishment is recounted in 37:11–21 and 38:1–13.

66 See the discussion in AB (1965), cviii–cx, pointing out that Jeremiah had many opportunities to escape, and rejected the chance to leave the city with the Babylonians after its fall. None of these arguments is conclusive, of course; the judgment of his innocence is based on what we know (or intuit) of his character.

67 Jeremiah 50:23; 51:11.

68 Jeremiah 37:17.

69 Jeremiah 38:4.

70 Jeremiah 31:33–34.

71 Jeremiah 31:30.

72 Jeremiah 31:3–4.

73 Jeremiah 32:39–40.

74 II Kings 25:3.

75 Jeremiah 52:10.

76 II Kings 25:8–12.

77 See, e.g., Finkelstein and Silberman (2001), 294–95.

78 The story of Gedaliah is recounted in Jeremiah 40:7–41:3. He was the son of Ahikam, who had helped save Jeremiah from execution after his Temple Sermon, and the grandson of Josiah's secretary of state.

79 For a well-imagined account of Jeremiah's last days, see Gottwald (1964), 286–93.

80 Jeremiah 41:1–2.

81 Jeremiah 32:6–15.
82 Jeremiah 42:10–11.
83 Jeremiah 44:24–30.

Chapter VI: *"I Will Make You the Light of the Nations"*

1 Jeremiah 50:23. See also 51:11, naming the "king of the Medes" as the destroyer—probably a later emendation, although written before the fall of Babylon. See McKenzie (1968), 359–60.
2 Jeremiah 50:2–3.
3 E.g., "[Babylon] will never be inhabited again, but remain uninhabited age after age. As when God overthrew Sodom and Gomorrah, with their neighboring towns—it is YHVH who speaks—no one will live there any more, no man will make his home there ever again." Jeremiah 50:39–40.
4 Isaiah 43:18–19.
5 According to D. J. Wiseman, "Babylonia 605–539 B.C.," in Boardman et al. (1991), 239–40, Nebuchadnezzar was as famous for his wise administration as for his military prowess.
6 Ibid., 240–44. See also Oates (1986), 130–32.
7 Oates (1986), 172, 176.
8 For conflicting interpretations, see Wiseman, op. cit., 246–47; Oates (1986), 133–34; Saggs (2000), 170–71; Roux (1992), 386.
9 See "The Mother of Nabonidus," in Pritchard (1975), 104–8 (ANET 560–62). Sin seems to have been considered the tutelary god of Harran.
10 "Nabonidus and His God," in Pritchard (1975), 109 ff. (ANET 562–63). The phrases in parentheses are the translator's interpolations. See also Oates (1986), 132–33, with photo of the cylinder recording his dream concerning the restoration of the temple of Sin (at 132).
11 Pritchard, ibid., uses the spelling "Tema" instead of "Taima." D. J. Wiseman (op. cit., 246–47) reads the monolith inscription as implying a "priest-led" rebellion against Nabonidus, although this reading does not seem compelled by the text.
12 Oates (1986), 133, remarks that "the verses in the Book of

Daniel . . . which attribute to Nebuchadnezzar a period of madness are clearly a corruption of the stories about Nabonidus," noting that the recently discovered Qumran scrolls ascribe a seven-year illness to the Babylonian king. She also states that "Nabonidus' religious and administrative reforms provoked great resentment, while the wars and extensive building programmes of his predecessors had proved a severe burden on the country's resources."

13 Wiseman (op. cit., 247) argues that the king traveled to Taima to gain control of the spice trade and to extend the Babylonian empire westward. To the same effect, see Saggs, op. cit., 171. Oates (op. cit., 134) does not believe that the evidence warrants imputing such motives to Nabonidus.

14 For Cyrus's rise and early career, see T. Cuyler Young Jr., "The Early History of the Medes and the Persians and the Achaemenid Empire to the Death of Cambyses," in Boardman et al., eds. (1988), 24–41; Amelie Kuhrt, "Babylonia from Cyrus to Xerxes," in Boardman et al. (1988), 120–29; Oates (1986), 132–38; and "Cyrus (557–529)" in Pritchard (1958), 206–8.

15 The war of 553–550 B.C.E. is sometimes said to have been started by a rebellion of Cyrus against his Median overlord, Astyages (thus, McKenzie, 1968, xxvii), but the Babylonian Chronicle states that the Medes marched against the Persians "for conquest": See T. Cuyler Young, Jr., op. cit., 30–32, which attempts to reconcile apparently conflicting sources.

16 T. Cuyler Young Jr., op. cit., 42, states that the Medes "were included almost as partners in the rise of the Iranians to imperial glory."

17 Young, ibid. See also Bright (1972), 362. On Cyrus's policy of religious toleration, see Mary Boyce, "Persian Religion in the Achemenid age," in Davies and Finkelstein (1984), 287–88. Oates (1986), 134, sees these measures as part of "a blatant propaganda campaign throughout the Babylonian Empire [to win] support for what were presented as his liberal policies." In "Cyrus II and the Political Utility of Religious Toleration," Cyrus Masroori (in Laursen, ed., 1999) agrees that "for him, religion was a means of rule by propaganda, as opposed to the Babylonian-Assyrian rule by terror" (at 127).

18 Young, op. cit., 33–35.

19 The precise dates and other details of Cyrus's conquests are not known. When he died in 530, he was said to be fighting in the area later known as Pakistan's northwest frontier. See Young, op. cit., 35–36; Henri-Paul Francfort, "Central Asia and Eastern Iran," in Boardman et al. (1991), 170–71.

20 Young, op. cit., 30–33, discusses a dream of Nabonidus occurring early in his reign and recorded in the so-called Dream Text, which predicted the fall of the Medes who were then besieging Harran. In interpreting the dream, Nabonidus identifies Cyrus as the figure whose liberation of that city would permit him to rebuild the temple of Sin. If the Babylonian king did collaborate with the Persians against the Medes, Young remarks, this was to prove a "bad bargain" (at 32).

21 See the "Cyrus Cylinder" in Pritchard (1958), 206–8 (ANET 315–16).

22 See the account of Babylon's fall in D. J. Wiseman, op. cit., 248–51. Wiseman attributes the city's quick surrender to "collaborators or dissident elements who assisted the invaders," noting Herodotus's story that a "commando-type group" entered the city "through the dried-up river bed or canals flowing through the city beneath the walls" (at 249).

23 "Cyrus (557–529)" in Pritchard (1958), 207–8 (ANET 315–16). The phrases in square brackets are the translator's restorations of the text. The phrases in parentheses are his interpolations.

24 T. C. Mitchell, "The Babylonian Exile and the Restoration of the Jews in Palestine (586–c. 500 B.C.)," in Boardman et al. (1991), 419. The Babylonian word, as transliterated, is *ia-a-hu-da-a-a,* which becomes the Aramaic *yehuday,* the Latin *Iudaeus,* the Old French *giu,* etc.

25 I. Eph'al, "Syria-Palestine under Achaemenid Rule," in Boardman et al. (1988), 151.

26 Ezra 1:2–4. II Chronicles 36:23 contains a shorter version of this passage, ending "let him go up." There is no extrabiblical source for this decree—see, e.g., Kuhrt, op. cit., 124–26—although the book of Ezra reports that it was republished by King Darius in the second year of his reign (520) to permit the rebuilding of the

temple to be completed despite obstructionist tactics by the Samaritans (Ezra 4–6). The phrase "the God of heaven" might seem to imply that Cyrus was a Yahwist, but, as would shortly become apparent, he was not. "He is the God who is in Jerusalem" more accurately represents his view that YHVH was the local deity of the Jews.

27 For estimates of numbers, see Ezra 2, Nehemiah 7, and the discussion in T. C. Mitchell, "The Babylonian Exile and the Restoration of the Jews in Palestine (586–c. 500 B.C.)," 430–31.

28 Cf. von Rad (1965), 246: "There can be no doubt that the prophet regards the exodus of the redeemed from Babylon as the counterpart in the saving history to Israel's departure from Egypt in the far past."

29 Isaiah 40:1–2. I have used the first four lines of the JPS translation, which is more familiar (and seems to me more beautiful) than the JB's idiosyncratic, "Console my people, console them. . . . Speak to the heart of Jerusalem." McKenzie (1968), 17, points out that "double punishment" was customary in the case of payments imposed on thieves and for breach of trust. Cf. Job 42:12–16.

30 Cf. Buber (1949), 208–9: "Deutero-Isaiah is, despite the teachings of Amos, Isaiah, and Jeremiah, the originator of a theology of world history, for he is the first to base his particular message again and again on declarations about the rule of God over the nations and his works among them, the first to found the particular on this universal and to deduce it, so to speak, from this."

31 Hanson (1995), 2: "We know nothing concerning the personal life of this prophet, neither name nor gender nor social class." Since most prophets were men, I assume that Isaiah of Babylon was, too, at least in the absence of any evidence that he was a woman.

32 Isaiah of Babylon (also known as Second Isaiah, Deutero-Isaiah, the Prophet of the Exile, and the Prophet of Consolation) is generally thought to be the author of chapters 40–55 of the book of Isaiah, and perhaps chapters 38 and 39 as well. According to McKenzie (1968), the distinction between First and Second Isaiah, which "has been made on the basis of vocabulary, style, and

thought ... is so widely accepted in modern scholarship that the argument against it need not be examined at length" (at xvi, xv). See also Blenkinsopp (1996), 184. Most modern scholars also believe that the last eleven chapters of the book, with a few possible exceptions, stem from another source, which Bernard Duhm called Trito- (or Third) Isaiah, and which others take to be either the work of a single anonymous author or several authors: See, e.g., Hanson (1995), 186–93, and the extensive discussion in Schramm (1995), 11–52. Compare Podhoretz (2002), 179, 267–68. It was earlier thought that Isaiah of Babylon might have been a member of an "Isaian" community of some sort, but Willey (1997), 37, points out that "the notion of a continuous school of Isaiah's disciples who not only helped edit and preserve the prophet's oracles, but who finally composed and added chapters 40–66 ... has few adherents today."

33 Most scholars, but not all, accept the idea that Second Isaiah resided in Babylon. For a dissent, see Barstad (1987), 90 ff.

34 For the prophet's affliction by disease, see Isaiah 53:2–3—the fourth Servant Song. In 49:7 (assuming that the second Servant Song is autobiographical), he describes himself as "the slave of despots." The problems of interpretation of the Servant Songs are discussed infra at 282, n. 509.

35 For speculation about the cultic assemblies, see T. C. Mitchell, "The Babylonian Exile and the Restoration of the Jews in Palestine (586–c. 500 B.C.)," in Boardman et al. (1991), 424–25; McKenzie (1968), xxv, xxxv; Blenkinsopp (1996), 189.

36 Isaiah 49:1.

37 Isaiah 49:4.

38 Isaiah 49:2.

39 McKenzie, op. cit., 131, 133. Leviticus 21:16–23 bars deformed or disfigured people from approaching the Holy of Holies; they are considered ritually unclean, although not necessarily accursed. On the other hand, some Middle Eastern cultures, Egypt in particular, viewed physical deformity as a sign of divine favor. See W. R. Dawson, "Pygmies and Dwarfs in Ancient Egypt." *J EgyptArch* 1938; 24:185–9.

40 For the dating of Isaiah's work, see McKenzie., op. cit., xviii ff.

41 Isaiah 10:5 describes Assyria as "the rod of my anger, the club brandished by me in my fury."

42 Jeremiah 27:6, and see discussion, supra, at 119–20.

43 Isaiah 45:1–3. Other references to the king as YHVH's chosen may be found at 41:1–5, 25 and 44:28 ("I am he who says of Cyrus, 'My shepherd—he will fulfill my whole purpose.'") Some commentators identified Cyrus with the servant of YHVH in the first Servant Song, 42:1–4, but this interpretation is fairly well discredited; see McKenzie, op. cit., xlviii.

44 Von Rad (1965), 238, comments on "the prophet whose mouth JHVH filled with words of an unparalleled splendor which charm the reader and carry him forward."

45 Cf. Isaiah 11, in which the virtuous Davidic king "shall stand as a signal to the peoples" and "will bring back the scattered people of Judah from the four corners of the earth." The meaning of the description of Cyrus as *mashiach* is much debated. Von Rad (1965), 244, fn. 16, calls the use of the term "remarkable," but adds, "this is no more than a rousing rhetorical exaggeration inspired by the actual situation. How could Deutero-Isaiah have meant more than this, since Cyrus was not of the line of David? Cyrus was YHVH's instrument in basically the same way as the Assyrians were this for Isaiah of Jerusalem." With respect to this renowned interpreter of Old Testament theology, this seems to miss the point. Hanson (1997), 189–90, explains the matter clearly: "God was designating a *pagan* king as his shepherd and anointed one and entrusting in his hands God's eternal purposes! . . . God's freedom could not be limited by a mythic/static concept of tradition that had distorted the creative-redemptive vocation of this nation."

46 Barstad (1987), 97–100, insists that the Cyrus Cylinder, which speaks of "grasping the hand" of Marduk, is not necessarily referential for Deutero-Isaiah. This is consistent with his overall view that Isaiah's audience was Judean, not Babylonian. He does, however, concede that "the particular idiom of 'holding one's hand' occurs more frequently in Deutero-Isaiah than in other texts of the Hebrew Bible" (at 100).

47 Isaiah 43:1. See Paul D. Hanson, "The Word of the Servant of the Lord in Isaiah 40–55," in Bellinger and Farmer (1998), 16, re-

marking that the substitution of Cyrus for the traditional Davidic king represented "a radical revision of the traditional view."

48 Isaiah 43:14. The JPS commentary paraphrases: "I send Cyrus to Babylon to conquer it" (at 870). I have replaced the JB's "Chaldeans" with the synonym "Babylonians." See also the scornful prophecy of Babylon's fall in chapter 47.

49 See Klein (1978), 201; McKenzie (1968), 78–79.

50 Cf. Isaiah 45:11: "Is it for you to question me about my children and to dictate to me what my hands should do?"

51 Isaiah 48:7.

52 Isaiah 54:10.

53 As Walter Brueggemann (2001), 68, puts it, Isaiah's "speaking depends on the reality and confession of God's radical freedom, freedom not only from the conceptions and expectations of his people, but from God's own past actions as well."

54 Isaiah 40:12.

55 Isaiah 45:12–13.

56 The creation poem is called *Enuma elish* after its first two words. See, e.g., Oates (1986), 169–70; Erica Reiner, "First-Millennium Babylonian Literature," in Boardman et al. (1991), 303–4. See also the valuable discussion in Blenkinsopp (1996), 187–89.

57 Isaiah 44:6 (see also 48:12); 45:18.

58 Isaiah 40:22–23.

59 Isaiah 45:7, 55:9. And see the discussion of "divine self-predication" in Barstad (1987), 101–10, which denies, contrary to the opinions of certain other scholars, that this mode of expression reflects Babylonian literary influence.

60 Cf. T. Cuyler Young Jr., "The Consolidation of the Empire and Its Limits of Growth under Darius and Xerxes," in Boardman et al. (1988), 79: "Borrowing methods and ideologies of government from the Medes and the Assyrians, the Persians took over the ancient bureaucracies of Babylon and Elam, and molded the whole thing into a new form and style of state organization. That organization perhaps became one of the most lasting Achaemenid contributions to the civilization of the Near East."

61 See Buber (1949), 209: "Deutero-Isaiah is, in spite of the teaching of Amos, Isaiah and Jeremiah, the originator of a theology of

world-history, for he is the first to base his particular message again and again on declarations about the rule of God over the nations and his works among them, the first to found the particular on this universal, and to deduce it, so to speak, from this." See also von Rad (1965), 240–41.

62 See, e.g., Isaiah 45:5: "Though you do not know me, I arm you that men may know from the rising to the setting of the sun that, apart from me, all is nothing." See also the discussion in Gottwald (1964), 338–39.

63 In "The Consolidation of the Empire," op. cit. at 99–103, T. Cuyler Young Jr. states that "the record is too sparse" to say anything about Cyrus's religion, but that his successors Darius and Xerxes "may well have been good Zoroastrians of their times." Gottwald (1964), 335, argues more positively that "another conceivable source of the prophet's sympathy for Cyrus is the Persian's adherence to a non-idolatrous religion. As a prince of Anshan, Cyrus was a devotee of Mithraism; as heir of the Median empire, he was a Zoroastrian."

64 T. Cuyler Young Jr., "The Consolidation of the Empire," op. cit., 103, remarks that the Persian policy "was good *Realpolitik.* . . . Given the enormous size and astounding ethnic diversity of the empire, probably no other policy would have worked." See also the discussion of Cyrus's worship of Marduk, supra at 137.

65 Isaiah 2:1–3, 19:24–25; and see the discussion supra, at 80–83. Gottwald (1964), 337, refers to Isaiah's defining "the task of Israel as the universal spiritual counterpart to the universal political dominion of Persia."

66 It is clear that Isaiah expected all the nations to recognize YHVH as the One God; he was sharply critical of "those who carry about their idol of wood, those who pray to a god that cannot save" (45:20). But whether he expected them to worship YHVH precisely as the Jews did is not at all clear. Speaking of the first Isaiah's vision of universal peace (2:1–4), Gottwald (1964), 200, remarks that "the terms of the oracle do not require that the confederated nations totally embrace Yahwism . . . in the manner expected by the later Isaiah of the exile." One wonders, however, whether the two visions are as different as Gottwald suggests, es-

pecially since he makes it clear that Deutero-Isaiah's vision does *not* include Judean political supremacy (at 341–46). Could not the "confederated nations" renounce false gods and embrace the ethics of Yawhism without adhering to every prescription of the oral and written law? This issue, of course, was raised 500 years later by Jesus and the apostle Paul.

67 Cf. McKenzie (1968), 31: "None of the peoples whom historical Israel had known, whether as friendly or hostile, had survived into the middle of the sixth century B.C. except Babylon; and Babylon's fate was already discernible in the figure of Cyrus."

68 Isaiah 52:10.

69 Isaiah 48:5: "And so I revealed things beforehand, before they happened. I announced them to you, so that you could not say, 'My idol was the one that performed them, it was my carved image, my image of cast metal, that decreed them.'" See also 41:25–29; 42:9; 46:10.

70 Isaiah 45:21–22.

71 Jeremiah 1:5.

72 Isaiah 51:4.

73 Cf. Gottwald (1964), 344: *"The establishment of the universal YHVH cult will be a triumph of imperial policy and of national conversion. The conversion will, however, not be due so much to what Israel says as to what Israel is.* To the prophet it means that the combination of what Israel has undergone both as a decimated people and as a restored people will awaken a recognition of YHVH's lordship among the people of the empire."

74 Isaiah 49:6. This passage is from the second Servant Song, which I interpret as at least partly autobiographical.

75 Gottwald, op. cit., 341, 343, states that although it is difficult to extract a theory of Israel's relationship to the nations from "poetic generalities," her prime role is to be "the priestly benefactor of the nations." To the same effect, Buber (1949), 215–17; Heschel (1962), 197–201; McKenzie (1968), lxiii, 82. Podhoretz (2002), 278, adds the qualification that when Isaiah "envisages a spiritual *imperium,* it is one that brings with it material benefits, together with the religious vindication that (the children of Israel being human) is not entirely free of the taste of revenge."

76 Isaiah 58:6–8. This passage is from the chapters usually attributed to Third Isaiah, but their sentiment is consistent with the thought of Isaiah of Babylon.

77 Jeremiah 29:21–23. See also Bright in AB (1965), 211.

78 Isaiah 50:6, a passage from the third Servant Song. The specific context of the passage remains unclear. McKenzie (1968), 117, notes that "what the Servant experiences is the vulgar insult which does no real physical harm, a type of insult common in the ancient Near East," adding that "the prophet need not be reflecting his own experience here."

79 Isaiah 44:10, 15–17. Similarly, see 40:19, 41:6, 45:20, 46:6–7.

80 Isaiah 46:1–2. Bel was another name for Marduk.

81 Isaiah 44:25.

82 Isaiah 47:12–14.

83 The Servant Songs, Isaiah 42:1–9, 49:1–26, 50:4–11, and 52:13–15 to 53:12, are poems whose subject, speaking in the first person, is an unnamed "servant of YHVH." The debates about the servant's identity would fill a small library; depending on the poem being interpreted and the interpreter's views, he has been identified as Israel (collectively), a historic individual, a person not yet born, a fictitious character, or Isaiah of Babylon himself. For summaries of and commentary on the various interpretations, see, e.g., Buber (1949), 217–35; North (1956); Mowinckel (1959), 187–260; von Rad (1965), 250–62; McKenzie (1968), xxxviii–lv. Blenkinsopp (1996), 184–93, discusses the theory that Isaiah was imprisoned for sedition by the Babylonians, and suggests that the author of the fourth Servant Song is a disciple (at 192–93). Miller (1970) argues convincingly that the second Servant Song reflects Isaiah's call, the third song the developing conflict between the exile community and the authorities, and the fourth Isaiah's persecution and execution by the Babylonians.

84 M. A. Dandamaev, "Neo-Babylonian Society and Economy," in Boardman et al. (1991), 257.

85 Isaiah 53:8–9. For an argument that the prophet was not executed, see Whybray (1978), 92–106. For the view that Isaiah returned to Israel with the second wave of exiles, see Podhoretz (2002), 267–69.

86 Isaiah 52:15, 53:2–3. The translation of these famous lines has long been a subject of some contention. The JB translates 53:3 as "a man of sorrows and familiar with suffering" (cf. the KJV and RSV: "a man of sorrows and acquainted with grief"), while the JPS says "a man of suffering, familiar with disease," and the AB (McKenzie, 1968) "a man of pains, familiar with disease." I have retained the JB translation for its familiarity.

87 McKenzie, op. cit., 133: "The person who suffered, according to the wisdom of the sages, was disclosed as a sinner, even if his sins were secret; the fact that he suffered was a manifest judgment of God upon his wickedness. Men avoid looking at him not only from repugnance but also from fear; it was dangerous to look upon one who lay under a curse." The "sages" are not identified here; it seems clear that this was a popular belief, not one enshrined in the law.

88 Isaiah 53:4–5. I use the JPS translation, which is consistent with the theme of the prophet's disease, rather than the JB ("He was pierced through for our faults, crushed for our sins"), which may reflect later Christian beliefs that Isaiah's punishment prefigured that of Jesus. Several scholars have pointed out that the preposition used in the passage, the Hebrew *min,* is most naturally translated "because of" rather than "for"; see, e.g., Morna D. Hooker, "Did the Use of Isaiah 53 to Interpret His Mission Begin with Jesus?", in Bellinger and Farmer (1998), 96. Hooker concludes, "In other words, the Servant suffered *as a result of* the sins of others. . . . We do not have someone who suffers *instead of* his guilty compatriots, but rather someone who *shares* in their sufferings, although he himself, unlike them, is innocent" (at 96–97). And, "What we have in Isaiah 53 is better described as *representative suffering* rather than *vicarious suffering:* as *inclusive* place-taking rather than as *exclusive* place-taking" (at 98). Hooker seems justified in pointing out that the idea of a purely substitutionary punishment has no parallel in the Old Testament.

89 Isaiah 53:7.

90 Isaiah 53:6.

91 See Buber (1949), 227–29, pointing out that "these iniquities, which [the servant] has borne, are not those of Israel, concerning

which it was publicly announced (40:2) that they were already atoned for by their affliction." Buber's view, which I share, is that the subject of the Servant Songs is both an individual and Israel, and that "the paradox of the two 'servants' cannot be solved or dispelled. It is intended to be a paradox" (at 223). See also Hanson (1995), 166–67.

92 Isaiah 53:12, 10 (JPS translation). See also 52:13–15. These lines were later interpreted as implying a resurrection from the dead, but most modern scholars believe that since the poem "is earlier than any attested belief in the resurrection... the prophet must therefore be expressing... his faith that the saving work of the Servant cannot end in the total defeat of death": McKenzie (1968), 135. Other current explanations are that the servant is "saved from a fate like death" (JPS commentary at 892), and that "he lives on in the prophetic following dedicated to perpetuating his message" (Blenkinsopp, 1996, 193). Hanson (1997, 192–93) states the general principle of the servant's power convincingly: "The Servant does not offer a model of acquiescence to the oppressor, but empowerment.... The servant, in being drawn into a cause larger than the individual, is both vindicated and empowered to become an agent of healing on behalf of others."

93 See St. Anselm's classic discussion of this issue in "Cur Deus Homo" (Why God Became Man), in Anselm (2003).

94 Isaiah 42:6–7 (from the first Servant Song).

CHAPTER VII: *"Now I Create New Heavens and a New Earth"*

1 Isaiah 7:14, 9:6; Matt. 1:23. See the discussion of the mistranslation of *almah* and other matters, supra at 48–49, fn. 31.

2 Jeremiah 31:31–34, 32:39–40; Hebrews 8:6–13. See also pages 125–28, supra.

3 The Gibson film begins with a quotation from Isaiah 53:5. See also Mark 15:28; Luke 22:37; Acts 8:30–35, and the discussion at 152–56, supra. See also Bellinger and Farmer, eds. (1998).

4 Von Rad (1965), 329–30. See also Seitz (1993), 1, stating that before the modern period, Christians interpreted Isaiah as "a book

that spoke of the future, generally, and of salvation through the agency of the Messiah, Jesus Christ, specifically. So it was that the church fathers . . . regarded Isaiah not just as the first and greatest prophet but as the first apostle and evangelist."

5 See Bright (1976), 467. Of course, there are also scholars who maintain the view that Jesus was the King whose coming was prophesied by the Old Testament prophets. See, e.g., Buzzard (2002), 13–23.

6 Some outstanding recent exceptions are Sanders (1985, 1993), Borg (1988), Meier (1994), Brueggemann (2001), Horsley (2002).

7 See the Holy Qu'ran, 2:135–141, 4:171–73.

8 On the Jewish rejection of Jesus's prophetic role, see Klinghoffer (2005), 159–71, passim. On Jewish reconsideration of Jesus's role, see Bruteau (2001).

9 T. C. Mitchell, "The Babylonian Exile and the Restoration of the Jews in Palestine," in Boardman et al. (1991), 430–31. See also Hayim Tadmor, "Judah," in Lewis et al. (1994), 261 ff.; Elias J. Bickerman, "The Babylonian Captivity," in Davies and Finkelstein (1984), 342 ff. Carroll (1978), 120, points out that no prophet predicted the continued existence of two Jewish communities, one in Yehud and one in Babylonia.

10 Abundant evidence of these problems may be found in the writings attributed to the Third Isaiah, esp. Isaiah 57–59, as well as in the books of Ezra and Nehemiah.

11 See Kaufmann (1960), 450, emphasizing the "ideological battle between Judaism and paganism" raging during the Second Temple period.

12 See T. Cuyler Young Jr., "The Consolidation of the Empire and Its Limits of Growth under Darius and Xerxes," in Boardman et al. (1988), 53–63.

13 Ibid., 78.

14 One aspect of this split was the "re-absorption" of most prophets into the temple cult. See Blenkinsopp (1996), 223. See also 228, where the author states that in the Second Commonwealth it became "increasingly apparent that prophecy is incapable of providing a firm basis for the ongoing life of the community."

15 Weber (1952), 380. This can be seen as an illustration of Weber's principle of "the routinization of charisma." Philip R. Davies, "The social world of apocalyptic writings," in Clements (1989), 251–71, questions whether an establishment / antiestablishment split took place, and disagrees with Hanson's (1985) assertion that apocalyptic prophecy emanated from antiestablishment conventicles (at 257–58).

16 See Bright (1976), 432–33; Podhoretz (2002), 309–10.

17 Brueggemann (2001), 21–37.

18 See Hanson (1975). See also Blenkinsopp (1996), 194–239, esp. "The Eschatological Reinterpretation of Prophecy" at 226–39. In "Iranian Influence on Judaism: First Century B.C.E. to Second Century C.E.," Shaul Shaked suggests that Jewish eschatology may be related to similar themes in Iranian religion (in Davies and Finkelstein, 1984, 321–24). See also Gunther Wanke, "Prophecy and Psalms in the Persian Period," ibid., at 162–83.

19 The apocalyptic style of prophecy is sometimes said to have begun with Ezekiel, a Jerusalemite priest taken into exile in Babylon. Some scholars believe that his work was heavily edited and revised by later members of his school. See, e.g., Blenkinsopp (1996), 165–71.

20 Bright (1972, 458) points out that although the Bible contains few examples of apocalyptic literature, "a host of similar writings were produced that did not gain admission to the canon."

21 For example, see von Rad (1965), 301 ff.

22 Isaiah 45:19. McKenzie (1968), 83, comments that the passage "denies that Yahweh has spoken by the occult art of divination. The revelation of Yahweh to Israel was given to an entire people; they did not need to seek it from professional revealers."

23 Bright (1972), 458.

24 The potency of human choice in the work of the prophets is emphasized throughout Buber's classic study (1949). See also Heschel (1962), 367–68 (on Jonah).

25 Von Rad (1965), 305. See also Frend (1984), 27–30.

26 Gottwald (1964), 228 (commenting on Isaiah 19:16–25).

27 See discussion of the "Qumran Covenanters" in Frend (1984), 27–30.

28 Cf. Bright (1976), 457: "We thus see that the expected *eschaton,* though still viewed in the context of history, was not conceived of as a continuation, or even a radical improvement, of the existing order, as was true in old Israel, but rather as a catastrophic divine intervention that would bring into being a new and different order."

29 See, e.g., the vivid description in Horsley (2003), 15–34.

30 The proportion of Jews in the population of the Roman empire is estimated (roughly) at about 10 percent: Johnson (1976), 11–12.

31 Horsley (2003), 28–30. See also 35–54 for a more detailed description of "resistance and rebellion in Judea and Galilee."

32 The locus classicus is Matt. 22:21: "Give to Caesar what belongs to Caesar—and to God what belongs to God." Horsley (2003), 98–99, argues that the implicit political message of this to the Jews was that the payment of tribute to Rome was not lawful according to Mosaic covenantal law, but there seems little doubt that Jesus was also eager to avoid a suicidal rebellion against Rome.

33 See the discussion of Augustan Peace and Pauline Peace in Crossan and Reed (2004), 70–75, passim. The authors are chiefly concerned to contrast the two concepts of peace, however, not to show their dialectical relationship.

34 Luke 21:20; Matt. 24:15. Daniel, quoted here, was almost certainly talking of the statue of Zeus set up by the Greek ruler, Antiochus Epiphanes, in the Jerusalem Temple. Jesus seemed to expect that the Romans would commit a similar sacrilege.

35 Luke 21:24.

36 Matt. 24:29–31. See also Luke 21:25–28. At 21:24, Luke quotes Jesus as foreseeing a preapocalyptic defeat and deportation of the Jews.

37 Sanders (1985), 319. The author asserts that the "kingdom" that Jesus had in mind was a restored Israel. He disagrees with others who emphasize Jesus's universalism on the grounds, inter alia, that they overstate the difference between Judaism and "universalistic" Christianity (see the discussion at 23 ff.). This seems to me a false dichotomy. Apocalyptic thinking frequently envisions the destruction of many and the saving of few, but there is no evidence that Jesus was less universalistic than, say, Isaiah of Babylon.

38 Luke 17:21.

39 See the extensive discussion in Sanders (1985), 150–56. "He may well have thought that 'the kingdom' in the sense of 'the power of God' was at work in the world, but that the time would come when all opposing power would be eliminated, and the kingdom of God in a somewhat different sense would 'come'—be ushered in" (at 152). The passage has also been interpreted as being self-referential; when Jesus says "the kingdom is among you," he is talking about himself. If this interpretation is correct (which seems unlikely), it illustrates the tendency of eschatological thinking to introject itself into the present.

40 E.g., Matt. 19:16–26; 23:23–24; Luke 6:20–26. Brueggemann (2001), 86–87, suggests that the prayer "Forgive our debts as we forgive our debtors" (Matt. 6:12, Luke 11:4) was "not likely metaphorical," but was responsive to "the weight of taxes, tithes, tolls, rents, and confiscation on the peasants of Galilee and Judea."

41 See, e.g., Mark 2:1–12, 15–17; 5:25–34; 7:24–30; Matt. 8:1–3; Luke 7:36–50; John 4:1–26. And see the discussion in Brueggemann (2001), 84–88.

42 See Horsley (2003), 121–22. Horsley also makes the point that Jesus's cures and exorcisms had significant political and social implications in addition to their demonstration of miraculous powers (at 99–103, 106–11).

43 Mark 11:15–17; 13:1–2; Matt. 21:12–13; Luke 19:45–46; 21:5–7.

44 Luke 6:27–28.

45 Luke 6:36–38; 15:11–24; 17:4. See also Brueggemann, op. cit., 88–94.

46 See Luke 19:1–10, in which the tax collector Zacchaeus repents and repays his victims because Jesus honors him.

47 Luke 22:37, quoting Isaiah 53:12; Matt. 20:28. An important collection of essays asking whether Jesus considered himself the suffering servant is Bellinger and Farmer's *Jesus and the Suffering Servant: Isaiah 53 and Christian Origins* (1998).

48 Cf. Luke 9:1–2.

49 Mark 10:42–44. See also the discussion in Horsley (2003), 108–25.

50 See the parables of the sower and the mustard seed, Mark 4:1–20, 30–32.

51 Cf. Podhoretz (2002), 310: "Little did [the prophets] realize, nor would they have expected . . . that the spoils of the spiritual triumph they had done so much to bring about would be reaped not by Judaism but by the new religion that would spring from it under the name of Christianity."

52 On the transformation of Christianity under Constantine the Great and his successors, see Carroll (2001), 155–207; Freeman (2002), 154–77; Rubenstein (1999), 48 ff.

53 See Luke 9:27: "I tell you truly, there are some standing here who will not taste death before they see the kingdom of God."

54 Revelation 19:11–21:8.

55 Isaiah 6:13.

56 Cf. Johnson (1987), 118–19: "Most of the Mediterranean and Near Eastern people prospered under Roman rule and judged it to be far preferable to anything else they were likely to get. This was the view of the six million or more Jews in the diaspora. . . . It is likely that even in the Jewish homeland, many, if not most, Jews did not see the Romans as oppressors or enemies of religion. . . . The real trouble with the Jews was that they were too advanced, too intellectually conscious to find alien rule acceptable."

57 The socioeconomic background to prophecy is discussed in a number of essays by Gottwald (1993). See esp. 131–64, 325–64.

58 Jeremiah 13:23.

59 Martin Buber, in Biemann (2002), 40.

60 http://www.nhtsa.gov/people/Crash/LCOD/index.htm.

61 Jeremiah 38:4.

62 Isaiah 5:28.

63 For the Jewish wars against Rome, see Flavius Josephus, *The Jewish War,* rev. ed. (Penguin Classics, 1984).

64 See, for example, John W. Burton, *Conflict: Resolution and Provention* and *Conflict: Basic Human Needs* (Macmillan, 1990); Richard E. Rubenstein, "Basic Human Needs: The Next Steps in Theory Development," *International Journal of Peace Studies,* 6:1 (2001); Johan

Galtung, *Transcend and Transform: An Introduction to Conflict Work* (Pluto Press, 2004).

65 See, for example, Peter Singer, *One World: The Ethics of Globalization* (Yale University Press, 2004); William Schweiker, "An Introduction to Ethics: Global Dynamics and the Integrity of Life," *Journal of Religious Ethics,* 32:1 (2004), 13–34; Marc Gopin, *Holy War, Holy Peace: How Religion Can Bring Peace to the Middle East* (Oxford University Press, 2005).

66 See Samuel F. Huntington, *The Clash of Civilizations and the Remaking of World Order* (Simon & Schuster, 1998). See also Richard E. Rubenstein and Jarle Crocker, "Challenging Huntington," *Foreign Policy,* Summer 1994.

Selected Bibliography

✳

Bibles and Bible Commentaries (with abbreviations)

Anchor Bible. Jeremiah: A New Translation with Introduction and Commentary by John Bright, 2d ed. Garden City, NY: Doubleday, 1965. (AB)

Anchor Bible. Second Isaiah: A New Translation with Introduction and Commentary by John L. McKenzie. Garden City, NY: Doubleday, 1968. (McKenzie)

Berlin, Adele, and Mac Zvi Brettler, eds. *The Jewish Study Bible, featuring the Jewish Publication Society TANAKH Translation.* Oxford and New York: Oxford University Press, 2004. (JPS)

Freedman, David Noel, ed. *The Anchor Bible Dictionary.* New York: Anchor Bible Commentary, 1992. (ABD)

Holy Bible, Containing the Old and New Testaments, King James Version. Philadelphia: National Publishing Company, 2000. (KJV)

Holy Bible, Containing the Old and New Testaments, Revised Standard Version. New York: Thomas Nelson & Sons, 1953. (RSV)

Jerusalem Bible, Reader's Edition. Garden City, NY: Doubleday & Company, 1968. (JB)

Mayes, James L., gen. ed. *The HarperCollins Bible Commentary,* revised ed. San Francisco: HarperSanFrancisco, 2000. (HC)

Books and Articles

Aberbach, David. *Imperialism and Biblical Prophecy, 750–500 B.C.E.* London: Routledge, 1993.

Anselm, Saint. *Proslogium; Monologium; An Appendix in Behalf of the Fool by Gaunilon; and Cur Deus Homo.* Eugene, OR: Wipf and Stock, 2003.

Armstrong, Karen. *A History of God: The 4,000-Year Quest of Judaism, Christianity and Islam.* New York: Ballantine Books, 1993.

Arnold, Bill T. *Who Were the Babylonians?* Leiden, the Netherlands, and Boston: Brill, 2005.

Atwell, James E. *The Sources of the Old Testament: A Guide to the Religious Thought of the Hebrew Bible.* London and New York: T & T Clark International, 2004.

Barstad, Hans M. "On the so-called Babylonian literary influence in second Isaiah." *Scandinavian Journal of the Old Testament* 2 (1987): 90–110.

Bartchy, S. Scott. "Who should be called father? Paul of Tarsus between the Jesus tradition and patria potestas." *Biblical Theology Bulletin,* Winter 2003.

Barton, John. *Oracles of God: Perceptions of Ancient Prophecy in Israel after the Exile.* New York: Oxford University Press, 1986.

Bellinger, William H., Jr., and William R. Farmer, eds. *Jesus and the Suffering Servant: Isaiah 53 and Christian Origins.* Harrisburg, PA: Trinity Press International, 1998.

Berrigan, Daniel. *Isaiah: Spirit of Courage, Gift of Tears.* Minneapolis: Fortress Press, 1996.

———. *Jeremiah: The World, The Wound of God.* Minneapolis: Fortress Press, 1999.

Biemann, Asher D., ed. *The Martin Buber Reader: Essential Writings.* New York: Palgrave Macmillan, 2002.

Blenkinsopp, Joseph. *A History of Prophecy in Israel,* rev. ed. Louisville, KY: Westminster John Knox Press, 1996.

———. *Sage, Priest, Prophet: Religious and Intellectual Leadership in Ancient Israel.* Oxford: Oxford University Press, 1997.

Bloom, Harold. *Jesus and Yahweh: The Names Divine.* New York: Riverhead Books, 2005.

Boardman, John, et al., eds. *Cambridge Ancient History,* 2d ed., Vol. III, Part 1, *The Prehistory of the Balkans; the Middle East and the Aegean World, Tenth to Eighth Centuries* B.C. Cambridge: Cambridge University Press, 1982.

———. *Cambridge Ancient History,* 2d ed., Vol. III, Part 2, *The Assyrian and Babylonian Empires and Other States of the Near East, from the Eighth to the Sixth Centuries* B.C. Cambridge: Cambridge University Press, 1991.

———. *Cambridge Ancient History,* 2d ed., Vol. IV, *Persia, Greece and the Western Mediterranean c. 525 to 479* B.C. Cambridge: Cambridge University Press, 1988.

Borg, Marcus J. *Jesus: A New Vision.* New York: Harper & Row, 1988.

Boring, M. Eugene. "The 'Third Quest' and the Apostolic Faith." *Interpretation* 50:4: (October 1996): 341–54.

Borowski, Oded. "Hezekiah's Reforms and the Revolt against Assyria." *Biblical Archaeologist* 58:3 (1995).

Bottéro, Jean. *Everyday Life in Ancient Mesopotamia.* Baltimore, MD: Johns Hopkins University Press, 2001.

Bright, John. *A History of Israel,* 2d ed. Philadelphia: Westminster Press, 1972.

———. *Covenant and Promise: The Prophetic Understanding of the Future in Pre-Exilic Israel.* Philadelphia: Westminster Press, 1976.

Brueggemann, Walter. *The Prophetic Imagination,* 2d ed. Minneapolis: Fortress Press, 2001.

———. *Interpretation and Obedience: From Faithful Reading to Faithful Living.* Minneapolis: Fortress Press, 1991.

———. *Theology of the Old Testament: Testimony, Dispute, Advocacy.* Minneapolis: Fortress Press, 1997.

Bruteau, Beatrice, ed. *Jesus Through Jewish Eyes: Rabbis and Scholars Engage an Ancient Brother in a New Conversation.* Maryknoll, NY: Orbis Books, 2001.

Buber, Martin. *The Prophetic Faith.* New York: Harper & Row, 1949.

———. *The Kingship of God,* 3d ed., trans. Richard Scheimann. New York: Harper & Row, 1967.

Butler, James T., Edgar W. Conrad, and Ben C. Ollenburger, eds. *Understanding the Word: Essays in Honor of Bernhard W. Anderson.* Sheffield, UK: JSOT Press, 1985.

Buzzard, Anthony F. *The Coming Kingdom of the Messiah: A Solution to the Riddle of the New Testament,* 3d ed. Atlanta, GA: Restoration Fellowship, 2002.

Carroll, James. *Constantine's Sword: The Church and the Jews.* Boston and New York: Houghton Mifflin, 2001.

Carroll, R. P. "Second Isaiah and the Failure of Prophecy." *Studia Theologica* 32 (1978): 119–31.

———. *When Prophecy Failed: Reactions and Responses to Failure in the Old Testament Prophetic Traditions.* London: SCM Press, 1979.

Childs, Brevard S. *Isaiah and the Assyrian Crisis.* London: SCM Press, 1967.

Clements, Ronald E. *Isaiah 1–39.* Grand Rapids, MI: William B. Eerdmans, 1980.

———, ed. *The World of Ancient Israel: Sociological, Anthropological and Political Perspectives.* Cambridge: Cambridge University Press, 1989.

Cogan, Morton. *Imperialism and Religion: Assyria, Judah and Israel in the Eighth and Seventh Centuries B.C.E.* Missoula, MT: Scholars Press, 1974.

Contenau, Georges. *Everyday Life in Babylon and Assyria.* London: Edward Arnold, 1954.

Cross, Frank Moore. *Caananite Myth and Hebrew Epic: Essays in the History of the Religion of Israel.* Cambridge, MA: Harvard University Press, 1973.

Crossan, John Dominic, and Jonathan L. Reed. *In Search of Paul: How Jesus's Apostle Opposed Rome's Empire with God's Kingdom.* San Francisco: HarperSanFrancisco, 2004.

Davies, Andrew. *Double Standards in Isaiah: Re-evaluating Prophetic Ethics and Divine Justice.* Leiden, the Netherlands: Brill, 2000.

Davies, Philip R. *In Search of "Ancient Israel,"* 2d ed. Sheffield, UK: Sheffield Academic Press, 1994.

Davies, W. D., and Louis Finkelstein, eds. *Cambridge History of Judaism.* Vol. I, *Introduction; the Persian Period.* Cambridge: Cambridge University Press, 1984.

De Vaux, Roland. *Ancient Israel: Its Life and Institutions.* Grand Rapids, MI: William B. Eerdmans, 1997.

Dever, William G. *What Did the Biblical Writers Know and When Did They Know It? What Archaeology Can Tell Us About the Reality of Ancient Israel.* Grand Rapids, MI: William B. Eerdmans, 2002.

———. *Did God Have A Wife? Archaeology And Folk Religion In Ancient Israel.* Grand Rapids, MI: William B. Eerdmans, 2005.

Finkelstein, Israel, and Neil Asher Silberman. *The Bible Unearthed: Archaeology's New Vision of Ancient Israel and the Origin of its Sacred Texts.* New York: Simon and Schuster, 2001.

Fishbane, Michael. *Biblical Interpretation in Ancient Israel.* Oxford: Clarendon Press, 1985.

Freeman, Charles. *The Closing of the Western Mind: The Rise of Faith and the Fall of Reason.* New York: Vintage Books, 2002.

Frend, W. H. C. *The Rise of Christianity.* Philadelphia: Fortress Press, 1984.

Garnsey, Peter D. A., and C. R. Whittaker, eds. *Imperialism in the Ancient World: The Cambridge University Research Seminar in Ancient History.* Cambridge: Cambridge University Press, 1979.

Gitay, Yehoshua, ed. *Prophecy and Prophets: The Diversity of Contemporary Issues in Scholarship.* Atlanta, GA: Scholars Press, 1997.

Goldin, Hyam E. *Hebrew Criminal Law.* New York: Twyford Press, 1952.

Goodspeed, George Stephen. *A History of the Babylonians and Assyrians.* New York: Charles Scribner's Sons, 1902 (Folcroft Library Editions, 1978).

Gordis, Robert. *Poets, Prophets, and Sages: Essays in Biblical Interpretation.* Bloomington: University of Indiana Press, 1971.

Gottwald, Norman K. *All the Kingdoms of the Earth: Israelite Prophecy and International Relations in the Ancient Near East.* New York, Evanston, and London: Harper & Row, 1964.

———. *The Hebrew Bible In Its Social World and In Ours.* Atlanta, GA: Scholars Press, 1993.

———. *The Politics of Ancient Israel.* Louisville, KY: Westminster John Knox Press, 2001.

Graetz, Henrich. *History of the Jews,* Vol. I, *From the Earliest Period to the Death of Simon the Maccabee (135 B.C.E.).* Philadelphia: Jewish Publication Society of America, 1891.

Grayson, A. K. "Assyria: Ashur-Dan II to Ashur-Nirari V (934–745 B.C.)," in Boardman et al. (1982): 238–81.

———. "Assyria: Tiglath-pileser III to Sargon II (744–705 B.C.)," in Boardman et al. (1991): 71–102.

———. "Assyria: Sennacherib and Esarhaddon (704–669 B.C.)," in Boardman et al. (1991): 103–41.

———. "Assyria 668–635 B.C.: the reign of Ashurbanipual," in Boardman et al. (1991): 142–61.

Hamilton, Mark W. "The past as destiny: historical visions in Sam'al and Judah under Assyrian hegemony." *Harvard Theological Review,* 91:3 (July 1998): 215 ff.

Hanson, Paul D. *The Dawn of Apocalyptic.* Philadelphia: Fortress Press, 1975.

———. "Conflict in Ancient Israel and Its Resolution," in *Understanding the Word: Essays in Honor of Bernhard W. Anderson,* edited by James T. Butler, Edgar W. Conrad, and Ben C. Ollenburger. Sheffield, UK: JSOT Press, 1985, 185–205.

———. *Isaiah 40–66. (Intepretation: A Bible Commentary for Teaching and Preaching).* Louisville, KY: John Knox Press, 1995.

————. "Divine Power in Powerlessness: The Servant of the Lord in Second Isaiah," in *Power, Powerlessness and the Divine: New Inquiries in Bible and Theology*, edited by Cynthia L. Rigby. Atlanta, GA: Scholars Press, 1997, 179–98.

Hardt, Michael, and Antonio Negri. *Empire.* Cambridge, MA: Harvard University Press, 2001.

Hawkins, J. D. "The Neo-Hittite States in Syria and Anatolia," in Boardman et al. (1982): 372–441.

Herzog, Chaim, and Mordechai Gichon. *Battles of the Bible.* London: Greenhill Books, 2002.

Heschel, Abraham J. *The Prophets.* New York: Perennial Classics, 2001.

Hill, John. *Friend or Foe? The Figure of Babylon in the Book of Jeremiah MT.* Leiden, the Netherlands, Boston, and Köln, Germany: Brill, 1999.

Hogenhaven, Jesper. "The Prophet Isaiah and Judaean Foreign Policy under Ahaz and Hezekiah." *Journal of Near Eastern Studies* 49:4 (October, 1990): 351.

Holladay, John S., Jr. "Assyrian Statecraft and the Prophets of Israel," in *Prophecy in Israel: Search for an Identity*, edited by David L. Petersen. Philadelphia: Fortress Press, 1997: 122–43.

Horsley, Richard A. *Jesus and Empire: The Kingdom of God and the New World Disorder.* Minneapolis: Fortress Press, 2002.

————. *Religion and Empire: People, Power, and the Life of the Spirit.* Minneapolis: Fortress Press, 2003.

Irvine, Stuart A. *Isaiah, Ahaz, and the Syro-Ephraimitic Crisis.* Atlanta, GA: Scholars Press, 1990.

Isserlin, B. S. J. *The Israelites.* Minneapolis: Fortress Press, 2001.

James, E. O. *The Ancient Gods: The History and Diffusion of Religion in the Ancient Near East and the Eastern Mediterranean.* New York: G. P. Putnam's Sons, 1960.

Johnson, Paul. *A History of Christianity.* New York: Atheneum, 1976.

————. *A History of the Jews.* New York: Harper & Row, 1987.

Kaufmann, Yehezkel. *The Religion of Israel: From Its Beginnings to the Babylonian Exile*, trans. and abridg. Moshe Greenberg. Chicago: University of Chicago Press, 1960.

King, Philip K. *Jeremiah: An Archaeological Companion.* Louisville, KY: Westminster John Knox Press, 1993.

Kirsch, Jonathan. *God Against the Gods: The History of the War Between Monotheism and Polytheism.* New York: Viking Compass, 2004.

Klein, Ralph W. "Going Home: A Theology of Second Isaiah." *Currents in Theology and Mission* 5 (1978): 198–210.

Klinghoffer, David. *Why the Jews Rejected Jesus: The Turning Point in Western History.* New York: Doubleday, 2005.

Kramer, Samuel Noah. *Cradle of Civilization.* New York: Time-Life Books, 1967.

Laursen, John Christian, ed. *Religious Toleration: "The Variety of Rites" from Cyrus to Defoe.* New York: St. Martin's Press, 1999.

Lewis, D. M., et al., eds. *Cambridge Ancient History.* Vol. V, *The Fifth Century* B.C. Cambridge: Cambridge University Press, 1992.

———. *Cambridge Ancient History,* Vol. VI, *The Fourth Century* B.C. Cambridge: Cambridge University Press, 1994.

Lindblom, J. *Prophecy in Ancient Israel.* Philadelphia: Fortress Press, 1962.

Lipschitz, Oded. "The Rural Settlement in Judah in the Sixth Century B.C.E.: A Rejoinder." *Palestine Exploration Quarterly* 136:2 (2004), 99–107.

Lloyd, Seton. *The Archaeology of Mesopotamia.* London: Thames & Hudson, 1978.

Lods, Adolphe. *The Prophets and the Rise of Judaism.* Westport, CT: Greenwood Press, 1971.

Machinist, Peter. "Assyria and Its Image in the First Isaiah." *Journal of the American Oriental Society* 103:4 (October–December 1983): 719.

Margalit, Avishai. "After Strange Gods" (Review of *The Prophets: Who They Were, What They Are,* by Norman Podhoretz). *New York Review of Books* L:15 (October 9, 2003): 29.

Matthews, Victor H. *The Social World of the Hebrew Prophets.* Peabody, MA: Hendrickson, 2001.

Meier, John P. *A Marginal Jew: Rethinking the Historical Jesus,* Vol. 2, *Mentor, Message, and Miracles.* New York: Doubleday, 1994.

Miller, John W. "Prophetic Conflict in Second Isaiah: The Servant Songs in the Light of their Context." *Wort, Gebot, Glaube: Beitrage zur Theologie des Alten Testaments.* Zurich: Zwingli Verlag, 1970.

Mitchell, T. C. "Israel and Judah until the revolt of Jehu (931–841 B.C.)," in Boardman et al. (1982): 442–87.

———. "Israel and Judah from Jehu until the period of Assyrian domination (841–c. 750 B.C.)," in Boardman et al. (1982): 488–510.

———. "Israel and Judah from the coming of Assyrian domination until the fall of Samaria, and the struggle for independence in Judah (c. 750–700 B.C.)," in Boardman et al. (1991): 322–70.

———. "Judah until the fall of Jerusalem (c. 700–586 B.C.)," in Boardman et al. (1991): 371–409.

———. "The Babylonian Exile and the restoration of the Jews in Palestine (586–c. 500 B.C.)," in Boardman et al. (1991): 410–60.

Moran, W. L., ed. *Towards the Image of Tammuz and Other Essays on Mesopotamian History and Culture.* Cambridge, MA: Harvard University Press, 1970.

Mowinckel, Sigmund. *The Spirit and the Word: Prophecy and Tradition in Ancient Israel.* Philadelphia: Fortress Press, 2003.

———. *He That Cometh: The Messiah Concept in the Old Testament and Later Judaism.* Oxford: Clarendon Press, 1959.

Newsome, James D. *The Hebrew Prophets.* Atlanta, GA: John Knox Press, 1984.

North, C. R. *The Suffering Servant in Second Isaiah.* Oxford: Oxford University Press, 1956.

———. *The Second Isaiah.* Oxford: Clarendon Press, 1964.

Oates, Joan. *Babylon,* rev. ed. London: Thames and Hudson, 1986.

Oded, Bustanay. "The Historical Background of the Syro-Ephraimite War Reconsidered." *Catholic Biblical Quarterly* 34 (1972): 153–65.

———. *Mass Deportation and Deportees in the Neo-Assyrian Empire.* Wiesbaden: Reichert, 1979.

Orlinsky, Harry M. *Studies on the Second Part of the Book of Isaiah.* Leiden, the Netherlands: E. J. Brill, 1967.

———. *Ancient Israel,* 2d ed. Ithaca, NY: Cornell University Press, 1960.

Petersen, David L., ed. *Prophecy in Israel: Search for an Identity.* Philadelphia: Fortress Press, 1987.

———. *Prophetic Literature: An Introduction.* Louisville, KY: Westminster John Knox Press, 2002.

Ploger, Otto. *Theocracy and Eschatology.* Oxford: Blackwell, 1968.

Podhoretz, Norman. *The Prophets: Who They Were, What They Are.* New York: The Free Press, 2002.

Postgate, J. N. "The Land of Assur and the yoke of Assur." *World Archeology* 23:3 (1992): 248–62.

Prior, Michael, CM. *The Bible and Colonialism: A Moral Critique*. Sheffield, UK: Sheffield Academic Press, 1997.

Pritchard, James Bennet, ed. *The Ancient Near East*. Vol. I, *An Anthology of Texts and Pictures*. Princeton, NJ: Princeton University Press, 1958.

———. *Ancient Near Eastern Texts Relating to the Old Testament with Supplement*, 3d ed. Princeton, NJ: Princeton University Press, 1969.

———. *The Ancient Near East*. Vol. II, *A New Anthology of Texts and Pictures*. Princeton, NJ: Princeton University Press, 1975.

Reade, Julian. *Assyrian Sculpture*, 2d ed. London: The British Museum Press, 1998.

Rigby, Cynthia L., ed. *Power, Powerlessness, and the Divine: New Inquiries in Bible and Theology*. Atlanta, GA: Scholars Press, 1997.

Roux, Georges. *Ancient Iraq*, 3d ed. Harmondsworth, UK: Penguin, 1992.

Rubenstein, Richard E. *When Jesus Became God: The Struggle to Define Christianity during the Last Days of Rome*. New York: Harcourt, 1999.

Sack, Ronald H. *Images of Nebuchadnezzar: The Emergence of a Legend*, 2d ed. London and Toronto: Associated University Presses, 2004.

Saggs, Henry W. F. *Everyday Life in Babylonia and Assyria*. New York: Dorset, 1987.

———. *The Greatness That Was Babylon*. London: Sidgwick & Jackson, 1962.

———. *The Might That Was Assyria*. London: Sidgwick & Jackson, 1984.

———. *Civilization Before Greece and Rome*. New Haven, CT: Yale University Press, 1989.

Sanders, E. P. *Jesus and Judaism*. Philadelphia: Fortress Press, 1985.

———. *The Historical Figure of Jesus*. New York: Penguin, 1993.

Scarre, Chris, gen. ed. *Past Worlds: Collins Atlas of Archaeology*. Ann Arbor, MI: Borders Press in association with HarperCollins, 2003.

Schwartz, Seth. *Imperialism and Jewish Society, 22 B.C.E. to 640 C.E.* Princeton, NJ: Princeton University Press, 2001.

Seitz, Christopher R. *Isaiah 1–39 (Interpretation: A Bible Commentary for Teaching and Preaching)*. Louisville, KY: John Knox Press, 1993.

Snell, Daniel C. *Life in the Ancient Near East, 3100–332 B.C.E.* New Haven, CT, and London: Yale University Press, 1997.

Smith, Mark S. *The Early History of God: Yahweh and the Other Deities in Ancient Israel,* 2d ed. Grand Rapids, MI: William B. Eerdmans, 2002.

Speiser, E. A., ed. *At the Dawn of Civilization: A Background of Biblical History.* New Brunswick, NJ: Rutgers University Press, 1964.

Spong, John Shelby. *The Sins of Scripture: Exposing the Bible's Texts of Hate in Order to Reveal the God of Love.* New York: HarperCollins, 2005.

Stein, Stuart D. "Ethnocide," in *Encyclopedia of Race and Ethnic Studies,* edited by Ellis Cashmore. London: Routledge, 2003.

Stulman, Louis. *Order Amid Chaos: Jeremiah as Symbolic Tapestry.* Sheffield, UK: Sheffield Academic Press, 1998.

Thomas, D. Winton. *Documents from Old Testament Times.* New York: Harper & Brothers, 1958.

Thompson, Michael E. W. *Situation and Theology: Old Testament Interpretations of the Syro-Ephramite War.* Sheffield, UK: Almond Press, 1982.

Twombly, Charles C. "The Mighty Shepherd: Diaphor in Deutero-Isaiah." Unpublished paper, 1985.

Van Ruiten, J., and M. Vervenne. *Studies in the Book of Isaiah.* Leuven-Louvain, Belgium: Leuven University Press, 1997.

Von Rad, Gerhard. *Old Testament Theology.* Vol. I, *The Theology of Israel's Historical Traditions,* trans. D. M. G. Stalker. New York: Harper & Row, 1957.

———. Vol. II, *The Theology of Israel's Prophetic Traditions,* trans. D. M. G. Stalker. New York: Harper & Row, 1965.

Walsh, Bryan J., and Sylvia C. Keesmaat. *Colossians Remixed: Subverting the Empire.* Downer's Grove, IL: InterVarsity Press, 2004.

Weber, Max. *Ancient Judaism,* trans. Hans H. Gerth and Don Martindale. Glencoe, IL: The Free Press, 1952.

Wellhausen, Julius. *Prolegomena to the History of Ancient Israel.* New York: Meridian Books, 1957.

Whitley, C. F. "The Call and Mission of Isaiah." *Journal of Near Eastern Studies* 18:1 (January 1959): 38 ff.

Whybray, R. Norman. *Thanksgiving for a Liberated Prophet: An Interpretation of Isaiah,* Chapter 53. Sheffield, UK: Sheffield Academic Press, 1978.

———. *The Second Isaiah.* London: T & T Clark International, 2004.

Willey, Patricia Tull. *Remember the Former Things: The Recollection of Previous Texts in Second Isaiah.* Atlanta, GA: Scholars Press, 1997.

INDEX

✳